Bagging
BIG BUGS

How to Identify, Collect and Display the
Largest and Most Colorful Insects of the
Rocky Mountain Region

Whitney Cranshaw and
Boris Kondratieff

Department of Entomology
Colorado State University

Fulcrum Publishing
Golden, Colorado

Library of Congress Cataloging-in-Publication Data
Cranshaw, Whitney.
    Bagging big bugs / Whitney Cranshaw and Boris Kondratieff.
        p.   cm.
    Includes bibliographical references (p. 303) and index.
    ISBN 1-55591-178-1
    1. Insects—Rocky Mountains Region. 2. Insects—Collection and preservation. I. Kondratieff, B. C. (Boris C.) II. Title.
QL475.R63C73   1995
595.70978—dc20   94–34085
                                                                        CIP

Printed in the United States of America
0 9 8 7 6 5 4 3 2 1

Fulcrum Publishing
350 Indiana Street, Suite 350
Golden, Colorado 80401-5093

Contents

Preface

The original idea for this project occurred while judging the 4-H projects at the Colorado State Fair. The collections made by the finalists are always outstanding and typically contain many insects that even professional entomologists rarely find. Predictably, mistakes in identification are made, many of which were consistently repeated.

Beginning bug-collectors, setting off with their peanut butter jar or cheesecloth and broomstick nets, usually are attracted to the larger, more conspicuous insects. When they subsequently attempt to learn more about what they have discovered, they find numerous insect identification guides. However, there are a *lot* of insects (more than 1.5 million species), and available references do not include many of those that are common in the Rocky Mountain region. The 4-H kids working on their collections tried to match what they found in their front yard with pictures in the available insect guides, but sometimes they were in error. The most commonly illustrated insects are typically species found in such locales as New York, Florida, southern California or even foreign countries. Some of these also occur in this part of the country, especially now that many insects have become cosmopolitan through their spread by human activities. However, the Rocky Mountain region, with its soaring mountains, arid plains, fast-running streams and deep canyons, hosts a great many insects that are unique.

Bagging Big Bugs features insects that are common in the Rocky Mountain region of North America, an area that includes northern New Mexico, Colorado, Utah, Wyoming, Idaho, Montana and sections of southern Canada. Since it would be difficult (and tedious reading) to feature all the insects that live here—in excess of fifty thousand species—emphasis was placed instead on the larger or more striking ones—those that attract attention and are of interest to the beginning bug-collector.

Furthermore, many people are intrigued by and wish to learn more about these fascinating and infinitely varied creatures. To merely identify the beetle or moth one has captured or observed is never an end in itself. Rather, it opens up endless questions: "What does it eat?" "How does it live?" "Why does it have those colors?" "Where can I find more?" "Why does it act like that?" Most entomology books, in attempting to cover all insects found over a large region, can provide few details in this respect.

Slightly more than one hundred insects, and several of their relatives, were chosen to be featured in this book. Generally these are the largest members of their family or order, including some of the smaller, but by no means insignificant, groups of insects such as aphids, scales and thrips. Several examples are included among the insects that are most striking, such as longhorned beetles, silk moths and other behemoths of the insect world. The distribution for each featured insect in the Rocky Mountain region is provided. Also included is a summary of its life history and habits, as well as collecting and rearing tips.

Acknowledgments

A great many people have assisted in writing and reviewing this publication. We would especially like to acknowledge the technical contributions of Paul A. Opler, Howard Ensign Evans, Michael Weissmann and David Leatherman. Pamela Harrell provided some excellent editing comments during final reviews, and the whole project would not have been possible without the crew at Fulcrum Publishing—David Nuss and Patty Maher being particularly involved in the development of this book.

We have used several publications to provide line drawings, with the University of Nebraska 4-H manual and USDA Miscellaneous Publication 1443, *Insects and Mites: Techniques for Collection and Preservation,* being most frequently used. A wide range of sources have been tapped to provide the photographs, including David Leatherman, John Capinera, Frank Peairs, Fred Kirchner and collections produced by Oregon State University and by Brigham Young University. For all these illustrative materials, which have been invaluable to the final product, we are very appreciative.

We would also like to acknowledge the efforts of Colorado 4-H members and other young students of entomology whose project displays and efforts in entomology helped inspire us to write this to further encourage their interests.

Collecting Insects

Where to Look

The good thing about starting an insect collection is that the subjects for your study can be found almost everywhere. Go to the highest peaks in the Rockies and you will find species that have adapted to the harsh alpine environment. Other insects thrive in the pine forests, aspen groves, along the mesas and throughout the dry grasslands of the plains. The lakes, rivers and streams support a tremendous number of unique insects. Although most insects are active during the warm seasons of the year (mid-June through early August is usually the time for greatest bug "action"), a few insects develop and are active even through the winter months. The following are good places to observe and capture insects.

> *On flowers.* Flowers are one of the best places to observe and capture insects. Many large and attractive species visit flowers to feed on nectar or pollen, including butterflies, flower flies, bees, wasps and certain beetles. Flowers also attract predators of these insects, such as ambush bugs and crab spiders.

> *On plant foliage.* A large number of insects feed on plants. Others visit plants to feed on the plant-feeding insects. Plants are also used as resting places by many insects. Thorough searching of plants will almost always yield some

insects to the collector or observer. Areas along fields and streams or open areas of a woodland are particularly good spots to find insects in abundance. An insect sweep net or a beating tray can be very helpful in capturing insects at these locations.

In or under decaying plant and animal materials. Many insects develop on decaying materials such as logs, animal manure and animal carcasses. Although these sites may not be very pleasant, they harbor some of the more unusual insects, such as carrion beetles, large rove beetles and many types of flies.

Under rocks in streams. Numerous insects live in streams under rocks or fallen logs. Nymphs of mayflies and stoneflies, and larvae of hellgrammites, caddisflies and many flies can be collected by lifting rocks and capturing the insects in an aquatic dip net or strainer as they drift downstream.

Under loose rocks or logs on the soil. Many large insects, such as ground beetles and crickets, hide under loose rocks during the day. Centipedes, millipedes and some spiders can also be found under rocks. Although collecting at these sites can be very productive, they should be searched with care in areas where rattlesnakes and scorpions exist.

Around evening lights. Many moths, antlions, May/June beetles and other insects fly only at night. These insects are often attracted to lights, particularly those that reflect high amounts of ultraviolet light waves. Collecting insects at lights on a warm summer evening can be very rewarding.

Insect Collecting Equipment
INSECT NET

An insect net can be your most important collecting tool. Although nets are often used to capture flying insects, they can be designed to sample insects in other types of environments, such as on shrubs or in water. The basic construction of a net is fairly simple.

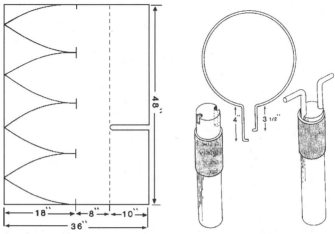

Plans for an insect net

It involves a handle, a metal loop attached to the handle and a collecting bag.

The handle should be lightweight and strong; a wooden dowel is a good choice. One end of the handle should have a groove cut on either side to attach the loop. Cut the grooves just deep enough to hold the loop, and drill a hole to help anchor the ends of the loop. For maximum strength, the ends of the loops should be slightly different lengths. For example, the hole in one groove should be 3 inches (7.6 cm) from the end of the handle, the other groove should be 2.5 inches (6.3 cm) in length.

The loop or ring of the net should be made of steel wire. Since the ring will receive a lot of wear, it should be sturdy. Piano wire or other wire about 3/8 inch (.9 cm) in diameter is just right. Twist the wire into a loop; most nets have a diameter of 12 to 15 inches (30.4–38.1 cm). The ends of the wire should be bent back sharply so that they are parallel to each other. Insert the ends of the wire into the grooves of the handle. The ring can then be kept in place by lashing with string or wire. Alternatively, a metal tube, the same circumference as the handle, can be used to attach the ring.

Your choice of material for the bag will determine the type of collecting to which the net will be best suited. Unbleached muslin or light duck is a good fabric for a net that will be used for sweeping plants. Dacron, nylon or another light, transparent material can be used to make an aerial net for capturing winged insects such as butterflies. Regardless of the type of net, the bag should be tapered and about twice as long as the diameter of the loop. The bag can be constructed from a single piece of cloth. A reinforced band should be sewn into the top of the net. There must be a hole in the band to allow threading of the ring. At the net opening, the bag is folded over and sewn to attach to the ring. In another design, a separate piece of cloth can be used to form a band that attaches to the loop. Since the edge of the bag attached to the loop receives a great deal of wear, a strong band will last longer. For this reason, bands are sometimes made of, or covered by, reinforcing materials such as canvas and even leather.

The *aerial net* (or butterfly net) is usually the first type of net to be used by a beginning collector. It is constructed with a light, thin, transparent material that lets air move through it freely, thus allowing it to be handled more easily and swiftly, which is useful for capturing fast-flying insects such as dragonflies and butterflies. This type of net also allows you to see the insects in the bag, which is especially important when you are removing a stinging insect or a delicate butterfly. An aerial net is poorly suited for sweeping plants, however, since it can be easily snagged and ripped.

Nets constructed with thicker fabrics such as muslin or canvas are known as *sweep nets* or *general-purpose nets*. These are excellent for sweeping plants, and can capture many insects that are not readily observed. They can also capture flying insects, although they are

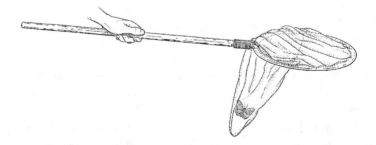

After you capture an insect, a twist of the net can prevent its escape.

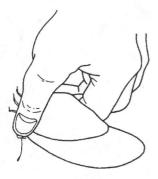

After being captured in a net, a butterfly can be stunned by pinching its thorax. This can prevent the insect from tearing its wings.

not as well adapted for this purpose because they are somewhat heavy and don't readily allow air flow. A *combination net* is a compromise between the aerial and sweep nets that suits some collecting purposes. With this design, most of the net is constructed similarly to a general-purpose net. However, the end of the net is made with mesh fabric, which allows captured insects to be observed and improves air flow through the bag.

For sampling insects in water, *aquatic nets* or *dip net*s are used. These are much sturdier in construction because they must support the weight of water and debris. They are used as a scoop and have a strong, screened bottom to allow water to drain. The edges are lined with a tough, canvas-type fabric, and sturdy mesh covers the bottom. Usually the front edge of the ring is straight rather than looped. Aquatic nets are more expensive to purchase or construct than other nets. For casual collectors a kitchen strainer is a good substitute for collecting aquatic insects.

Aquatic nets are constructed to help filter insects out of water and mud.

A kitchen strainer can also serve to collect aquatic insects.

INSECT KILLING JAR

To preserve insect specimens for a collection it is important that they be captured and killed in a manner that prevents them from being damaged. One useful method for insects collected around the home is to immediately place the insect in a freezer for a few days. It is advisable to remove the insect within a week to prevent drying. After thawing, the frozen insect can be pinned and mounted.

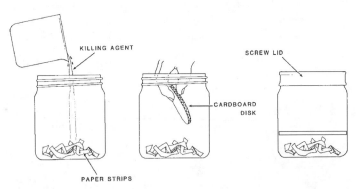

This simple design for an insect killing jar can be improved by substituting plaster of paris for the paper strips.

A *killing jar* is the primary means used to collect large numbers of insects or to collect insects during a trip. It may be useful to prepare several jars, particularly for collecting delicate insects like moths or butterflies, which are easily damaged by other insects, such as beetles.

Killing jars can be of various sizes and shapes. For beginning collectors, it is best to use a jar with a fairly wide opening, such as a peanut butter jar.

Insects are killed by an agent that produces lethal fumes. Ethyl acetate (an ingredient in nail polish remover) is the safest of the common killing agents and the best for beginning collectors. Furthermore, insects kept in a jar with ethyl acetate may remain soft for days. However, ethyl acetate killing jars require frequent recharging if they are used a lot. Also, ethyl acetate can stain specimens and dissolve plastic. Although insects are rapidly stunned by the fumes, it may take awhile for them to die, so they should be kept in the jar for at least a half-hour before removal. Ethyl acetate can be acquired from suppliers of insect-collecting equipment, some chemical supply outlets and even at supermarkets (as nail polish remover).

Insect being placed in a kill jar

The simplest method involves putting some sort of absorbent material in the jar and soaking it with the killing agent. Cotton balls or paper strips are effective for this purpose, provided they are covered with cardboard, screening or paper toweling to prevent the insects from becoming entangled. For a more permanent killing jar, mix plaster of paris with water and pour enough to fill the jar about 1 inch (2.5 cm). This provides an absorbent surface that can soak up the liquid ethyl acetate and slowly release fumes into the jar. The surface of the plaster of paris should be covered with cardboard or thick paper to slow down the release of the killing fluid and to prevent the insects from lying directly on the plaster surface.

INSECT TRAPS AND BAITS

Traps

Many night-flying insects are attracted to light, so various *light traps* are widely used for insect collecting. Many types of bulbs are available for attracting insects, although some, such as black light, ultraviolet and mercury vapor, are much more attractive than regular incandescent bulbs. Insect flights are usually greatest on calm warm evenings without too much moonlight.

Insects can be simply collected as they visit existing porch lights. Visitations are most frequent during the first few hours following dusk. A brighter surface can be produced by shining a light on a white sheet, a useful way to collect some of the larger moths.

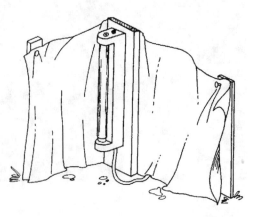

Light and sheet

Traps that physically collect the visiting insects can also be constructed. These attract insects to a light suspended over a collecting funnel. The addition of baffles next to the light improves this design. Flying insects attracted to the light hit the bulb or baffles, and drop down the funnel into the collecting container. The trapped insects can then be killed by use of a "pest strip." Light traps should be checked daily to prevent the insects from becoming badly damaged. During periods when large numbers of beetles are present, particularly May/June beetles, the collected insects may become badly scratched.

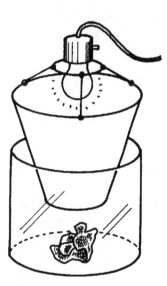

Light trap

Pitfall traps are useful for collecting insects that move over the soil surface, such as ground beetles and crickets. These involve sinking a cup or can into the ground so that the upper lip is flush with the soil surface. Most insects that attempt to crawl across the cup fall in and are trapped. A small amount of soapy water in the bottom can prevent escape by those that climb well, but such traps need to be checked daily.

The most difficult problem in collecting soil insects may be extracting them. Extracting can be accomplished easily, however, with a *Berlese funnel,* a simple method based on the tendency of most soil insects to avoid light and drying. A soil sample or debris suspected of containing insects, such as leaves or pine litter, is placed on a holding screen within a fairly long funnel. Ideally, a light should be suspended over the surface to accelerate the drying of the soil sample. As the surface of the sample dries, the insects move lower, ultimately falling down the funnel. They can then be collected in a collecting jar, containing alcohol or another preservative, from the base of the funnel.

Baits

Many insects can be collected with baits that are attractive to them. These can be used to lure the insects into a trap or concentrate them for easy collection.

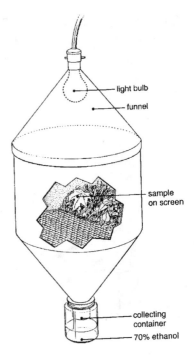

light bulb

funnel

sample on screen

collecting container

70% ethanol

Berlese funnel

One of the more common techniques of baiting involves *sugaring*. Many species of moths are attracted to sugary materials, particularly those that have fermented. Fruit (especially bananas or peaches) mixed with sugar makes a particularly good base for a bait. Such baits should be made into a thin paste and allowed to ferment for a couple days, ideally until the bubbling associated with fermentation is complete. Alternatively, beer and molasses mixtures can be used. Regardless of which bait is used, the mixture should be painted onto tree trunks or other surfaces in the early evening in bands several inches (centimeters) wide. As it gets dark, the baited site can be visited and carefully checked with a flashlight. Try not to startle the insects by shining the light directly on them. Moths or other insects feeding on the mixture can be easily picked off and collected. The baited areas should be checked repeatedly, since new insects may visit the bait. (*Note:* Some kinds of moths do not begin to become active until after midnight, although most will be active shortly after dusk.)

Dry *oatmeal baits* can be effective for concentrating various types of crickets, including camel crickets. This involves scattering the oatmeal in various locations in the early evening and then visiting the sites during the evening as the insects become active.

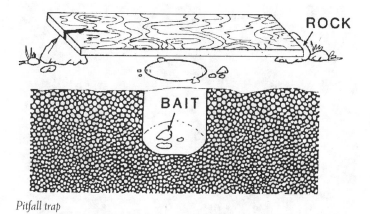

Pitfall trap

Insects often use chemicals, known as *pheromones*, to communicate with each other. For example, females of many moths produce sex pheromones that attract males of the same species from very long distances. Recently there has been a tremendous amount of research on insect pheromones and how they might be adapted for use in monitoring and managing insect pests. Pheromone traps are frequently used for these purposes: the pheromone lure is combined with some sort of trap, usually one with a sticky surface. Pheromone traps are most widely used to trap insects that damage fruit crops, such as the codling moth (adult of the common "apple worm") and various borers such as the peach tree borer. The traps can be purchased from specialty garden supply catalogs or agricultural supply companies.

Preserving and Displaying Insects
PINNING

Pinning is the most common means of preserving and displaying insects. Adult stages of all the large insects can be pinned directly. With smaller insects, it is usually best to glue them to a cardboard point, which is then mounted on a pin. Immature stages of insects (larvae, nymphs) and all stages of the other arthropods (spiders, centipedes, ticks, etc.) should be placed in alcohol-filled vials.

Special *insect pins* should be used whenever possible. These pins are very sharp and narrow to prevent damage to the insect and are

Some of the supplies useful for pinning an insect include pins, pinning block, points for small insects and labels.

rust- and corrosion-resistant. However, insect pins can be rather expensive, costing several cents each.

Insect pins come in a wide range of thicknesses, indicated by a numbering system. Thinner pins are given low numbers, for example, 00, 0 and 1. Thick pins, used for very large insects with tough body coverings, are ranked as no. 3 or no. 4. The no. 2 pin is standard for most commonly collected insects.

It is always best to pin insects either the same day or the morning after they are caught, before they have become dry and brittle. Any insect large enough to be pinned should be held firmly between the thumb and forefinger of the left hand, with its back upward. Then push the pin through the body.

A *pinning block* is a very useful aid to proper pinning; it helps to hold the insect while pinning and helps to place the insect at the proper level on the pin. Pinning blocks are also helpful for properly leveling the various labels used for insect collections. All insects should be pinned at the same height. In a correctly mounted collection, the upper surface of all the insects should appear at the same level. This leaves about 3/8 inch (.9 cm) of the pin showing above each insect.

Because it is best to display certain features useful for identification and allow for a more uniform appearance among insect

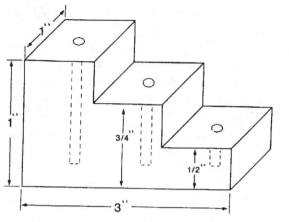

Design for a pinning block

collections, the proper location of the pin varies according to insect type. Beetles, cockroaches, crickets and mantids should be pinned through the right wing cover near its base. The pin should appear on the underside between the middle and hind legs. Grasshoppers and katydids should be pinned through the base of the prothorax, the large shieldlike plate behind the head. For the true

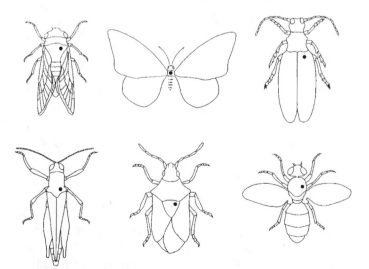

Proper pin placement for different insects

bugs (order Hemiptera) the pin should pass through the upper right corner of the triangular scutellum, which is located at the base of the front wings. For most other large insects, such as bees, wasps, butterflies, dragonflies, cicadas, flies and lacewings, the pin should be placed through the middle of the body (thorax) and should pass between the bases of the wings, slightly to the right side of the midline of the insect.

If an insect has dried, it may break or tear when it is pinned. It is therefore wise to use a *relaxing jar* to soften the insect. A simple design for a relaxing jar involves placing moistened sand in the bottom of a jar and covering the sand with cardboard. It is important not to leave insects in the relaxing jar too long or they will mold—two days is the maximum unless kept in a refrigerator. This problem can be reduced somewhat by moistening the sand with antiseptic mouthwash instead of water. Small insects may become relaxed in as little as a couple of hours, while large moths or butterflies may take a day or more.

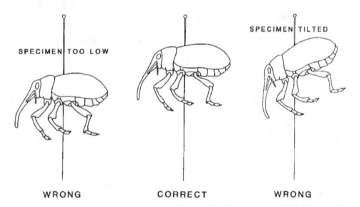

Correct and incorrect ways to pin an insect

POINTING

Insects that are too small to be mounted directly on an insect pin without injury are best mounted on *points*. Points are small triangular pieces of stiff white paper. They can easily be cut out or made rapidly and uniformly by means of a special "point-punch" available from entomology supply stores. The pin is pushed through the broad

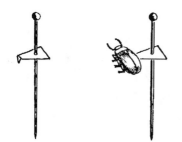

part of the point and the insect is glued crosswise on the tip. The insect should be mounted so that the small end of the point is directed toward the left. When properly mounted, the insect should be pointed away from you.

Use of points to display small insects

Mounting insects on points can be as easy as pinning them if the proper techniques are used. Place the insect on its back and touch the tip of the point into a drop of clear glue or clear nail polish. Touch the glued point to the proper spot on the underside of the insect. Usually the insect can be picked up immediately and oriented in place for the glue to dry.

SPREADING

Certain insects, such as butterflies, moths, dragonflies and damselflies should be mounted with their wings spread. Proper spreading helps to display the wing features useful for identification. Spreading also helps to give the specimens a more uniform and attractive appearance.

Spreading is most easily accomplished with the aid of a *spreading board*, which has a center groove for the body of the pinned insect, bordered by raised flat areas for the wings to rest and dry. Spreading boards can be constructed out of soft materials such as balsa wood, styrofoam or cork, or they may be purchased from biological supply houses.

To spread an insect, first pin it in the usual way. Place the insect in the center groove at a height at which the wings are parallel to the flattened surfaces. It is very important that the insect be fresh and flexible.

For butterflies and moths, gently work the front wings forward until the back edge is in a straight line at a right angle to the body. Once the wing is in place, fasten it to the board by overlaying a strip of paper (or waxed paper) on the wing and fastening the paper with pins. Do not pin directly through the wing. After properly

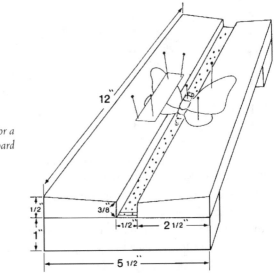

*Design for a
spreading board*

placing the front wing, position the hind wing so the front edge is in a straight line at a right angle to the body. The two wings should be just touching. Fasten the hind wing with a paper strip. Repeat with the other pair. Blunt forceps are useful for handling butterfly and moth wings and will not damage them.

Properly spreading butterflies and moths can be difficult and frustrating. With practice and patience, however, your ability to properly spread insect wings will improve. The end result is worth it: A well-prepared butterfly or moth collection is one of the most attractive parts of an insect collection.

PRESERVING

Soft-bodied arthropods, including the immature stages of insects, cannot be well displayed by pinning because they dry and shrivel. These should be placed in vials of alcohol.

Ethyl alcohol (ethanol) is the best preservative, although it can be difficult to obtain. Isopropyl alcohol (rubbing alcohol) is an alternative, although it is considerably more poisonous if ingested. The alcohol concentration should be about 70 percent. If large

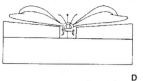
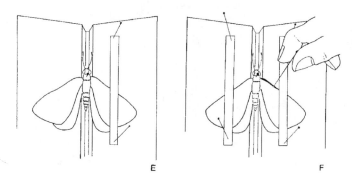

Spreading an insect

insects are to be preserved, larger vials containing greater amounts of alcohol should be used.

Vials should be airtight to prevent evaporation of the alcohol. Rubber stoppers are effective, as are screw-top vials with plastic inserts. However, most screw-top vials and cork stoppers will allow alcohol to evaporate. These require that the alcohol be continually replaced.

Insects preserved in alcohol often darken because of the chemicals (enzymes) that are not rapidly inactivated by the alcohol. This problem can be minimized by first boiling the insect, which breaks down the enzymes.

LABELING

Properly labeling an insect collection is extremely important. Certain collection information must be included with any insect specimen if it is to be of value to insect museums or to individuals studying insects. Proper labeling is also important in the judging of 4-H collections.

The most important information tag is the *locality label.* This label should include:

1. detailed information on the locality of the collection so that someone else could later re-collect specimens from the same area
2. date of the collection
3. collector's name or initials

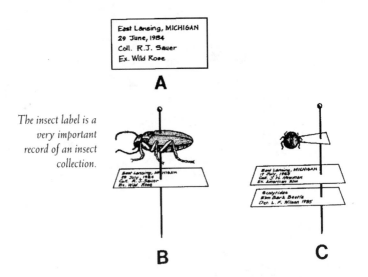

The insect label is a very important record of an insect collection.

The importance of a proper locality label cannot be stressed enough. Amateur collectors are always finding new or unusual specimens that may be of great interest and use to entomologists. However, to be of any use for study, the insects must have collection information.

When the insect can be identified, an *identification label* should be prepared. Ideally, an identification label will include the genus and species of the insect, for example, *Leptinotarsa decemlineata* (Say).

Beginning collectors may only be able to determine the family name, (such as Chrysomelidae) or the common name (Colorado potato beetle) of the insect.

Each label should be pinned at a different height. The locality label should be on top, immediately underneath the insect. This is followed by the identification label. A pinning block with holes of multiple depths is very useful for uniform labeling.

PRESERVING AN INSECT COLLECTION

If an insect collection is to be kept for an extended period of time, some maintenance is required to protect it. Dermestid beetles (carpet beetles) are the most common cause of damage or destruc-

The adult and larva of a common dermestid (carpet) beetle can damage insect collections; photograph courtesy of USDA.

tion to insect collections. These are very common insect scavengers found throughout the region, and feed on a wide variety of animal materials such as woolens and animal skins. In insect collections, small piles of brownish dust beneath the preserved insects are the most common evidence of infestation by dermestid beetles. Carrot-shaped, hairy larvae, or their old skins, are another indication.

Tight construction of the storage box will help to exclude dermestid beetles, but even well-constructed boxes may become infested. Most professionally maintained insect collections include a small amount of a fumigant insecticide in each display box. This may be a small piece of plastic impregnated with the insecticide DDVP (dichlorvos), sometimes sold as "fly strips."

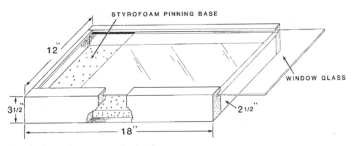

STYROFOAM PINNING BASE

12"

WINDOW GLASS

3 1/2"

2 1/2"

18"

Sample design for an insect display box

Moth crystals, which contain paradichlorobenzene (PDB), can also be used. PDB crystals are usually kept inside a small box in the corner of the collection. This confines the crystals and prevents them from directly contacting the bottom of the display box. Some plastics can be damaged by contact with PDB crystals. *Note:* Both dichlorvos and paradichlorobenzene are poisonous to humans. Treated insect collections should be stored in an area where exposure is minimized. Never store them in a refrigerator with food.

For small collections, a simple alternative is to periodically freeze the collection. Carpet beetles are fairly slow to develop, and if collections are put into a freezer once a year, damage by carpet beetles can be prevented. Do not store in the freezer or refrigerator any collection that contains moth crystals or "fly strips"; these will contaminate food.

Classifying Insects

Millions of species of animals and plants exist, and new species are discovered daily. For example, more than 1.5 million species of insects have been described, but it is estimated that probably less than 25 percent have yet been identified and named.

To help understand and identify the tremendous number of different organisms that exist, a method has been developed to classify all animals and plants in a systematic manner. *Taxonomy* is the science of classification of species in categories based on their similarities and differences. The foundation of taxonomy involves a *hierarchical system*, which allows the grouping of different species into a series of progressively more specialized and smaller categories. These categories include:

Kingdom
Phylum
Class
Order
Family
Genus
Species

At the end of the hierarchical system is the *species*, a group of organisms that is similar in structure and physiology and—most important—is capable of interbreeding to produce fertile young. The scientific name of a species is made up of two parts (binomial nomenclature): the *genus* name and the *species* name. For example, the scientific name for the housefly is *Musca domestica*. The classification of the housefly is as follows:

Kingdom: Animalia (all animals)
Phylum: Arthropoda (all arthropods—the "jointed-foot" animals)
Class: Insecta (all insects)
Order: Diptera (the two-winged or true flies)
Family: Muscidae
Genus: *Musca*
Species: *domestica*

The name of the person who originally described the insect usually follows the genus/species name. For example the housefly may be written as *Musca domestica* Linnaeus (or L.) because it was originally described by Linnaeus. If there has been a change in the genus name since the original description, the name of the describer will be in parentheses. For example, the complete scientific name of the Colorado potato beetle is *Leptinotarsa decemlineata* (Say). Thomas Say described this species and classified it as *Chrysomela decemlineata* at that time.

In addition to recognizing the individuals who originally helped to classify these insects, the inclusion of the human descriptor at the end of the scientific name is of great importance in categorizing the various insect species. Sometimes an insect has been separately identified by two or more individuals. (Although the great majority of insects appear to have never been described at all!) The accepted scientific name gives precedence to the first description and synonymizes the other names into those that are currently accepted worldwide. Although it may seem a bit awkward in the text, the complete scientific names, including that of the descriptor, are included in this book for greatest accuracy.

Insects and other arthropods often have a *common name*, the name used in normal conversation. However, even this term is standardized, since different insects may be given the same name in different areas of the country. For example, the common name "armyworm" correctly belongs only to the species *Pseudaletia unipuncta* (Haworth), a type of cutworm that damages wheat and barley crops and sometimes moves in large bands across fields during outbreaks. In northern Minnesota and Wisconsin, people commonly refer to the forest tent caterpillar, *Malacosoma disstria* (Hubner), as "armyworm," since it also moves in bands during outbreaks. Similarly, the term "miller moth" is applied worldwide to any type of moth that becomes so abundant that the scales from the wings may cover objects, like flour covering the smock of a miller. Without some standardization, the use of common names would not allow people to be confident that they were discussing the same insect. A committee of the Entomological Society of America is the referee for what should be the accepted common name. These names are used whenever possible in this book. However, many of the insects that are prominent in the Rocky Mountain region have never been given recognized common names. As a result, scientific names often must be used by default.

Characteristics of Insects and Insect Relatives

Insects comprise one group of animals within a larger group called the *Arthropoda* (meaning "jointed foot"). All arthropods possess the following combination of characteristics:

1. a segmented body
2. jointed appendages
3. a skeleton on the outside of the body (exoskeleton) made of chitin
4. growth that involves molting
5. a dorsal heart
6. a ventral nerve cord

Insects, as a distinct class of arthropods, also possess the following combination of characteristics:

1. three body regions (head, thorax and abdomen)
2. three pairs of legs (restricted to the thorax)
3. one pair of antennae
4. wings (usually) in the adult stage

Insect Growth

All insects begin their development as eggs produced by the adult female. Although some insects, such as aphids, may appear to give live birth, they produce eggs that hatch within the mother.

After eggs hatch, insects grow in a series of distinct stages. Each stage has a period of growth that is limited by the size of the exoskeleton. When maximum size has been reached, the insect sheds, or molts, its exoskeleton. During molting, a new exoskeleton is produced, which is larger than the previous one. A few hours following a molt, the new exoskeleton becomes hardened, and no further change in body size occurs until the following molt. Each intermediate stage between molts is called an *instar*. Body parts that remain soft, such as the thorax and abdomen of caterpillars, may expand somewhat during the course of an instar. All growth ceases following the final molt to the adult stage of the insect. (A small beetle will remain a small beetle and is not a "baby" large beetle.)

As insects develop, they also undergo changes in form, called *metamorphosis*. The kinds of changes vary among different insect groups, but there are two general types of metamorphosis: *simple metamorphosis* (hemimetabolous) and *complete metamorphosis* (holometabolous).

Characteristics of Common Arthropod Groups (Classes)

Arthropod Class (Common Name)	Distinguishing Characteristics	
Crustacea (shrimp, crayfish, sowbugs, pillbugs, etc.)	Five to 7 pairs of legs; 2 body regions (cephalothorax and abdomen); 2 pairs of antennae.	*A crustacean (sowbug)*
Arachnida (spiders, mites, ticks, daddy longlegs, scorpions, etc.)	Four pairs of legs; 2 body regions (cephalothorax and abdomen); no antennae.	*An arachnid (scorpion)*
Diplopoda (millipedes)	Elongate, usually rounded bodies; numerous body segments (typically about 50); appear to have 2 pairs of small, jointed legs at each segment.	*Millipedes*

Characteristics of Common Arthropod Groups (Classes)

Arthropod Class (Common Name)	Distinguishing Characteristics	
Symphyla (symphylans, garden centipedes)	Slender, pale-colored, small [1–8 mm]) soil-dwelling arthropods with 10 to 12 pairs of legs and 15–22 body segments.	*A symphylan*
Chilopoda (centipedes)	Elongate, usually flattened bodies; 14 to 20 body segments; appear to have 1 pair of legs at each segment.	*A centipede*
Insecta/Hexapoda (insects)	Three distinct body regions (head, thorax, abdomen); 3 pairs of legs; adults of many species are winged; single pair of antennae.	*An insect (lady beetle)*

Insects undergoing simple metamorphosis (also called *incomplete* or *gradual metamorphosis*) have three basic life-forms: *egg*, *nymph* and *adult*. Nymphs typically molt three to five times. Nymphs and adults often live in the same habitat, with the principal changes being size, body proportion and the development of wings during metamorphosis. Insects that undergo simple metamorphosis include grasshoppers, crickets, earwigs, the "true" bugs (Hemiptera), aphids and related insects.

Insects that undergo complete metamorphosis pass through four basic life-forms: *egg, larva, pupa* and *adult*. Caterpillars, maggots and grubs are typical examples of larvae. During the larval stage there may be three to seven instars (sometimes more) that usually feed. The pupal stage that follows (cocoon, puparia, chrysalid) is a nonfeeding stage during which the insect changes to the adult form. Adults are usually winged and may differ from the larval form in a number of ways, including type of legs, mouthparts and feeding habits. Adults of insects undergoing complete metamorphosis are very different in form from the larvae and may be found in very

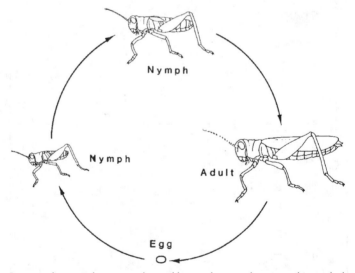

Insects such as grasshoppers, crickets and bugs undergo simple metamorphosis, which involves three life stages: egg, nymph and adult.

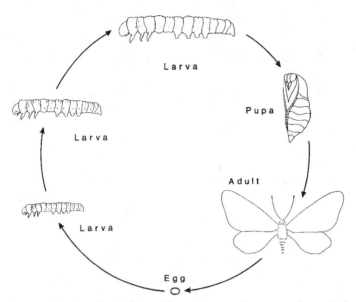

Insects such as butterflies, beetles and flies undergo complete metamorphosis, which involves four life stages: egg, larva, pupa and adult.

different habitats. Insects with complete metamorphosis include butterflies, moths, beetles, flies and lacewings.

Some variations of the pattern of metamorphosis occur with other insects. Some of the oldest orders that have primitive characteristics (for example, bristletails, firebrats, proturans) show very little change in external features from immature to mature stages, other than an increase in size. These are known as ametabolous insects. Several of the aquatic insects with simple metamorphosis, such as the dragonflies, stoneflies and mayflies, typically have aquatic immature stages, called nymphs or naiad, that do not resemble the winged adults. Thrips, scales, whiteflies and some other insects have nonfeeding stages that resemble the pupal stage found in complete metamorphosis.

Outline of Insect Orders

(Based on classification scheme of Borror, Triplehorn and Johnson, 1989.)

Order (Common Name)	Type of Metamorphosis
Protura (proturans)	Primitive type with little change in features, other than size, between immature and mature stages.
Diplura (diplurans)	Primitive type with little change in features, other than size, between immature and mature stages.
Microcoryphia (bristletails)	Primitive type with little change in features, other than size, between immature and mature stages.
Thysanura (silverfish, firebrats)	Primitive type with little change in features, other than size, between immature and mature stages.
Ephemeroptera (mayflies)*	A variation on simple metamorphosis with immature, aquatic forms.
Odonata (dragonflies and damselflies)*	A variation on simple metamorphosis with immature, aquatic forms.
Orthoptera (grasshoppers and crickets)*	Simple.
Grylloblattaria (rock crawlers)*	Simple.
Phasmida (walkingsticks)*	Simple.
Mantodea (mantids)*	Simple.
Blattaria (cockroaches)*	Simple.
Isoptera (termites)*	Simple.
Plecoptera (stoneflies)*	A variation on simple metamorphosis with immature, aquatic forms.
Dermaptera (earwigs)*	Simple.
Embiidina (webspinners)	Simple.

* Orders included in this book.

Outline of Insect Orders

(Based on classification scheme of Borror, Triplehorn and Johnson, 1989.)

Order (Common Name)	Type of Metamorphosis
Psocoptera (psocids)	Simple.
Phthiraptera (lice)*	Simple.
Zoraptera (zorapterans)	Simple.
Hemiptera (true bugs)*	Simple.
Homoptera (cicadas, hoppers, some aphids, psyllids, white-flies, scale insects)*	Simple, but some species show features that are intermediate with complete metamorphosis.
Thysanoptera (thrips)*	A variation on simple metamorphosis including nonfeeding stages prior to adult emergence.
Neuroptera (alderflies, dobson-flies, snakeflies, fishflies, lace-wings, antlions and owlflies)*	Complete.
Coleoptera (beetles)*	Complete.
Strepsiptera (twisted-wing parasites)	Complete.
Mecoptera (scorpionflies)	Complete.
Siphonaptera (fleas)*	Complete.
Diptera (flies, gnats, mosquitoes, etc.)*	Complete.
Trichoptera (caddisflies)*	Complete.
Lepidoptera (butterflies, moths, skippers)*	Complete.
Hymenoptera (sawflies, ichneu-mons, chalcids, ants, wasps and bees)*	Complete.

* Orders included in this book.

The Big Bugs
of the Rockies

ORDER: ORTHOPTERA
Grasshoppers, Crickets and Katydids

The order Orthoptera includes some of the most familiar and easily collected insects in the region: the grasshoppers and crickets. As a group they are generally recognized by having a front pair of thickened and leathery wings (the tegmina) and membranous hind wings. However, some species of Orthoptera are wingless or have very reduced wings, such as the Mormon cricket (actually a type of longhorned grasshopper related to katydids). Grasshoppers and crickets are also usually characterized by large hind legs designed for jumping. Orthoptera have mouthparts designed for chewing. Most species feed upon plants; many are predators or scavengers.

Most older entomology books have included a wide variety of insects within the order Orthoptera, such as grasshoppers, mantids, cockroaches and many other insects that have chewing mouthparts, leathery forewings and threadlike antennae. In recent years, however, most scientists working with the classification of insects (insect taxonomists) have agreed that there are enough differences to separate the order Orthoptera (grasshoppers, crickets, etc.) from other groups of insects such as walkingsticks (Phasmida), mantids (Mantodea), cockroaches (Blattaria) and rock crawlers (Grylloblattaria). The latter classification scheme is used in this book. The larger local species of these other orders are discussed in following sections.

Many Orthoptera are capable of "singing," by making chirping or buzzing noises, creating the "chorus of the night." The crickets and longhorned grasshoppers produce noise by rubbing the sharp edge of one forewing (called the scraper) against a filelike edge (the file) of the other wing. Other groups produce noises by snapping the hind wings or by rubbing the hind legs on the front wings. Usually the male produces these sounds, primarily to attract females for mating.

Orthoptera have simple metamorphosis. Grasshoppers usually lay eggs in masses or pods in the soil, while others lay eggs in small groups, such as the conspicuous flattened eggs many katydids deposit on twigs. Some species, such as the Mormon cricket, have different forms and colors that are produced in response to environmental conditions such as crowding.

Grasshopper egg pod

Orthoptera are best displayed by pinning. The pin should be placed through the upper right wing cover of the prothorax. Most Orthoptera can be easily maintained for a limited time in captivity, and some, such as house crickets, can even be reared.

Largest Grasshopper—Plains Lubber/Homesteader
Brachystola magna (**Girard**)

Order: Orthoptera

Family: Acrididae (sometimes Romaleidae)

Distribution: Short-grass prairie and rangeland areas from Montana south to Mexico.

Life History and Habits: Winter is spent in the egg stage. Eggs are laid in pods in the soil and hatch in late spring. The young grasshoppers feed on various broadleaf plants, such as wild sunflowers and shrubs. The plains lubber does not feed on grasses.

A plains lubber grasshopper, also known as the homesteader

Development is completed in approximately two months, with adults first appearing in early July. They continue to feed and lay eggs until early fall, dying out with the occurrence of killing frosts. There is one generation per year.

Related Species: Close to one hundred species of grasshoppers are recorded from the region. These show a wide range in life cycles, with various species overwintering as either nymphs, adults or eggs. Most are not considered destructive, restricting their feeding to plants that do not cause economic losses. However, there are several serious pest species, primarily in the genus *Melanoplus*. This includes the differential grasshopper, *M. differentialis* (Thomas); the migratory grasshopper, *M. sanguinipes* (Fabricius); the two-striped grasshopper, *M. bivittatus* (Say); and the redlegged grasshopper, *M. femurrubrum* (De Geer).

A differential grasshopper feeding on a leaf

A pair of twostriped grasshoppers rest on a leaf. The abdomen of the large female is swollen with eggs.

Several other large grasshoppers occur in the grasslands and foothills from New Mexico through Montana. Perhaps most striking is the giant crested grasshopper, *Tropidolophus formosus* (Say). This large (1.5 to almost 2 inches [3.8–5 cm]) green species is marked with a prominent toothed crest behind the head. It has a similar life cycle to that of the lubber grasshopper, but feeds on various plants in the mallow family. It is not considered to be a pest species.

The red shanks, *Xanthippus corallipes* Haldeman, rivals the lubber grasshopper in size. Markings of this grasshopper can be quite variable and differ with the habitat in which it is found, ranging from the plains to nearly timberline. All are marked with orange and red legs and red, yellow or orange hind wings. The red shanks feeds on grasses and occasionally is a destructive species. The complete life cycle takes two years to complete, with winter spent during the first year as an egg, the second year as a nymph.

Collecting Tips: Lubber grasshoppers have short wings and do not fly. Instead they move by walking and jump only short distances. Consequently, lubber grasshoppers can be difficult to see while they are on the ground. They are more easily collected while resting on shrubbery or plants such as wild sunflowers, or while crossing roads. The best time to look for lubber grasshoppers is from mid-July through early September.

Some types of lubber grasshoppers are commonly sold by biological supply houses. Because of their large size, they are very useful for dissection in biology classes. If large numbers are known to occur in your area, you may wish to contact a biological supply house or high school biology teachers for possible sale.

Rearing Tips: Grasshoppers can be fairly easily maintained in a small aquarium, large glass jar or cut plastic bottle. Most grasshoppers will survive well on a diet of lettuce, fresh grass and other vegetable matter, although it is a good idea to supplement this with some bran or wheat germ. A supply of additional water is not necessary when raising grasshoppers, as they get moisture from food. Conditions within the rearing container should be on the dry side. Most grasshoppers will lay eggs if provided with a cup of moist sand, although eggs usually will not hatch until they have gone through a chilling period.

A Large Grasshopper—Green or Lined Bird Grasshopper
Schistocerca alutacea (Harris)

Order: Orthoptera

Family: Acrididae

Distribution: This grasshopper is found throughout the region, with a range that extends into the northeastern United States. Three subspecies occur in the Rocky Mountain region, each of which tends to occur in different habitats. For example, the whitelined bird grasshopper, *Schistocerca alutacea albolineata* (Thomas), is most often found in mountainous areas; the lined bird grasshopper,

Lined bird grasshopper

S. a. lineata Scudder, mostly in sand-hill areas and the green bird grasshopper, *S. a. shoshone* (Thomas) along riverways.

Life History and Habits: These grasshoppers spend the winter in the egg stage, massed in bunches of about thirty to sixty eggs laid in soil. Eggs hatch in May and June, and the grasshoppers begin to feed on various herbaceous plants such as legumes and large weeds. They will also feed on grasses but are not considered a pest species since they are never sufficiently abundant to cause much injury. Adult stages are present from the middle of summer through the killing frosts in fall.

There is one generation per year. Eggs are laid as masses in dry undisturbed sites, such as around tunnels of burrowing rodents or areas of drifted sand, at the end of the growing season.

The adults are strong fliers, capable of covering one hundred yards or more in a single flight.

Related Species: Several species of grasshoppers can be found in the region, all of which are large. In northern areas of the region, the spotted bird, *Schistocerca emarginata* (Scudder), can be found. In southern areas the gray bird grasshopper, *S. nitens* (Thunberg), is sometimes encountered, while the American grasshopper, *S. americana* (Drury) is widespread. This genus includes *S. gregaria* (Forskal), the notorious "locusts" that periodically occur in devastating swarms throughout northern Africa and the Mideast.

Collecting Tips: The adult grasshoppers rest on the foliage of large weeds or shrubs during the night and are most easily collected in the morning before they warm up and become active. They can be difficult to collect since they are strong fliers. They are most commonly associated with areas of lush plant growth.

A Common Large Grasshopper—Carolina Grasshopper
Dissosteira carolina (Linnaeus)

Order: Orthoptera

Family: Acrididae

Distribution: Widespread throughout much of North America. Apparently some of its distribution is due to human activities, which have allowed it to follow railroads and other roadways.

Carolina grasshopper

Life History and Habits: The overwintering stage is eggs laid in pods in exposed areas of undisturbed soil in late summer and early fall. Eggs hatch in spring and develop during May, June and July. It feeds on a variety of plants, most often a mixture of grasses and broadleaf weeds. However, it is rarely abundant enough to cause any significant damage to desirable plants. Some grasshoppers begin to mature to the adult stage by early July and are present until killed by frosts.

These familiar large grayish grasshopper have striking bands hind wings. They are capable fliers and make zigzag flights of escape when disturbed. During mating the males may hover in the air and create an audible "click-a-click" sound.

Related Species: A native species of the Rocky Mountain region is the High Plains grasshopper, *Dissosteira longipennis* (Thomas). It is primarily found in plains areas east of the Rocky Mountains and occasionally is reported to damage corn, sorghum and other summer grain crops. It is separated from the Carolina grasshopper by having more mottled forewing and a less pronounced dark banding on the underwings.

Collecting Tips: This insect can be found along roadsides, next to parking lots and railroad rights-of-way. The adults are quite agile and are one of the most difficult species to capture with a net.

Largest Longhorned Grasshopper— Mormon Cricket
Anabrus simplex Haldeman

Order: Orthoptera

Family: Tettigoniidae

Distribution: Distributed throughout the region, particularly west of the Continental Divide. In most areas, however, populations are very low and individuals are difficult to find. In recent years, large outbreaks of the Mormon cricket have been particularly frequent around Dinosaur National Monument in Colorado.

Life History and Habits: Mormon crickets spend the winter as eggs laid in the soil. Eggs are laid in midsummer not in masses, but sin-

A female Mormon cricket, solitary phase

gly, in firm but not hard soil that is free from roots (such as barren hillsides). Eggs hatch in mid- to late spring.

Mormon crickets can develop very different physical features and habits depending on the density of populations. Normally they occur in the "solitary phase," generally green or pale brown in color. During outbreaks they transform to a "gregarious phase" that is dark brown to black and slightly larger in size than the solitary-phase Mormon crickets. Gregarious-phase Mormon crickets band together and move in masses.

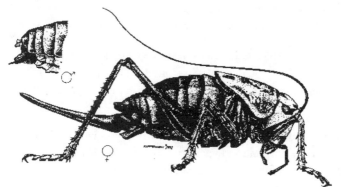

This detailed drawing of a female Mormon cricket highlights the difference between the hind end of the female and the male (upper left); drawing by Mike Kippenhan.

During outbreaks Mormon crickets may form large bands in the day time. These may move several hundred yards (meters) per day and 25 to 50 miles (40–80 km) during a single season. Because of this migratory habit, they may be present in a single location for only a few days.

The Mormon cricket is a general feeder, being particularly fond of various shrubs and broadleaf plants, especially flowers. It is also highly cannibalistic and readily feeds on other Mormon crickets that are wounded, killed or vulnerable during molting.

Mormon crickets can damage cropland when the migrating bands move into fields. They are also a concern to ranchers, although most of their feeding is restricted to shrubs and flowering plants, rather than grasses. The common name is derived from the threat they posed to the crops of early Mormon settlers in Utah.

Despite their name, Mormon crickets are actually a species of longhorned grasshopper or shieldbacked katydid (Tettigoniidae family), rather than a true cricket (Gryllidae family).

Collecting Tips: In most areas, Mormon crickets are uncommon and are infrequently collected. However, during outbreaks they are very easily collected in large numbers. In recent years these outbreaks have been most common in the area around Dinosaur National Monument in Colorado. During early morning and evening, they may be found in "roosts" on sagebrush, serviceberry and other shrubs. In the day, gregarious-phase Mormon crickets can be found moving in bands of various size. They produce an unpleasant odor and may give a mildly painful pinch with their mouthparts if handled carelessly.

LARGEST KATYDID—BROWNWINGED DECTICID
Capnobotes fuliginosus (Thomas)

Order: Orthoptera

Family: Tettigoniidae

Distribution: Associated primarily with piñon-juniper habitats of New Mexico, Utah and southern Colorado, particularly west of the Continental Divide.

Life History and Habits: Eggs are laid on plants and hatch the following spring. The young katydids develop during the season,

Brownwinged decticid

becoming full grown in late summer. The brownwinged decticid eats a variety of plant and animal foods, and is partially carnivorous on other small insects. Mating and egg laying occur primarily in August and September. There is one generation per year.

Related Species: A somewhat smaller green species, *Capnobotes occidentalis* (Thomas), shares much of its distribution with the brownwinged decticid and is even found farther north through Idaho. The broadwinged katydid, *Microcentrum rhombifolium* (Saussure), is common throughout much of the region. This is a large green species that feeds on the leaves of various trees. Several other large katydids are native to southern areas of the region, including *Neoconocephalus robustus* (Scudder) and several species in the genus *Scudderia*.

A true katydid

Recently, the true katydid, *Pterophylla camellifolia* (Fabricius), has become established in parts of the Front Range area of Colorado. The males of this large insect, present in late summer and early fall, are night singers that make loud mating calls, described as "lisps" and "ticks." The females lay flat brown eggs on smaller twigs in overlapping double rows.

Collecting Tips: Despite its large size, the brownwinged decticid is uncommon and not often collected. The males, which rest in trees and shrubs, make mating calls at night and can be collected at lights. Mating calls are made in late summer. Adults can sometimes be found on roads after a late afternoon thunderstorm.

The broadwinged katydid, and many other related species, can be collected during searches of trees and shrubs at night. They make distinctive clicks or buzzing sounds and can be located by aid of a flashlight.

Largest Field Crickets—*Gryllus* Species
Gryllus pennsylvanicus Burmeister
Gryllus veletis (Alexander and Bigelow)

Order: Orthoptera

Family: Gryllidae

Distribution: Widespread and common throughout the region.

Life History and Habits: Both species of these common field crickets are extremely similar in appearance, being black with fine gray hairs on the area behind the head (pronotum). However, they can be easily distinguished by the time of the season when they are active. Adults of *Gryllus veletis* are present in the spring, whereas *G. pennsylvanicus* occurs in midsummer through fall.

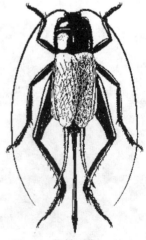

Field cricket

Overwintering stages of the two species differ. *G. veletis* spends this period as a nearly full-grown nymph within a soil burrow and molts to the adult stage in spring. The female lays eggs in late spring and early summer. The eggs are inserted in small groups into slightly damp soil with her swordlike ovipositor. The developing nymphs are present throughout the remainder of the year.

The life cycle of *G. pennsylvanicus* parallels that of *G. veletis*, but is shifted so that most stages occur later in the season and are completed more rapidly. It spends the winter in the egg stage, hatching in May and June. Developing nymphs are usually present throughout early summer, with adults first appearing in midsummer. Overwintering eggs are laid at this time.

Males and females can easily be distinguished by the presence or absence of the prominent ovipositor, used by the females to lay eggs. Field crickets are also well known among the "singing" insects, producing the familiar "chirp, chirp, chirp" noises of the night. Only the males produce this noise, which is used to attract mates and defend territories.

Field crickets eat a wide variety of plant materials. They have occasionally caused damage to various crops such as alfalfa, tomatoes and beans. They also may be an annoying nuisance when they move into homes and chirp, which happens most commonly late in the season, when cool weather causes them to seek shelter.

Related Species: Several species of tree crickets (*Oecanthus* species) are common in the region. These are delicate, pale green insects that are less commonly seen than heard. Tree crickets are among the noisiest of the night-singing insects, making their evening calls from trees and shrubs.

Tree cricket; photograph courtesy of Oregon State University Cooperative Extension

The house cricket, *Acheta domesticus* (Linnaeus), is an introduced insect not common in the wilds of the region. However, this cricket is a familiar one: It is reared for use as food for pets such as lizards and snakes and for school science projects.

Collecting Tips: Field crickets are common insects that are fairly easily collected in most areas. One of the better ways to capture them is to overturn rocks, boards or other materials under which they hide during the day.

Rearing Tips: Field crickets and house crickets are among the most easily reared insects, although regular maintenance is important. The bottom of the container should be covered with dried grass clippings, shredded paper or straw; some shelter should be provided, such as an old pinecone or corrugated cardboard.

Crickets need a supplemental water source, which can be provided by wetting tissue paper or a cotton ball every couple of days, changing the water source if any molds develop. Crickets generally like a dry environment, so the water source should be protected to avoid leakage into the rearing container.

Crickets will feed on a wide variety of plant and animal materials. Dried pet foods, fish flakes, wheat germ and bran make a good basic diet. Cut pieces of apple, carrot, potato or other vegetables may be useful to further vary the diet. Uneaten foods, soiled bedding material and dead crickets should be cleaned out regularly.

Crickets will lay eggs in moist sand or slightly wetted cotton. The eggs are pale colored and cylindrical.

LARGEST GRYLLACRIDID GRASSHOPPER— JERUSALEM CRICKET
Stenopelmatus fuscus Haldeman and Other Species

Order: Orthoptera

Family: Stenopelmatidae (or subfamily Stenopelmatinae of the Gryllacrididae)

Distribution: Generally distributed in western North America, particularly west of the Continental Divide

Life History and Habits: Jerusalem crickets, sometimes called "Children of the Earth," are primarily predators or scavengers of insects,

Insect Songsters

Many insects attract our attention by their production of audible noises. Some of these are so common that they help define seasons for us, such as the daytime buzzing of dog day cicadas in midsummer or the song of tree crickets at night.

Insects can produce noises by various means, of which only a few have been studied. Some insects have special structures for noise production, while others produce noise as a by-product of other activities such as flying. A summary of the noise-production mechanisms of some of the more common regional songsters is provided below.

Field crickets and katydids produce noise by raising and then rubbing their wings together. One wing is a raised ridge (known as a file) across which another ridge (known as a scraper) is drawn. This produces a rapid series of chirping noises that are amplified by a resonating membrane in the wing. These are among the loudest insects and will sometimes produce coordinated, pulsing choruses. Only the males produce sounds, which are used to attract females as mates.

The noises produced by grasshoppers differ slightly in that one of the ridged surfaces they use consists of a series of pegs that are rubbed against a raised surface on the forewing. Other grasshoppers and the Jerusalem cricket can make audible noises by rubbing or beating the ground with their legs or abdomen.

Male cicadas produce sound by means of air vibrations. These insects have a pair of drumlike organs, known as tymbals, on the sides of the thorax. By alternately contracting and releasing their muscles, they can produce a rapid series of clicking that is perceived as a buzzing. An associated air cavity acts to resonate the sound.

Flies and mosquitoes produce noises during flight; the tones are related to the frequency of the wing beat. For most species, these sounds are not audible to humans, although the whine of the **Culex tarsalis** mosquito at night is familiar to most. It is the females that produce these noises, and males are attracted to them. Furthermore, only sexually mature female mosquitoes produce noises to which males respond; the frequencies used by immature females differ and are not attractive.

Insects may also make noises with small movements of their wings, even when not in flight, as occurs when a bumblebee is gathering pollen.

A Jerusalem cricket or "Child of the Earth"; photograph courtesy of Brigham Young University

spiders and other small arthropods. Occasionally they will also feed on plant material such as roots and tubers.

Jerusalem crickets are active at night, living within burrows constructed under rocks and other cover during the day. They may inadvertently enter homes, usually basements, or be encountered under porches. Both adult and immature (nymph) stages overwinter in the soil. They have a very prolonged life cycle and take about four to five years to mature.

Related Species: Several species of Jerusalem crickets apparently occur in the region. However, they can be distinguished only by differences in the songs produced by the adult males.

Collecting Tips: Jerusalem crickets are best collected at night using lights to search areas of bare ground. They will also feed on baits of oatmeal spread out during the evening, and can be concentrated on these oatmeal baits during the night searches. During the day they may be found hiding under rocks, wood and other debris.

Jerusalem crickets will readily bite if handled carelessly, giving a painful pinch.

Edible Insects

Insects once made up an important part of the diet of the Native Americans that lived in the Rocky Mountain region. A variety of species were used, primarily those that were easily collected in large numbers, such as grasshoppers, Mormon crickets and certain caterpillars. Less commonly, other insects, such as shore flies, cicadas, salmonflies, yellow jackets and ants, were eaten, when they occurred in sufficient abundance that their food value exceeded the effort to collect them.

Grasshoppers were perhaps the most important of the insect foods eaten by Native Americans in the West. They were sometimes collected by digging a deep pit and driving the insects into it, resulting in the capture of bushels of grasshoppers at a time. The grasshoppers were usually prepared by roasting, but sometimes were immediately eaten raw or saved for winter stores, since they preserved well. Most often they were ground into flour and eaten in cakes mixed with other foods, such as sunflower seeds, or added to soups. Mormon crickets were often captured and prepared in a similar manner.

Two of the most highly prized caterpillars were those of the pandora moth and the whitelined sphinx, both of which are large and often abundant. Regular journeys were made to the pine forests that supported the pandora moth. The larvae or pupae were parched in fires and eaten immediately or stored after air drying. These foods were frequently traded among tribes.

One of the best sites for collecting and eating insects was along the shores of the Great Salt Lake. Large numbers of grasshoppers would land on the lake and later be swept ashore in windrows. Shore flies (Ephydridae family) fed on the organic debris along the shoreline and sometimes occurred in spectacular concentrations that could easily be collected. These insects not only were readily available for foraging but also stored well because of the salt.

The food value of most insects is very high. For example, grasshoppers and crickets are typically at least 50 percent protein, while caterpillars are rich in fats and calories. Several vitamins, notably A and D, may be concentrated in insects.

Western culture is highly biased against the idea of eating insects; when the practice occurs, it is usually considered to be a novelty rather than a substantial food source. (Yet, various crustaceans—such as lobsters, crabs, crayfish and shrimp—are considered delicacies.) Using insects for food is still a widespread practice in cultures throughout the world, however. Insects are being seriously proposed by many researchers as an excellent future source of protein that is currently underutilized.

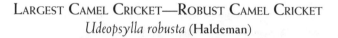

Largest Camel Cricket—Robust Camel Cricket
Udeopsylla robusta (Haldeman)

Robust camel cricket

Order: Orthoptera

Family: Gryllacrididae

Distribution: Generally distributed in the region, especially around sand blowouts. Populations are often restricted to fairly small areas of loose or sandy soil.

Life History and Habits: The robust camel cricket is primarily a predator of other insects, although it also takes some plant foods and other organic debris. It hunts at night, returning to shelter during the day. Most produce a semipermanent burrow under the sand, 1.5 feet (.45 m) or more in length, to which they return and rest during the day. The males, distinguished by very enlarged hind legs, are more active foragers than the females, which tend to stay in the vicinity of the burrow.

The life history of these insects has been little studied. Eggs are inserted in the sand. The insects appear to require a year or more to become full grown.

Related Species: Several other large camel crickets occur in the region. The Great Plains camel cricket, *Daihinia brevipes* Haldeman, occurs in eastern Colorado and New Mexico and has habits similar to those of the robust camel cricket. Perhaps the most unusual species is the giant sand treader, *Daihinibaenetes giganteus* Tinkham, which is found only in three highly localized areas, including the Great Sand Dunes National Monument in the San Luis Valley of Colorado.

The giant sand treader is found only in areas where large sand dunes occur.

Smaller species of camel crickets commonly invade cellars and crawl spaces of homes. One abundant species west of the Continental Divide is the Utah camel cricket, *Ceuthophilus utahensis* Thomas. This cricket is attracted to moisture sources; large numbers have been reported to collect in wells.

Collecting Tips: Robust camel crickets can be found under rocks or logs or around rodent burrows. Since they hunt at night, they are most easily collected using lights at night. They will also gather around and feed on piles of oatmeal baits placed out during periods when they are active. However, they sometimes emerge in afternoon after a light rain. Adults are most commonly collected in June and July.

If the sand is undisturbed, the tracks left by the crickets may lead to burrows, which can then be dug out. This is best accomplished by inserting a straw into the hole and excavating around it with a small hand shovel.

Since the insects are cannibalistic, they should not be kept together in collecting jars.

ORDER: GRYLLOBLATTARIA
Rock Crawlers/Ice Crawlers

Rock crawlers are one of the most unusual and obscure groups of insects, with only twenty known species in the world. All are adapted to cold environments, such as around glaciers or ice caves. Indeed, the optimal temperature for one species was calculated to be around 38.5°F (3.75°C). They are pale-colored, elongate insects that reach only about 1/2 to 3/4 inch (1.3–1.9 cm) when full grown. Only one species is known from the region covered in this book.

LARGEST ROCK CRAWLER—
GRYLLOBLATTA CAMPODEIFORMIS E. M. WALKER

A rock crawler; photograph courtesy of Brigham Young University

Order: Grylloblattaria

Family: Grylloblattidae

Distribution: Found within the Rocky Mountains from Alberta south to Yellowstone National Park. Several related species are found in alpine areas of the northern Rockies as well as the Cascade and Sierra Nevada mountain ranges.

Life History and Habits: The biology of these insects is very unusual in that they are adapted to live in areas that remain at or below freezing temperatures throughout most of the year. If summer temperatures become too warm, they retreat deep into the ground. In winter, rather than hibernate, they move upward to find sites that are just above freezing.

Rock crawlers feed at night, foraging on the ground or snow surfaces. Most of their diet consists of dead and dying insects, with winter craneflies (*Chionea* species) being one of their most important foods. Some plant material may also be eaten.

Eggs are laid singly, in soil crevices or moss, and may take a year to hatch. Nymphs can take up to five years to develop, molting eight or more times. The entire life cycle may require seven years to complete, making rock crawlers some of the most long-lived insects.

Related Species: Thirteen species of rock crawlers are known to occur in North America, all classified in the genus *Grylloblatta*. Within the region, these insects are rare, and *G. campodeiformis* is the only species found.

Collecting Tips: These insects are most commonly found on mountain slopes of loose debris or talus, near the edge where vegetation occurs.

Order: BLATTARIA
Cockroaches

The order Blattaria is a rather infamous group of insects, as many species of cockroaches have adapted extremely well to human-altered environments and thrive in dwellings and other structures. However, these introduced pest species, such as the German cockroach, are of subtropical origin and cannot survive outdoors under the environmental conditions of the Rocky Mountain region. The few species of cockroaches native to the region, the wood roaches (*Parcoblatta* species), have innocuous habits and are usually found around fallen leaves and other sites where there is moist plant debris. They can sometimes be collected when they fly to lights on warm summer evenings.

As a group, cockroaches are generally recognized as having an oval shape, with the head concealed—when viewed from above—by a shieldlike plate (pronotum). Most cockroaches are winged, with thickened front wings and more membranous hind wings. However, several important species have very reduced wings, such as the oriental cockroach and brownbanded cockroach. Cockroaches have very long filamentous antennae and conspicuous tail-like cerci.

Cockroaches undergo simple metamorphosis. Eggs are laid in distinctive capsules, called oothecae, that are dropped or carried by the female.

Cockroaches are best displayed by pinning. The pin should be placed through the upper right wing cover of the thorax.

An American cockroach feeds on a cracker; photograph courtesy of USDA.

LARGEST COCKROACH—AMERICAN COCKROACH
Periplaneta americana (**Linnaeus**)

Order: Orthoptera/Blattaria

Family: Blattidae

Distribution: Distributed worldwide, except in the extreme northern areas. They are usually found in man-made structures where they have been introduced, often by transporting egg pods (oothecae).

Life History and Habits: This large (1.5-inch [3.8-cm]) brown cockroach is easily identified by its yellow-brown pronotum marked with two large chestnut-brown spots. Eggs of the American cockroach are laid in oothecae typically containing about sixteen eggs. The oothecae are most commonly glued by the female into cracks or crevices, soft wood or other soft materials. Eggs hatch in about thirty to forty-five days.

American cockroaches are relatively slow-growing insects, requiring one to two years for the immature nymph stages to become completed. During this time they may molt as many as thirteen times. After mating, the female produces and lays egg capsules at intervals of about one week. Adult American cockroaches have been known to live as long as two and a half years in captivity, but survival is typically less than a year.

The American cockroach, and some other large species common in the southern United States, are frequently referred to as "palmetto bugs."

Related Species: The oriental cockroach, *Blatta orientalis* Linnaeus is another large species of cockroach that rivals the American cockroach in size. It is dark chestnut or brown in color, and the wings are very

Oriental cockroach; photograph courtesy of USDA

much reduced in size on the males and nearly absent on the females. Oriental cockroaches are particularly common in dark, damp basement areas and near sources of water, including sewage. Because of these habits, this insect is sometimes known as a "waterbug."

Far more common cockroach species found in the region are the smaller German cockroach, *Blattella germanica* (Linnaeus), and the brownbanded cockroach, *Supella longipalpa* (Fabricius).

Collecting Tips: The American cockroach is most commonly found near sources of moisture, such as water pipes and sewers. Their numbers are often highest during warmer months. Since cockroaches avoid well-lit areas, they may be difficult to collect. Use of sticky cockroach traps in areas of suspected cockroach activity are probably one of the easiest means to collect them.

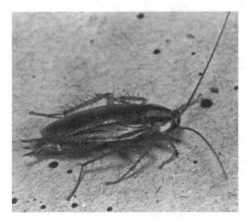

The German cockroach is the most common species found in buildings; photograph courtesy of USDA.

ORDER: ISOPTERA
Termites

Termites are social insects that develop a significant colony structure including reproductive stages (kings, queens), a predominant worker caste and other specialized forms (such as soldiers). They also feed on cellulose, a common product of plants that most insects cannot digest. This is usually made possible through the symbiotic relationship of termites with certain bacteria that grow in the termite gut and break down the cellulose.

Almost all termites found in the region are subterranean termites in the genus *Reticulitermes*. These maintain an underground colony, sometimes several feet (meters) below the soil surface. Foraging workers create tunnels through the soil in search of wood or other cellulose-rich materials, such as cow manure. Because termites are extremely sensitive to drying and light, tunneling is done either within the soil or the wood.

Termite colonies can be long-lived, lasting decades, with queens being replaced as needed. Reproduction of the colony occurs when winged, reproductive stages are produced that issue from the colony in periodic swarms. An individual pair of termites (king and queen) attempts to initiate a colony, usually starting around the edge of a

Subterranean termite workers

buried piece of wood or rock. Colony size builds slowly during the first few seasons, but may ultimately contain several thousand individuals when fully developed.

Termites develop through simple metamorphosis. They are sometimes included in the same order as cockroaches, since they share many physical and behavioral features.

Termites are soft-bodied and are best preserved in alcohol (70 percent).

Rearing Tips: Small numbers of workers and soldiers can be maintained in captivity if provided with a high-humidity environment that contains some wood for food.

MOST COMMON TERMITE—ARID-LAND SUBTERRANEAN TERMITE
Reticulitermes tibialis Banks

Order: Isoptera

Family: Rhinotermitidae

Distribution: The arid-land subterranean termite is found throughout the region, up to elevations of about 7,000 feet (2,133 m).

Life History and Habits: The arid-land subterranean termite develops on a wide variety of organic materials such as cattle manure and scrub brush. The cellulose within these materials is then broken down by aid of microscopic protozoa that grow in the hind gut of the insect to produce usable nutrients for the termites. *Reticulitermes tibialis*, and other subterranean termites, are highly sensitive to drying and produce colonies in soil rather than wood.

Colonies are established by a single pair of the reproductive stages (queen and king). Winged reproductive stages typically emerge from colonies in late winter, usually during the first warm period. Large numbers of winged-stage termites then issue from the colony and may be seen later as they drop on snow or soil. During these flights of the reproductive stages, the queens pair with a single king and initiate a colony, constructing a small chamber under a rock or in cracks in the soil. They then mate and continue colony construction.

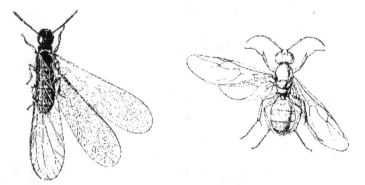

Comparison of a winged termite (left) and a winged ant (right)

Termites are social insects that produce different forms or castes. During colony initiation, the female first rears infertile female forms, known as workers. These conduct the majority of colony chores, such as rearing young, foraging for food and constructing tunnels for the colony; the queen then concentrates on laying eggs. Other forms are produced, including soldiers, which have a greatly enlarged head and a powerful mandible that helps protect the colony from ants and other predators.

During its establishment, a colony may include less than one hundred individuals after the first few years. Later, mature colonies expand sufficiently to allow production of winged reproductive forms (queens, kings) that leave the colony and attempt to form new colonies. The original queen remains in the colony and may live for a decade or more. (Workers may live for three to five years.) If she dies, some "supplementary reproductives" may be reared from among the young to continue egg production. Colonies can thus maintain themselves for a very long time and usually die out only after being devastated by ants or some other severe disruption.

The arid-land subterranean termite feeds on cellulose-containing materials, as do all termites. Despite its abundance in the region, however, it does not usually damage buildings or other wooden structures. Damage does occur in some locations where subsoil conditions, notably the presence of adequate moisture, favor colony development. Termite damage in the region has increased in recent years primarily because of the establishment of the eastern subterranean termite,

R. flavipes (Kollar), which far more aggressively attacks buildings than does the native arid-land subterranean termite.

Related Species: The eastern subterranean termite, *Reticulitermes flavipes* has become established in parts of the region and is a locally destructive species in many areas, particularly in Colorado. *R. flavipes* is more sensitive to drying than is the native species, but apparently has adapted well to areas where there is regular watering, such as irrigated landscapes, that provide sufficiently high soil moisture. In southern areas of the region at least two other species of subterranean termites occur, *R. virginicus* (Banks) and *R. hageni* Banks. In the western areas of the region to the Pacific coast, the western subterranean termite, *R. hesperus* Banks, may be the predominant subterranean termite.

The western drywood termite, *Incisitermes minor* (Hagen), occurs in isolated areas along the Utah-Colorado border. Drywood termites nest directly in wood and do not form a subterranean nest. Very uncommon in the region, they are major pests in buildings and other wood-constructed materials in the southwestern United States and Mexico.

Areas in the northwestern part of the region that receive the most moisture, such as eastern Idaho, sustain some populations of the common dampwood termite, *Zootermopsis angusticollis* (Hagen). One of the largest termites, it is found in decaying wood.

Collecting Tips: Termite workers are most easily collected by turning over wood, cattle manure or other cellulose-rich materials that have settled into the surface of the soil. Adult termites are typically seen in late winter as they emerge from colonies for mating flights, and are sometimes found on the surface of snow.

ORDER: MANTODEA
Mantids

The order Mantodea is a very familiar group of insects, distinctive in form and habits and with many conspicuous members. All mantids are predators; their beneficial habit of killing plant-destructive species is well recognized, contributing to their purposeful distribution throughout North America. Although both of the largest species of mantids found in the region are introduced species, there are native species in the genus *Stigmomantis* that reach almost 3 inches (7.6 cm) in length. In addition, there are the small, wingless ground mantids, *Litaneutria minor* (Scudder), that are very common but rarely observed.

The most striking feature of mantids is their grasping front legs, well-designed for grabbing and holding prey. (Some other groups of insects have also developed this feature independently, notably the mantidflies in the order Neuroptera.) To support the prominent forelegs, the prothorax of mantids is very elongated. Mantids also have the remarkable ability to turn their triangular heads so that they can see in all directions. Most mantids are winged and the adult males frequently fly.

Mantids have simple metamorphosis. Eggs are laid in a distinctive styrofoamlike capsule, called an ootheca, that is glued to plants, rocks, buildings and other surfaces.

Mantids are best displayed by pinning. The pin should be placed through the upper right wing cover of the thorax.

LARGEST PRAYING MANTIDS—CHINESE MANTID AND EUROPEAN MANTID
Tenodera aridifolia sinensis Saussure—Chinese Mantid
Mantis religiosa Linnaeus—European Mantid

Chinese mantid

A European mantid feeds on grasshopper prey.

Order: Mantodea

Family: Mantidae

Distribution: The Chinese mantid is native to Asia and the European mantid is native to Europe. Both have been introduced into North America for purposes of biological control. Regional introductions have originated from mail-order purchases of egg masses (oothecae), which are widely available through garden catalogs. These mantids appear to be imperfectly adapted to the environmental conditions in much of the region, and often die out after being introduced. Fairly good survival does occur in some of the southern parts of the region that experience milder winter and spring conditions. The European mantid is more widely distributed in the region than the Chinese mantid.

Life History and Habits: Eggs of the mantids are laid in papery oothecae containing several hundred eggs. These masses are light brown and are attached to thick twigs or flat surfaces.

Eggs hatch in late spring, and the newly hatched young begin to hunt insects. Since they are highly cannibalistic, many of the mantids are eaten by each other around the time of egg hatch. They then scatter, usually hunting on shrubs or in dense grass by remaining motionless and capturing prey that moves within reach. As they develop, they molt repeatedly (six to nine times) before reaching the adult stage in late July or August.

Adult mantids are winged and occasionally fly. Mating occurs after the male successfully locates the female, approaching her carefully from the back. Sometimes, however, the female captures the male during the mating process and eats him, a protein source that helps mature more eggs. This does not necessarily interrupt the matings, since the male can continue to actively copulate even after the head is eaten.

Females are considerably larger and fatter than the males, particularly as they swell with eggs, and thus often cannot fly, unlike the slender males. The sexes can usually be distinguished by color after they have produced wings: females are green and males are brownish.

Females typically produce one to three oothecae at the end of summer. The eggs are laid within a frothy mixture, which is soft when first laid, later hardening to produce a protective cover. The females die at the end of the year following killing frosts.

The Chinese mantid, almost 4 inches (10.2 cm) long, is considerably larger than the European mantid, which is about 2.5 inches (6.3 cm) long, and has a green stripe running along the edge of its wing. European mantids are distinguished by their dark-ringed "eyespot" near the base of the forearm.

Related Species: Several other native mantids occur in the region. West of the Continental Divide in Colorado, New Mexico and Utah, the California mantid, *Stagmomantis californica* Rehn and Hebard, is fairly common. A related species, the Carolina mantid, *Stagmomantis carolina* (Johannson), is found throughout the eastern United States and is sometimes collected in eastern Colorado. Both are smaller than the European mantid but are still fairly large insects, about 3 inches (7.6 cm) in length. They can be distinguished from the European mantid by the absence of the distinctive eyespot under the

foreleg; in addition, the wing covers of the females do not completely cover the tip of the abdomen.

By far the most common mantids in the region are ground
mantids, *Litaneutria minor* (Scudder). These lack wings and are quite
small, rarely exceeding 1.5 inches (3.8 cm) in length. They are often found running rapidly across rocks and soil, although their gray-
brown coloration blends in well with the background. The life history of these mantids is generally similar to that of the European
mantid, although in the southern part of the region, some of the
ground mantids produce a second generation.

The mantidflies (Mantispidae family) also have grasping forelegs and resemble miniature praying mantids. However, these are
very different insects, belonging to the order Neuroptera (see "Largest Mantidfly").

Collecting Tips: Mantids are most commonly found in dense grass
or on shrubs in August and September, when the adults are present.
The larger species are not often caught using a sweep net, but this
technique is useful for capturing ground mantids.

Rearing Tips: Egg cases of the European mantid and the Chinese
mantid are sold in mail-order catalogs. The young can be reared
easily, but they should be kept in separate containers because of
their cannibalistic habits. Small active insects, such as leafhoppers
and fruit flies, are good foods for younger mantids. As they get
older, larger foods can be provided, such as grasshoppers or crickets. Mantids need some additional water, which can be provided by
misting the inner surface of the container once a week. If fertilized
adult females are being reared, they should be given a stick or rock
on which to lay the egg case.

ORDER: PHASMIDA
Walkingsticks/Stick Insects

The order Phasmida includes some of the most bizarre insects in
appearance, the walkingsticks. All walkingsticks are markedly elongated in most every feature, allowing them to blend in with their sur-
roundings, sticks and branches. Most walkingsticks have no wings,
and only short antennae and cerci. They are slow-moving and feed on

plants, usually at night. Because of their inconspicuous appearance in natural settings, they are infrequently collected, although they may be very abundant in parts of the region.

Walkingsticks undergo simple metamorphosis. Eggs are scattered singly, rather than laid in masses or glued to surfaces.

Walkingsticks are best displayed by pinning. The pin should be placed through the upper right wing cover of the thorax. Because they are very fragile when dried, however, it is a good practice to also mount them on a solid card to support their legs.

LARGEST WALKINGSTICK—PRAIRIE WALKINGSTICK
Diapheromera velii velii **Walsh**

A female prairie walkingstick; males are somewhat smaller and are light brown rather than green.

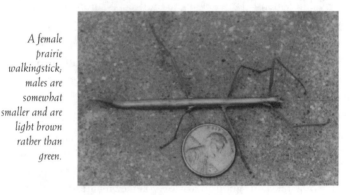

Order: Phasmida (Cheleutoptera)

Family: Heteronemiidae

Distribution: Eastern New Mexico, Colorado and Utah, particularly the southeastern area of this region.

Life History and Habits: The prairie walkingstick spends the winter in the egg stage, in sandy washes where the female dropped the eggs. Heavy spring rains move the eggs, and they often collect in pockets where the water flow slows, which typically results in a highly localized abundance of walkingsticks.

Eggs hatch in late spring. The young walkingsticks feed on various shrubby plants and grasses. Several legumes are most commonly eaten, but the prairie grass big bluestem is also reported as a food source. Almost all feeding occurs at night after dark. The young walkingsticks are green, but males turn darker as they get older.

Walkingsticks develop rapidly and adults can be found by late June and early July, when they mate. The sexes are readily distinguished: females tend to be green and larger than the brown males. As the female feeds, she periodically drops single eggs to the ground. Walkingsticks can be found until a killing frost.

Related Species: A closely related walkingstick, *Diapheromera femorata* (Say), has also been collected in eastern Colorado and New Mexico. This walkingstick is much more common in the Midwest, where it occasionally damages oak forests. Two smaller walkingsticks also occur in the region: *Pseudosermyle straminea* (Scudder) can be collected along the Western Slope of Colorado and Utah and is most easily found on roads following a rain. In eastern Colorado, Wyoming and New Mexico, the Colorado walkingstick, *Parabacillus coloradus* (Scudder), is present.

Collecting Tips: The common walkingsticks are most easily collected at night by aid of a flashlight. They tend to concentrate in dry riverbeds, particularly in shrubbery. Walkingstick populations are usually greatest in July and early August.

Rearing Tips: Prairie walkingsticks can be easily reared by feeding them leaves of certain legumes. Black locust (*Robinia*) is a very good food to provide.

ORDER: DERMAPTERA
Earwigs

Earwigs are an order of insects that includes few species in North America but is almost universally recognized because of the common European earwig, found in yards and sometimes in homes. Earwigs are distinguishable by their prominent forceps (or cerci) at the tip of the abdomen, which are used primarily to hold the mate during mating.

The term *Dermaptera* means "skin wing," referring to the short, leathery forewings. A membranous pair of hind wings is tucked underneath; some species of earwigs can fly.

The derivation of *earwig* is from the old English for "ear creature." Old superstitions persist about earwigs entering ears or causing other harm. Although they do enjoy hiding during the day in tight, dark places, these superstitions are without basis. Earwigs can, however, give a noticeable pinch with their mouthparts if handled.

Earwigs undergo simple metamorphosis, and the young nymphs resemble miniature adults. Some earwigs are semisocial, with the mother providing substantial care for the young.

LARGEST EARWIG—EUROPEAN EARWIG
Forficula auricularia Linnaeus

Order: Dermaptera

Family: Forficulidae

Distribution: Common throughout the region.

Life History and Habits: Adult earwigs spend the winter under rocks or similar protected sites and may become active during warm periods in winter. The females live within a small chamber they have created and lay their eggs in late winter. Eggs are laid in groups, numbering about

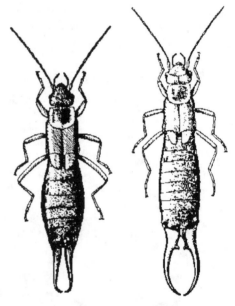

A comparison of a female (left) and male (right) European earwig shows the male to have a more bowed cerci; line drawing courtesy of Washington State University Cooperative Extension.

forty to sixty, and the mother carefully guards them.

Eggs hatch in early spring around the time that fruit trees start to blossom. During the early stage of their life, the mother continues to care for the young, periodically leaving the nest to collect food. Only after the nymphs have molted do they leave the nest, although they may continue to return to it for several weeks. The females may then produce a second, smaller group of eggs.

Earwigs are active at night and feed on a wide variety of foods. Soft parts of plants, such as corn silks and flower petals, are common foods, so earwigs can damage garden plants. However, they feed primarily on other insects and can be important natural controls of many garden pests. During the day they seek cover, preferring tight, dark locations. Earwigs also appear to like the presence of other earwigs, and groups of them often gather together.

Most of the overwintered earwigs die by late spring. The young earwigs become full grown in about two months and continue to be active throughout the summer. There is one generation a year, although nymphs may be found for much of the season, since many overwintered females rear a second brood.

Earwigs have wings tucked under their leathery wing covers. The small native earwig *Labia minor* (Linnaeus), can fly. However, the European earwig rarely, if ever, flies.

The European earwig is a species that was introduced into the region during the late 1940s and 1950s.

Related Species: Two other earwigs occur in the Rocky Mountain region. The ringlegged earwig, *Euborellia annulipes* (Lucas), nearly equals the European earwig in size but is only rarely collected and is restricted to southern areas of the region. A much smaller species of earwig, *L. minor*, occurs in the plains areas east of the Continental Divide. They are most commonly found under cow manure, where they feed on other insects.

Earwigs are sometimes confused with rove beetles (Staphylinidae), since both insects have short forewing covers and are generally elongate in form. Rove beetles, discussed later in this book, lack the distinctive hind forceps that earwigs possess throughout their development.

Collecting Tips: Earwigs hide during the day, seeking tight, dark cover. Curled leaves and ear tips of sweet corn are common places in the garden where they can be found. They will often gather in shelters that are purposely placed around the yard, such as a moistened rolled newspaper or a board.

Earwigs have fairly powerful jaws and can give a noticeable nip if handled. However, the pincers are not strong enough to cause injury and are used only during mating. Male earwigs have bowed pincers; those of the female are more elongated.

Order: EPHEMEROPTERA
Mayflies

Mayflies are a rather small order of insects (about 614 North American species) that develop in water. The immature nymphs are elongate and generally flattened, with two or three conspicuous "tails" (caudal filaments) on the hind end. They breathe by means of feathery or leaflike gills along the sides and/or back of the body.

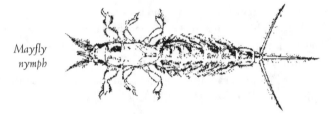

Mayfly nymph

Most often mayfly nymphs are found in moving water, such as rivers or streams; occasionally they also occur in ponds or lakes. Nymphs of some species are very active and are best collected with a dip net; others make burrows in the bottom of water bodies. All mayflies are plant feeders or scavengers, feeding on algae and decaying organic matter.

The life cycle of mayflies is unique. When the nymph stage is completed, they move to the surface or edge of the water and molt into a winged dark form (subimago) that flies to the shore. Shortly thereafter—usually within a day—they molt again to the adult form. Mayflies are the only insects that have two winged developmental stages. Emergences of mayflies can be spectacular, often occurring over a short period of a few weeks during the summer. Adult mayflies mate in flight and the female drops eggs over the water surface or attaches them to vegetation. Adult mayflies live only a short time, a few days at most, which gives rise to the name of the order: from the Greek *ephemera* ("short-lived" or "day") and *ptera* ("winged").

Mayflies are a very important food for fish and other wildlife. They are also useful as indicators of water-quality changes, since many mayflies are highly sensitive to pollutants.

Mayfly nymphs and most mayfly adults are best preserved in 70 percent alcohol. Some of the larger species can be pinned through the thorax, although they are very fragile. Alternatively, mayfly adults can be stored in envelopes.

LARGEST MAYFLY—
HEXAGENIA LIMBATA SERVILLE

Hexagenia limbata, *a large mayfly commonly found in the region; photograph courtesy of Brigham Young University*

Order: Ephemeroptera

Family: Ephemeridae

Distribution: Throughout the region in lakes and slow-moving rivers. They are introduced into some areas as a food for fish. Among the places where they are reported to be particularly abundant are Flathead Lake in Montana and Hayden Lake in Idaho. In Colorado, they are most common in the eastern part of the state.

Life History and Habits: Immature stages (nymphs or naiads) occur in water, where they live in shallow burrows on the bottom. They feed by filtering small food particles using their hairy mouthparts and legs. Development requires one year, or more often two years, to complete. When full grown, the nymphs emerge from the water and molt to a winged, grayish subimago stage that typically lasts a single evening (often termed the "dun" stage by fly fisher-men). They molt again, this time to the adult form (the "spinner" stage). Mating and egg laying occur over the course of a few nights, after which the insects die. Eggs are dropped onto the water surface and sink to the bottom.

This species is known as the "lead-winged" drake by anglers.

Related Species: Several other species of *Hexagenia* occur in neighboring states. Another large and important genus of mayflies is *Drunella*. One species, *D. grandis* (Eaton), is known as the "western green drake." Hatches of this species are a favorite with western anglers because they produce the best dry fly action of the year, usually in late June and early July. This group also includes the Colorado mayfly, *D. coloradensis* (Dodds), a species restricted to small streams at high elevations, above 9,000 feet (2,743 m).

Collecting Tips: Emergence of adults occurs from May to July. At this time they can easily be collected at lights near the bodies of water where they develop. Sweeping streamside vegetation during periods of adult emergence is another method of capturing adults. Nymphs are best collected by use of a "kick" net that captures them after they are disturbed and swim up from their feeding sites on the water bottom. They can then be preserved in alcohol.

Rearing Tips: Most developing mayflies require clean, cool running water to survive. They are therefore difficult to rear and will not survive for long in an aquarium that reaches room temperature.

ORDER: ODONATA
Dragonflies and Damselflies

The dragonflies and damselflies are fairly large and easily recognized insects. Adult stages have four membranous wings and are skillful fliers. The head is large owing to a distinctive pair of compound eyes and a powerful set of mandibles. The legs form a basketlike arrangement used for capturing insects.

Adult dragonflies and damselflies are predators of smaller insects that they capture during flight. Much of the time they will be found perching on grass or other objects near water from which they fly off swiftly in pursuit of passing prey. Adult males spend much time set-

Insects and Water Quality

The quality of surface waters, on which the very survival of the human species is so dependent, has become an increasing concern. An integral part of efforts to protect and improve water quality is monitoring. Various methods are used to describe the quality of water and the chemical, physical and biological changes to which it is subject. For example, chemical analyses are frequently used in water-quality testing. Aquatic insects are also very useful indicators of the impact of pollution on stream, lake and reservoir ecosystems.

Insects that live in water can be very sensitive to changes in oxygen, organic matter, temperature and chemicals that affect water quality. Therefore, sampling aquatic insects in the vicinity of a suspected pollution source can give an indication of the severity of the pollution. Indeed, the relative sensitivity of different insect families to pollution (particularly pollution by organic matter) has been quantified and is widely used in water-quality assessments.

For example, aquatic insects that are most sensitive to organic pollution include essentially all species of stoneflies, mayflies (Ephemeroptera) and many of the caddisflies (Glossosomatidae and Rhyacophilidae families). These insects will be found only where water quality remains high.

Where water quality has begun to deteriorate, other groups of insects can no longer survive. Moderately pollution-sensitive species include many of the mayflies (Baetidae, Ephemeridae and Tricorythidae families) and caddisflies (Hydropsychidae, Leptoceridae and Limnephilidae families) and aquatic species of crane flies (Tipulidae). Where pollution has progressed even further (poor water quality), only a few types of mayflies may be found (Caenidae and Siphlonuridae families) as well as various midges (Ceratopagonidae and most Chironomidae) and blackflies (Simuliidae). Streams or rivers in the worst condition may be able to support only the blood-red midges of the family Chironomidae or no insect life at all.

ting up territories that they defend by driving away other males. During mating the males and females fly coupled together.

Eggs are laid in or near water, and the immature nymph (or naiad) stages live under water. The nymphs are predators of small aquatic organisms captured with an unusual hinged jaw that they can thrust forward. The nymphs crawl but can also move rapidly by means of a type of jet propulsion that involves drawing in and rapidly expelling water. When full grown, the nymphs climb out of the water and molt to the adult stage.

Dragonflies and damselflies are a closely related group of insects, but can be easily distinguished in the adult stage. Dragonflies are larger, often heavy-bodied and hold out their wings horizontally at rest. They are adept fliers and can be very difficult to catch. Damselflies are much more delicately built and hold their wings above their back when resting.

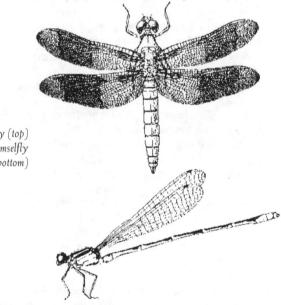

Dragonfly (top) and damselfly (bottom)

Dragonflies survive winters as immature nymphs in the water; the nymphs can be collected year-round. Damselflies spend the winter in the egg stage, which is inserted into the stems of plants along the water's edge.

Adult dragonflies and damselflies preserve well and are displayed by pinning through the thorax and spreading the wings. An alternative preserving method is to place them in clear envelopes. Nymphs should be preserved in alcohol.

Rearing Tips: Most dragonflies can survive well in aerated aquariums. They should be provided with small insects, or even large prey such as small minnows. Their unusual means of locomotion and of capturing prey make them fascinating to observe. Emerged adults can be released and enjoyed.

Largest Dragonflies—Blue Darner and Green Darner
Aeshna Species—Blue Darner
Anax junius Drury—Green Darner

A blue darner oviposits at water's edge.

Order: Odonata

Family: Aeshnidae

Distribution: Usually found in the vicinity of permanent water throughout the region, even reaching alpine and subalpine areas. The green darner is a particularly common species, found throughout most of North America.

Life History and Habits: Adult darners feed on a wide variety of flying insects that they capture in flight using their long legs as a basket. Mosquitoes and various midges are common prey, leading to the reputation of dragonflies as "mosquito hawks." Eggs may be dropped into the water during flight or pushed into mud or plant stems as the adult female sits on vegetation or debris at the edge of the water.

Green darner

Immature stages (nymphs or naiads) that hatch from the eggs live on the bottom of pond edges and streams, clinging to stems of plants or debris. The nymphs are predators that capture their food with a hinged, extensible mouthpart that grabs prey. They will feed on almost any animal of the proper size, including various insects as well as small fish. Development takes two to three years to complete.

Related Species: Most dragonflies are quite large; several other large species occur in the region, including the ten spot, *Libellula pulchella* (Drury), a common spotted-winged species, and the closely related species *L. luctuosa* Burmeister, known as "the widow."

Collecting Tips: Blue darners are present throughout the summer, usually around bodies of water. They are extremely adept fliers and can be difficult to capture. In the early morning, when temperatures are cool, they may be resting and are more easily captured. In particular, they are found on vegetation that received the last rays of direct sun the previous evening. Sweep nets used to capture dragonflies should allow easy air flow to capture these fast-moving insects.

Nymphs can be captured with a strainer or aquatic net around the edges of ponds or in still areas of larger rivers. The larvae are discovered after scooping the debris from the bottom and sifting through it.

Insects and Fishing

As every western trout angler knows, the diet of trout and many other prized game fish of the region consists largely of insects. An ability to understand the habits of insect prey and to mimic them to the satisfaction of the wary trout is the foundation of successful fishing, and a well-known concept since the appearance of the 1676 book, **The Compleat Angler.** At that time, Charles Cotton, the "father of modern fly-fishing," emphasized the importance of aquatic insect biology to fly-fishing and explained how to use the artificial fly to enhance fishing success.

Most of the "flies" used in trout fishing are based on the insects found in streams, and anglers often use special names for the insects they try to create in fly-tying patterns. For example, the "giant dark stone" is the term used to describe the salmonfly (willowfly). Mostly stoneflies or mayflies are used for these lures. Among the stonefly patterns used by anglers and the insects they attempt to mimic are the following:

- The giant dark stone (the salmonfly or willowfly, **Pteronarcys californica**)
- Tiny winter blacks (the winter stoneflies of the Capniidae family)
- Medium browns (the springtails and stripetails of the Perlodidae family)
- Little greens and yellows (the green stoneflies of the Chloroperlidae family)
- Big goldens (the common stoneflies of the Perlidae family)

This gray quill is an artificial fly designed to mimic a small species of mayfly.

Some special terms are used by anglers to describe mayfly life stages. When full grown, nymphs emerge from the water and molt to a winged, grayish intermediate stage that usually lasts a single evening. This is often termed the "dun" stage by fly fishermen. Shortly thereafter, they molt again this time to the adult form, known as the "spinner" stage. Following are some of the common mayfly patterns used in the region as artificial flies:

- Gray lead-winged drake **(Hexagenia limbata)**
- Western green drake **(Drunella grandis)**
- Great lead-winged coachman (**Isonychia** species)
- Quills (**Baetis, Rhithrogena, Epeorus** and **Heptagenia** species)

The green drake, an artificial fly, is designed to mimic the mayfly Isonychia.

Anglers can improve their chances for success by "matching the hatch" and choosing fly patterns based on the insects that are present in the stream, particularly those that are emerging and laying eggs. A little further knowledge of the insect's biology can also improve the chance that a fish will strike. All the aquatic insects have peak activity periods, such as emergence from the stream or egg laying, and fish feeding cycles are correlated to these. Therefore, salmonfly dry fishing is best from noon through the afternoon, since this is when females deliberately descend to the surface of the stream to lay eggs, often in great numbers.

ORDER: PLECOPTERA
Stoneflies

Stoneflies develop in streams or lakes, and adults are usually collected near water. They have chewing mouthparts, and immature nymphs of most stonefly species feed on algae or plant material; many are predators. These nymphs are typically found under rocks (the basis for their name) but also actively move around. They are recognizable by their two "tails" and the two claws on their legs, distinguishing them from the Ephemeroptera (mayflies), which usually have three tails and a single claw.

Stoneflies undergo simple metamorphosis. The final molt occurs after full-grown nymphs climb out of the water. Adult stoneflies are winged and often do not feed. Common species emerge and mate during the early summer months. However, the winter stoneflies (Taeniopterygidae and Capniidae families) emerge during winter months, completing their life cycle in cavities beneath the ice of streams.

The name of the order comes from the Greek *pleco*, ("folded") and *ptera* ("wings"). This refers to the way that adult stoneflies fold their wings over their back when at rest.

LARGEST STONEFLY—SALMONFLY/WILLOWFLY
Pteronarcys californica **Newport**

Salmonfly, Pteronarcys californica; photograph courtesy of Brigham Young University

Order: Plecoptera

Family: Pteronarcyidae

Distribution: Most commonly found around fast-flowing rivers and larger streams above 5,000 feet (1,522 m) throughout the region.

Life History and Habits: Emergence of adult stages occurs from late May to mid-June. The full-grown immature (nymph) stages climb vegetation or structures along the edge of streams and molt to the winged adult stage, leaving the old cast skin behind.

Adults are active for two to three weeks, during which time mating and egg laying occurs. Eggs are laid by the female as she touches the tip of her abdomen to the water surface while in flight. These egg-laying flights typically occur from noon through the afternoon. Immature stages of the salmonfly develop in the water, feeding on decaying organic matter, moss and some small arthropods. During the day, feeding is intermittent and occurs only when water temperatures are optimal, usually early in the day and again in early evening. Development of the nymphal stage may take three to four years to complete.

Salmonflies are eagerly fed on by trout during periods of adult emergence. The presence of the insects is commonly used by anglers as a guide to time periods and locations for above-average trout fishing.

Collecting Tips: Adult salmonflies are easily collected on vegetation and structures adjacent to streams from which they emerge in May and June. A beating net may be useful to collect the insects if populations are low. Immature stages can be collected with a sieve from under rubble and other debris in shallow, fast-flowing areas of a stream.

ORDER: PHTHIRAPTERA
Lice

The order Phthiraptera contains species that are external parasites of mammals or birds, feeding on blood, feathers or skin. Several are significant pests of medical or veterinary importance, such as the chicken body louse, *Menacanthus stramineus* (Nitzsch); the hog louse, *Haematopinus suis* (Linnaeus); and the head louse, *Pediculus humanus capitis* (De Geer). One species in particular, the body louse, *Pediculus humanus humanus* (Linnaeus), has indirectly had a tremendous influence on human history owing to its ability to transmit a human disease: typhus.

The order Phthiraptera includes insects that have been divided into two orders, the chewing lice (Mallophaga) and the sucking lice (Anoplura). The sucking lice are blood feeders that nearly always must remain closely attached to their host or they will die within hours because of their sensitivity to small changes in temperature. Most chewing lice are also found on the body of their host (usually birds), feeding on skin or feathers, occasionally surviving for brief periods in animal nests.

Lice develop through simple metamorphosis. Eggs are almost always laid on hairs or feathers of the host. Usually there are three nymphal instars before the adult stage is reached.

Largest Louse—Hog Louse
Haematopinus suis (**Linnaeus**)

Hog louse;
photograph
courtesy of
USDA

Order: Phthiraptera (Anoplura)

Family: Haematopinidae

Distribution: Generally distributed throughout the United States, in association with hog production.

Life History and Habits: Hogs are the only host of the hog louse, which does not voluntarily leave the body except when moving to another animal. Adult and nymphal stages feed on blood, which they suck with specialized mouthparts (stylets). When they are not feeding, the stylets are retracted into the head.

Adult females glue eggs to the hairs of the hog, close to the skin, often laying several eggs at a time. The eggs hatch after two to three weeks. The young lice begin to feed on hog blood, grasping the hairs of the animal with their clawlike legs. They periodically feed during the course of about two weeks as they develop, becoming an adult after three molts. Adults live for about one month, although they cannot survive more than a few days off the hog. Several generations are completed during a year.

During warm weather, hogs more actively dust themselves or exhibit other behaviors detrimental to hog lice. Therefore, louse populations are highest in the winter months.

The hog louse can be a serious parasite. Large populations are highly irritating to hogs and lead to weight loss caused by scratching and general restlessness. The skin of infested animals may become reddened and inflamed.

Related Species: The most common louse infesting humans is the head louse, *Pediculus humanus capitis*, a species adapted to living on hairs of the human head. Outbreaks of head lice often occur in the region, most commonly among schoolchildren. Although the head louse feeds on blood, it does not transmit diseases. Fortunately the closely related body louse, *P. humanus humanus*, is rare in the region, and is largely restricted to indigent individuals who do not launder their clothing regularly. The body louse is found on clothing and is notorious for its ability to spread typhus, formerly an extremely important disease that killed millions. Both of these species are in the Pediculidae family.

The crab louse, *Pthirus pubis* (Linnaeus), or "crab," is adapted to coarse hairs such as those of the pubic area. It is usually spread by sexual activity.

Collecting Tips: Hog lice are found by searching infested hogs. The lice are a dirty gray or blue-gray color and may be almost 1/4 inch (.6 cm) when full grown. In winter, when populations are highest, they are concentrated around skin folds of the neck, the upper area of the front legs or the ears.

Our "Lousy" English

Lice have had an unusually important role in human history. Until recent times, they were almost universally associated with many human populations. More important, they can transmit a lethal disease, typhus, which has changed the course of civilizations, particularly through outbreaks in the midst of wars. As a result, this group of parasitic insects has contributed much to vernacular English. Among these contributions are the following:

Cootie—A common name associated with the body louse, also called the "seam squirrel," during World War I.

Lousy—A person who is heavily infested with lice is "lousy," and often feels somewhat ill as a result.

Nit-picking—Louse eggs attached to hairs are known as "nits." Their removal during grooming, which is a common practice where lice infestations persist, is known as "nit-picking."

ORDER: HOMOPTERA
Aphids, Hoppers, Scales, Cicadas, Psyllids and Whiteflies

The order Homoptera is one of the most diverse in form and one of the hardest insect groups to learn. All are plant feeders; the order contains many of the most serious plant pests. Insects in this order feed by means of a sucking mouthpart similar to that found on the Hemiptera. Some insect taxonomists consider the Homoptera and Hemiptera to be so similar that they combine them. In the Homoptera, the mouthparts appear to originate from the back of the head below the eyes or even between the front pair of legs; mouthparts in the Hemiptera are more prominent and form a distinctive "beak" from the front of the head.

The Homoptera undergo simple metamorphosis. In some groups, notably the aphids, the eggs hatch inside the mother and bear living nymphs. Male stages are infrequent and even absent in many groups. This means of reproduction (parthenogenesis) does not involve mating, and all the young are usually females.

There are several ways to preserve and display the Homoptera. The very large species, such as cicadas, can be pinned through the thorax in a manner similar to that for other large insects. Smaller Homoptera, such as leafhoppers and treehoppers, should be mounted on card points. Very small groups that are soft-bodied, such as aphids, whiteflies, soft scales and psyllids, should be put in alcohol. Hard scales should be left with a small amount of their host plant, usually a twig or needle, or placed in alcohol.

LARGEST HOMOPTERAN—DOG DAY CICADAS
Tibicen dorsata (Say)
Tibicen dealbatus (Davis)

A dog day cicada emerges from its nymphal skin.

Order: Homoptera

Family: Cicadidae

Distribution: Both species are recorded from Montana to New Mexico, with highest populations east of the Continental Divide. They are particularly common in the southeastern areas of the region.

Life History and Habits: Immature stages (nymphs) of the dog day cicadas develop by feeding on sap from the roots of various trees. Boxelder and cottonwood trees in fairly loose, moist soils are common hosts. Development probably takes two to three years to complete.

When full grown, the immature nymphs emerge from the soil and climb onto a nearby upright object; this typically occurs from mid-July to mid-August. There they molt and change to the adult form, leaving their old skin attached to the surface on which they transformed to the adult stage. Immediately after emergence they are quite soft and usually pale green.

After several hours, during which the newly emerged adults darken and harden, they fly and feed on the sap of leaves and twigs. Mating occurs in trees, and the females insert their eggs into twigs, leaving wounds that may cause the twigs to die back, producing a "flag" of dead leaves. Dog day cicada adults may be present for several months, finally dying out with killing frosts.

Males of the dog day cicada produce a high-pitched buzzing noise, used primarily to attract the female cicada, by vibrating a special membrane (tymbal) along the sides of the abdomen, which creates a resonating sound in an internal chamber. Other cicadas "sing" by producing clicking noises with their wings. Female cicadas produce little or no noise.

Related Species: Approximately twenty-eight species of cicadas occur in the region. The most common genera of cicadas (species of *Okanagana* and *Platypedia*) reportedly have life cycles of three to seven years, but their biology is largely unknown. *Okanagana magnifica* Davis is one member of this group that is particularly large; it is black with red markings and occurs in Colorado, New Mexico and Utah.

Periodical cicadas (*Magicicada* species), such as the seventeen-year and thirteen-year "locusts," are very long-lived insects. They emerge during synchronized periods, often in spectacular numbers. Periodical cicadas are restricted largely to areas east of the Mississippi and do not occur in the Rocky Mountain region.

Collecting Tips: Cicadas are most easily collected with a sweep net and by following singing male cicadas in low-growing vegetation. By slowly approaching a singing cicada, its location can usually be determined before it stops making noise. If disturbed, cicadas may fly only a short distance and can be captured at this time. Cicadas sometimes can be found on the ground after rainstorms have knocked them out of trees. Late July and early August are particularly good times to search for adult dog day cicadas, although other species may be out by June. Cicadas are harmless to humans, although they often startle a collector.

Miscellaneous: Cicadas are sometimes mistakenly called "locusts," a term properly used to describe certain migratory grasshoppers. This error originated when early settlers encountered large infestations of periodical cicadas and likened them to the locusts described in the Bible.

Dog day cicadas have several natural enemies. Perhaps most spectacular are the cicada killer wasps, which resemble huge yellow jackets (see "Largest Hunting Wasp—Cicada Killer"). Another insect enemy is a large (approximately 1-inch [2.5-cm]) cedar beetle of the Rhipiceridae family, *Sandalus niger* (Knoch), which is a parasite of cicada nymphs in the southeastern part of the region. The Mississippi kite, a large predatory bird normally found along the Gulf Coast, has expanded its summer range into the Arkansas Valley of Colorado, where it subsists almost entirely on cicadas.

Despite their large size, cicadas cause very little injury. They develop slowly and their feeding on roots causes no detectable harm to the plants. The greatest injury occurs when a large number of certain cicadas, such as Putnam's cicada, *Platypedia putnami* (Uhler), insert eggs into tree stems and cause twig dieback during outbreaks, which are infrequent.

Putnam's cicada is one of the most common cicadas found in the region.

LARGEST SCALE INSECT—OAK KERMES SCALE
Allokermes gillettei (Cockerell)

Order: Homoptera

Family: Kermesidae

Distribution: Infrequently collected, but may occur throughout the region in association with its host plant, the red oak.

A colony of kermes scale on pin oak

Life History and Habits: The overwintering stage of the oak kermes scale occurs as a very small, first-instar nymph on branches and twigs of oak trees. They move from these areas in spring to the new growth and feed on sap. In late spring and summer, the scales develop, becoming full grown in July and August. Females become very large, almost the size of a marble, and are filled with eggs. Males are much smaller and form small white cocoons on branches before they emerge to fly and mate with the females.

Eggs hatch in September and October. The newly emerged scale "crawlers" move to overwintering sites on twigs for shelter, and remain dormant through winter. There is one generation per season.

Although uncommon, oak kermes scale can cause local damage to oak trees. One sign of injury is dieback (flagging) of twigs on infested oaks, which occurs because the scale feeds so much on the sap that the twigs suffer from drought. At this time the scales may also produce a sticky wax.

In fall, yellowjacket wasps often visit kermes scale–infested trees, feeding on the sticky wax and sometimes cracking open the scales to eat their eggs. Fox squirrels also eat scales.

A colony of mature cottony maple scale with egg sacks

Related Species: The most frequently encountered large scale insect is the cottony maple scale, *Pulvinaria innumerabilis* (Rathvon), which produces a large cottony egg sack that is quite visible in late June and early July. Cottony maple scale can be found on a wide variety of trees, such as honey locust, maple and hackberry. It belongs to a different family of scale insects, the Coccidae, or soft scales.

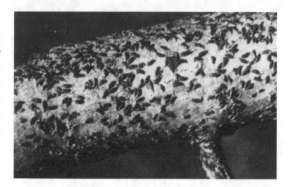

Oystershell scale is one of the most common and damaging scale insects found in the region.

Several scale insects can be important pests of trees and shrubs. Probably the most damaging scale insect in the region is the oystershell scale, *Lepidosaphes ulmi* (Linnaeus). Oystershell scale can be seriously destructive to aspen, ash, lilac, various fruit trees and many other woody plants. It is a member of the armored scale family, Diaspididae.

Collecting Tips: Oak kermes scale is most readily observed in late summer, when the females become full grown and filled with eggs. Oak tree branches must be examined carefully; the insects are difficult to see because their colors camouflage well. Often the bases of oak twigs that die back in late summer are infested by this scale.

LARGEST APHID—GIANT WILLOW APHID
Tuberolachnus salignus (**Gmelin**)

Order: Homoptera

Family: Aphididae

Distribution: Throughout the region, particularly west of the Continental Divide, in association with stands of willow.

A colony of giant willow aphids

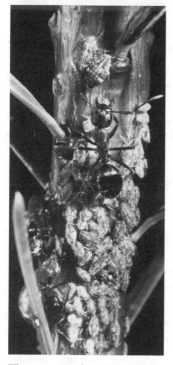

These giant conifer aphids are being tended by a carpenter ant; photograph courtesy of USDA Forest Service.

Life History and Habits: Little is known about the giant willow aphid. Willow appears to be its only host. Eggs are laid on the twigs in fall and hatch after new growth forms on the trees in spring. There are continuous, multiple generations throughout the growing season.

Giant willow aphids are usually most abundant late in the season, at which time they can be found in masses on twigs and smaller branches. Adults sometimes leave or are blown off trees, and can be found on sidewalks, porches and buildings near infested trees. Adults also have been observed walking on snow in early winter.

The giant willow aphid, and most other species of aphids, may produce either winged or wingless adult stages. Winged stages are produced most commonly when colonies are large; these individuals disperse to other trees.

Related Species: The giant conifer aphids (*Cinara* species) are quite large and are extremely common on various pines, spruce, junipers and Douglas fir. Because of their large size, they are sometimes confused with ticks. Another large aphid found on twigs of willow is the black willow aphid, *Pterocomma smithiae* (Monell), which is differentiated from others by its orange cornicles and legs.

Approximately three hundred species of aphids occur in the Rocky Mountain region. Almost every plant is host to aphid species; several aphids are important pests of crops such as wheat, potatoes, tomatoes, cabbage and alfalfa.

Collecting Tips: Carefully search willow twigs in late summer. The presence of sticky honeydew on leaves is usually a good indication

A colony of black willow aphids on a twig

that aphids are present. The large, black, overwintering eggs are fairly conspicuous in winter and can be used to identify branches that will be infested in early spring.

Aphids should be preserved in alcohol since they quickly dehydrate and lose their shape when pinned. Giant willow aphids will turn the alcohol preservative purple.

Miscellaneous: Giant willow aphids have been used as a source of dark natural dye.

Most Common Gall-making Insect—
Cooley Spruce Gall Adelgid
Adelges cooleyi (Gillette)

A Cooley spruce gall adelgid adult and nymph emerge from a gall.

Order: Homoptera

Family: Adelgidae

Distribution: Found throughout the region in association with the host plants on which it develops (spruce and Douglas fir).

Life History and Habits: The Cooley spruce gall adelgid uses two hosts, spruce and Douglas fir, to complete its development,

Nymphs of the Cooley spruce gall adelgid develop within chambers in the gall that forms on spruce.

alternating between them through the season. Overwintering forms of the insect occur on both plant species and exist as a partially grown female on the underside of twigs. Development ceases in the winter and typically resumes in April, at which time the females complete their development and produce a large sack containing hundreds of eggs.

On spruce these eggs hatch in synchrony with the budding of new growth. The newly hatched nymphs migrate to the base of the emerging needles and feed. In the process of feeding, they cause

Distortion of the new growth of spruce produced by the Cooley spruce gall adelgid

the tissues of the terminal to swell, forming small chambers at the base of each needle. This distortion of the terminal growth is known as the Cooley spruce gall. Within the chambers the insects develop and become full grown by late June or early July. At this time, the gall starts to dry, allowing the chambers to open. The insects crawl out onto the needles and molt to a winged form, then leave the spruce, flying to Douglas fir, where they survive during the summer. Late in the season some of the insects fly back to spruce and lay eggs that develop into the overwintering female form. The old galls on spruce dry to a light brown color and remain attached to the plant, but are no longer used by the insect.

On Douglas fir, continuous generations can occur during the growing season. Galls are not produced, but aphids feeding on the emerging needles may cause them to become slightly distorted and crooked.

Related Species: The Cooley spruce gall adelgid is one of the "woolly aphids" that occur in the region. These cover their bodies with threads or powders of wax. Several other species occur, mostly in the genus *Pinus*, and are almost all associated with pines, spruce and other conifers.

Collecting Tips: This insect is most easily collected by examining developing galls during May and June. Winged adult stages may be observed for a couple of weeks on the needles of the drying galls. The insects are soft-bodied and should be preserved in alcohol, although alcohol dissolves the waxy covering of the woolly aphids. The galls remain hard and are easily displayed.

Insects That Make Plant Galls

One of the amazing things about some species of insects is their ability to alter plant growth to form a unique shelter, surrounded by plant cells, on which the insects then feed. These changes in plant growth are called "galls."

Many kinds of insects (and other arthropods such as the eriophyid mites) can change plant tissues into galls. Sometimes this is caused by feeding in a certain pattern, which causes the undamaged tissues to grow faster and form curls or thickenings. During feeding, gall-making insects may also secrete saliva that actually changes the types of tissues that plants form. Chemicals closely related to the hormones used in plant growth have been detected in the saliva of insects.

Galls produced by insects can be very unusual, as the

Eriophyid mite gall

tissues of the plant may be changed to a radically different form to accommodate the gall maker. For example, one family of insects known as the gall wasps (Cynipidae) form a variety of ornate balls or mossy growths on leaves and stems of oaks and roses in which

Woody galls on oak are produced by gall wasps.

the developing gall wasps may be found. Despite their bizarre manipulations, however, gall-making insects rarely cause any serious damage; most attract attention merely because the galls they produce are so bizarre.

Several hundred gall-making arthropods occur in the region, including insects and mites from many orders. The most common groups of gall-making arthropods in the region, and the types of galls they make, are summarized below.

Common Groups of Regional Gall-making Insects

Common Name	Family Name	Types of Galls Produced
Gall wasps	Cynipidae	Most abundant group of gall-making insects in North America, including more than 800 species. Almost all make galls on either oak or rose. Galls produced by this group of insects are often bizarre, typically involving major change of plant growth so that leaves or stems are transformed into balls, mosslike growths or spines in which the gall wasps develop.

Common Name	Family Name	Types of Galls Produced
Gall midges	Cecidomyiidae	A very common group of gall-making insects, which includes some species that damage plants. Most gall midges produce fairly simple galls that involve thickenings or stuntings of plant growth to produce a chamber in which the developing insects live. The more common species include the honey locust podgall midge (makes a thickened curl of developing leaflets of honey locust), piñon spindlegall midge (makes a thickened swelling at base of piñon needles) and the chokecherry gall midge (infests and thickens developing chokecherry fruit).
Woolly aphids	Adelgidae, Eriosomatidae	These are known as "woolly aphids" because of the production by some stages of waxy threads or powder that may cover their body. One particularly common gall-making species is the Cooley spruce gall adelgid, which produces a conelike gall on terminals of Colorado blue and Englemann spruce. Related species curl leaves of elm in spring and form galls that appear as knots in the stem of poplars and cottonwoods.
Psyllids	Psyllidae	Psyllids, more commonly

Common Name	Family Name	Types of Galls Produced
		known as "jumping plant lice," occur on many plants; some are important plant pests of the region. However, few make galls on plants, and all of these infest a single plant: hackberry (**Celtis** species). In most areas of the region, at least two species of psyllids infest hackberry: the hackberry nipplegall psyllid, **Pachypsylla celtidismamma** (Fletcher), makes a prominent raised swelling on hackberry leaves, and the hackberry blistergall psyllid, **Pachypsylla celtidisvesiculum** Riley, makes a small dimpled swelling on leaves. Other species of psyllids make galls in buds, leaves and branches.
Eriophyid mites	Eriophyidae	Possibly the most common gall makers in the region are eriophyid mites. Because of their extremely small size (generally microscopic) they are little studied, however. Among the many galls that eriophyid mites create are "finger gall" growths on leaves of chokecherry and wild plum; hairy coverings on the surface of mountain maple, aspen and box elder; and distortions of flowers of ash and cottonwood.

Order: HEMIPTERA
True Bugs

The order Hemiptera ("half wing") is distinguished by a forewing that is thickened at the base and more membranous toward the tip. Mouthparts have evolved to pierce plant or animal tissues and suck fluids. Members of the order undergo simple metamorphosis (egg-nymph-adult).

Many species of Hemiptera are economically important to agriculture. The family known as the plant bugs contains several species that attack developing seed pods and fruit; squash bugs are serious pests of pumpkins and squash. Certain species in the stink bug family damage plants also, although many other stink bugs are predators of insects. Damsel bugs and minute pirate bugs are two groups of bugs that are highly beneficial because they feed on many pest species.

Adult Hemiptera are best preserved and displayed by pinning through the scutellum, a V-shaped area at the base of the wing covers. Small species may be mounted on a card point. Nymphs will shrink if pinned, and are best preserved in alcohol.

Largest True Bug—Giant Water Bug
Lethocerus americanus (Leidy)

Order: Hemiptera

Family: Belostomatidae

Distribution: Found primarily in southern areas of the region, in small permanent ponds. This insect is a strong flier and sometimes migrates long distances, occasionally being found at high elevations. It is not common.

Life History and Habits: Giant water bugs overwinter in the adult stage in ponds. Eggs are laid in spring on submerged wood and other organic debris.

The immature nymphs develop under water and are ferocious predators. Giant water bugs will eat anything they can subdue, including various insects, fish, reptiles and amphibians. They grasp their prey by the front legs and with their mouthparts inject the prey with a powerful digestive enzyme. After the body of the prey

Giant water bug, Lethocerus species; photograph courtesy of Brigham Young University

is digested by these enzymes, the water bug sucks up the fluid materials. Nymphs become full grown within a few months. There is one generation of the insect per year.

Related Species: Many species in the Belostomatidae family can be quite large. Among the larger are individuals in the genera *Abedus* and *Belostoma* that are more common than *Lethocerus americanus*. These species of giant water bugs also have the unusual habit of laying masses of eggs on the back of the male, which are then carried until they hatch. Nymphs and adults may be collected around slow-moving streams and are particularly abundant in the southwestern part of the region.

Many giant water bugs lay eggs that are carried on the back of the male; photograph courtesy of Brigham Young University.

Collecting Tips: Giant water bugs are most easily captured by seining or dip-net sampling along the edges of small ponds with a lot of vegetation. Adults are most common from late August until May. Nymphs predominate during the summer.

Adult giant water bugs can sometimes be collected at lights. They have been known to fly considerable distances from breeding areas.

Giant water bugs can inflict a very painful bite owing to the injection of their digestive saliva. They are sometimes called "toe-biters."

LARGEST BACKSWIMMER—
NOTONECTA UNDULATA SAY

Order: Hemiptera

Family: Notonectidae

Distribution: Widespread and common throughout the region.

Life History and Habits: To biologists and casual bug-watchers the backswimmers are a familiar sight in open water of ponds, stock

A comparison of a backswimmer Notonecta undulata *(left) with a water boatman (right) shows many similarities. These two kinds of aquatic bugs are sometimes confused.*

tanks, ditches and canyon pools. The adults are winged and highly dispersive and often will colonize swimming pools, where they can become an annoyance to swimmers.

The backswimmers get their name from their habit of swimming with the dorsal surface down. Their boat-shaped body allows them to move through the water easily as they use their long hind legs in an oarlike fashion. Backswimmers are predators of other insects and small fish, which they paralyze with a toxic saliva injected through piercing-sucking mouthparts.

Winter is spent in the adult stage; they can sometimes be observed swimming beneath the ice. Eggs are attached to or inserted into underwater plants. When these hatch, the nymphs are free-living and hunt small arthropods, passing through five instars before reaching full development. Typically two generations are produced per year.

During courtship the males produce chirping sounds while under water.

Related Species: Approximately thirty-two species of backswimmers are recognized in North America, nine of which occur within the region, all in the genera *Buenoa* and *Notonecta*. Most species of *Buenoa* are white, whereas the larger *Notonecta* are marked with orange, red and black. Among the most common regional species are Kirby's backswimmer, *Notonecta kirbyi* Hungerford, and *Buenoa margaritacea* Torre-Bueno.

Another family of swimming bugs often associated with the backswimmers are the water boatmen (Corixidae). Both families have hind legs that are adapted for paddling through water. Most water boatmen are smaller, lack the curved body of the backswimmer and have a darker-colored back.

Collecting Tips: Backswimmers are easily collected with an aquatic net in still waters or by sweeping adjacent vegetation. Pools without fish often support the highest populations of these insects. Backswimmers in the genus *Buenoa* are more gregarious and prefer open waters. Adult backswimmers can be captured throughout the year.

Backswimmers (and water boatmen) are highly attracted to lights at night, particularly ultraviolet light. Day-flying adults may be attracted to shiny surfaces, including car finishes.

Backswimmers can produce a painful bite and should be handled with caution.

LARGEST WATER STRIDER—
AQUARIUS REMIGIS (SAY)

The largest water strider, Aquarius remiguis

Order: Hemiptera

Family: Gerridae

Distribution: Generally distributed throughout the region in aquatic habitats ranging from isolated canyon pools to edges of large rivers and lakes.

Life History and Habits: Water striders are predators that capture prey with their grasping forelegs and subdue them with a paralyzing saliva injected with their piercing-sucking mouthparts. Insects that fall on the surface of the water comprise their main diet, but small fish near the surface may be "harpooned" by the insect's slender beak.

Adults hibernate during the colder months under logs, in mud, in piles of debris or in sheltered areas along the shore. They may become active shortly after ice melts, and have been found in early April. Eggs are laid on floating objects such as plants or debris and develop over a period of about two weeks before hatching occurs. The immature stages have habits similar to those of the adults and become full grown by early summer. Adult stages are winged and can disperse over long distances.

The long middle and hind legs of water striders are well adapted for walking on water. The tarsi at the tip of the legs are covered with fine hairs that resist water, allowing them to skate across the surface. This unusual habit has led to their common names, "pond skaters" and "Jesus bugs."

Related Species: At least six other species of water striders occur in the region, most in the genus *Gerris*. All are slightly smaller and darker than the reddish brown *Aquarius remigis*.

Collecting Tips: Water striders are found in almost any aquatic habitat, from small pools and lakes to rivers and streams. They tend to collect in quiet, protected areas of water and occasionally can be quite abundant. Other surface-feeding insects, such as whirligig beetles (Gyrinidae family), may share these pools with them.

LARGE LEAFFOOTED BUGS—CONIFER SEED BUGS
Leptoglossus occidentalis Heidemann
Leptoglossus clypealis Heidemann

Order: Hemiptera

Family: Coreidae

Distribution: Throughout the region, but most common near pine forests.

Life History and Habits: Leaffooted bugs in the genus *Leptoglossus* feed and develop primarily on seeds. Seeds of pines, Douglas fir

Conifer seed bug,
Leptoglossus
occidentalis;
*photograph
courtesy of*
USDA

and other conifers are preferred, but developing seeds and fruits of a wide variety of plants may be used.

Adults spend the winter in protected cover near plants on which they earlier fed. They emerge in mid-spring, and females lay rows of eggs on leaves and needles. The young seed bugs feed for several months before becoming full grown in summer. Only one generation is produced per year.

Often the adult bugs move into homes in fall, seeking winter shelter. They are a common nuisance invader of homes in Colorado, particularly at higher elevations. During winter they do not feed or reproduce, however, and cause no significant problems. Many other insects, such as boxelder bugs and elm leaf beetles, share this habit of wintering in homes.

Related Species: A slightly smaller species that is similar in appearance is *Narnia snowi* Van Duzee, commonly associated with cholla cactus in the southern areas of the region. Rarely, *Acanthocephala terminalis* (Dallas) and *Acanthocephala declivis* (Say) may be collected from the extreme southern areas of the region. This species is actually the largest member of the family found in the region, but is rarely collected.

An important leaffooted bug in the more southern areas of the region is the squash bug (see following section), which regularly causes severe damage to pumpkin and winter squash in many areas. The squash bug is slightly shorter in length and somewhat stouter in shape than the conifer seed bugs.

The conifer seed bugs (Coreidae) are commonly confused with assassin bugs (Reduviidae). Members of both families possess prominent piercing mouthparts that project from the front of a narrow head. Assassin bugs are predators of other insects, with a three-segment beak and enlarged forelegs for grasping prey, whereas plant-feeding seed bugs have four-segment beaks and often have hind legs with enlarged leaflike structures.

Collecting Tips: Immature conifer seed bugs can be seen during summer developing on young pine cones or seeds of various trees and shrubs. They hide when disturbed but can be dislodged and collected if infested branches are shaken over a cloth or tray. Adults are usually observed during September and October when they rest on the sides of buildings or move indoors for winter shelter.

Insects That Share Our Homes

One form of western wildlife that often chooses to share our homes is insects. Many kinds of insects that are casual visitors move into homes seeking shelter, food or moisture. Few are capable of reproducing indoors.

Usually the most conspicuous of the household invaders are insects that use homes as a winter shelter. Movements into homes occur in late summer and fall, during which time they may be little noticed. However, after spending several months indoors, these visitors begin to awaken from their winter dormancy and move about. Those that have taken a wrong turn and find themselves in a house may be seen in late winter and early spring in large numbers. Among the more common winter guests are boxelder bugs, elm leaf beetles, leaffooted bugs and cluster flies.

Other arthropods move into homes following certain weather patterns. Periods of cool, wet weather in spring and early fall cause millipedes, sowbugs and pillbugs to migrate indoors. Hot weather in summer contributes to indoor migrations of insects that are drawn to moisture, such as strawberry root weevils, centipedes, scorpions, springtails and camel crickets.

Sometimes we inadvertently build homes that are extremely attractive to insects. For example, many ants move to prominent points in the landscape to aggregate in mating swarms, and an isolated building in a prairie setting quickly becomes the "action spot" for male and female winged ants to meet. A sun-exposed wall of a building near a creek full of boxelder trees becomes highly attractive to boxelder bugs searching for winter shelter. High, sunny surfaces, such as tall buildings, are used by cluster flies looking for cover; they aggregate on the uppermost stories and especially plague residents of penthouse apartments and high-priced office space.

A LARGE LEAFFOOTED BUG—SQUASH BUG
Anasa tristis (DeGeer)

Order: Hemiptera

Family: Coreidae

Distribution: Found primarily in the southern areas of the region, being particularly common in the Arkansas Valley

A mating pair of squash bugs

and Western Slope areas of Colorado, northern New Mexico and eastern Utah.

Life History and Habits: Squash bugs spend the winter in the adult stage in protected sites around previously infested plantings, occasionally entering nearby homes. They become active and first begin to appear and feed in June, shortly after plant emergence. At this time they mate, and females lay masses of shiny brown eggs on leaf undersides. After hatching, the nymphs feed together in groups, usually on the shaded undersides of the plant. The nymphs of the first generation mature by early July. A second generation follows, which is often much more numerous and destructive than the first generation.

Newly hatched nymphs and eggs of the squash bug

    Adults that develop late in the season do not lay eggs, and leave the field for overwintering shelter. During warm seasons in southern areas of the region, some of the second-generation adults may continue to develop and lay eggs, producing a third generation.

    Adults and nymphs of the squash bug feed on most vine crops (Cucurbitaceae), particularly winter varieties of squash and pumpkins. During feeding they cause extensive damage to tissues around the feeding site, which causes areas of the stems and leaves to wilt—a condition sometimes described as "Anasa wilt of cucurbits." Plants may be killed by midsummer. Late in the season, fruits may be directly fed on, producing wounded areas that allow rotting organisms to enter. The squash bug is a very serious garden pest in much of the southern area of the region.

The opuntia bug is also known as the prickly pear bug.

Related Species: A leaffooted bug that resembles the squash bug is the prickly pear bug (or Opuntia bug), *Chelinidea vittiger* Uhler. This insect feeds on prickly pear cactus (*Opuntia*), sometimes causing plants to wither and die back.

Collecting Tips: Adults are easily collected on pumpkins and winter squash in late summer and fall. They often hide around the base of the plant during the day. They can sometimes be concentrated under boards or other cover placed around the plants.

LARGEST ASSASSIN BUG—WHEEL BUG
Arilus cristatus (**Linnaeus**)

A wheel bug feeds on a leafminer; photograph by David Leatherman.

Order: Hemiptera

Family: Reduviidae

Distribution: Found primarily in southeastern Colorado and less commonly in parts of New Mexico, southern Utah and southwestern Colorado.

Life History and Habits: As the name suggests, all assassin bugs, including the wheel bug, are predators of other insects. They feed on almost any prey they can overpower, piercing and immobilizing it with their sucking mouthparts. Large species of assassin bugs, such as the wheel bug, can even kill grasshoppers and large caterpillars. The wheel bug gets its common name from the large, cogwheel-like enlargement on the back of the thorax.

The overwintering stage of the wheel bug is eggs glued to tree bark and shrubs. Eggs hatch in spring, and the nymphs immediately begin to hunt small insects such as aphids and leafhoppers. Prey are immobilized rapidly with a paralyzing toxin injected through its piercing-sucking mouthparts. The wheel bug's forelegs help to further grasp and manipulate their prey. As wheel bugs get older, they can capture most large insects that land on twigs and branches, where they lie in ambush. These include wasps, flies, bees and a variety of other insects that are captured at this time. Wheel bugs become mature by early to midsummer; the adults are also predaceous. Eggs are laid in mid- to late summer, and there is one generation per year.

Related Species: Several other species of assassin bugs occur in the region, and most are moderately large. A large, black and fairly common species found around homes is *Reduvius personatus* (Linnaeus), known as the "masked hunter." This insect gets its name from the nymphs' habit of covering themselves with dust or other debris. Other common large species of assassin bugs include those of the genus *Apiomerus*, known as the "bee assassins." These bright red and black bugs commonly feed on bees or flies, captured as they visit flowers.

Although almost all assassin bugs feed solely on insects and many are highly beneficial, a few species occasionally bite humans (including the masked hunter), and members of the genus *Triatoma* ("conenoses" or "kissing bugs") feed on blood and may transmit Chagas' disease. However, assassin bugs have never been associated with transmitting disease in the region, although this has occurred in the more southwestern areas of the country.

Masked hunter, adult; photograph by Frank Peairs

Collecting Tips: Assassin bugs are found in a wide variety of plants and are most easily collected with a sweep net. However, the wheel bug usually restricts its hunting to trees and shrubs. Careful examination of the plants and use of a beat net can help with collection of this uncommon species. Adults are most common in midsummer.

Most assassin bugs will bite when handled carelessly and can cause a very painful reaction. The wheel bugs also may evert an orange gland from their hind end, which releases ammonium-based chemicals that some predators find distasteful.

Rearing Tips: Wheel bugs are easily maintained and reared in a terrarium if fed a variety of insects, such as crickets or mealworms. A moisture source should also be provided.

LARGEST AMBUSH BUG— *PHYMATA AMERICANA* (MELIN)

The ambush bug, Phymata americana; slide courtesy of Oregon State University

Order: Hemiptera

Family: Phymatidae (sometimes considered to be a subfamily, Phymatinae, of the assassin bugs, Reduviidae)

Distribution: Common throughout the region.

Life History and Habits: The common name of the ambush bugs was earned by their ability to lie concealed in flowers, ready to ambush and subdue unwary visiting insects. The ambush bugs are often well camouflaged in such sites and can seize prey such as bees, flies and small moths with their enlarged grasping forelegs. Once captured, the prey is drained of body fluids via the piercing mouthparts of the ambush bug.

Winter is spent in the egg stage. Eggs are laid in July and August in small, froth-covered masses on plant stems. The eggs hatch the following spring, and the nymphs develop rapidly through early summer. Adults are present for most of the summer months. There is one generation per year.

Related Species: Other species of ambush bugs in the genus *Phymata* that occur in the region are *P. vicinca* Handlirsch and *P. borica* Evans. All the members of this group are similar in appearance.

Certain crab spiders, especially those in the genus *Misumena*, also commonly wait on flowers to capture visiting insects and are often seen by collectors searching for ambush bugs.

Collecting Tips: Adult ambush bugs can usually be found by carefully searching flowers from late July through September. Among the flowers on which they are most commonly found are those produced by rabbitbrush (*Chrysothamnus* species) and goldenrod (*Solidago* species).

Misumena crab spiders often hide in flowers and ambush insects.

LARGE STINK BUGS—ROUGH STINK BUGS
Brochymena sulcatas **Van Duzee**
Brochymena quadripustulata **(Fabricius)**

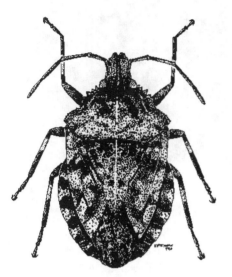

Rough stink bug,
Brochymena *species;*
drawing by Mike
Kippenhan

Order: Hemiptera

Family: Pentatomidae

Distribution: Generally distributed throughout the region and moderately common.

Life History and Habits: Although rough stink bugs are common species in the region, their coloration allows them to blend in well with the background; they are thus difficult to see. They are perhaps most commonly encountered when they enter homes in fall for winter shelter, or are carried indoors on firewood. Winter is spent in a dormant state in the adult stage, often under the bark of trees or logs. They become active in late April and June.

They feed on leaves of a wide variety of trees at this time, but do not appear to cause any significant injury. After mating, the females lay elongate, pearly white eggs in masses of ten to twenty. The overwintered bugs usually die before the end of June, but the

The harlequin bug is a brightly patterned stink bug that sometimes damages garden plants in the southern areas of the region.

pale-colored nymphs hatch from these eggs about two weeks after egg laying. The nymphs feed and develop throughout July; adults typically are first found in August. There is one generation per year.

Rough stink bugs feed primarily on leaves and developing seeds of trees, and have been recorded on ash, walnut, willow, boxelder and many other tree species. They are also often predatory and have been found feeding on caterpillars and leaf beetle larvae.

Related Species: Other species of rough stink bugs may be found at the extreme edges of the Rocky Mountain region. *Brochymena arborea* (Say) and *B. parva* Ruckes may be found in the southern areas of the region, while *B. affinis* Van Duzee may be collected in parts of the region.

Most stink bugs are large insects of distinctive round or ovoid shape. This group gets its name from their scent glands, which can produce a strong odor for defensive purposes. A few other groups of insects also share this habit, so stink bugs are frequently confused with the "stink beetles" (species of *Eleodes*), a common group of darkling beetles that also produce a strong odor as a defense (see "Largest Darkling Beetles— 'Skunk,' 'Stink' or 'Circus' Beetles"). Approximately two hundred species of stink bugs occur in North America; many of them are important pests of plants, while others are predators useful for biological control of other insects.

A mating pair of twospotted stink bugs

Among the larger stink bugs in the region are members of the genus *Chlorochroa*, which most closely rival rough stink bugs in size (see next section). Other large stink bugs that are frequently collected are brightly colored species, including the harlequin bug, *Murgantia histrionica* (Hahn), a brilliantly patterned orange, black and white species that feeds on plants in the mustard family in the southern half of the region. Another colorful species is the twospotted stink bug, *Perillus bioculatus* (Fabricius), which has a characteristic horseshoe pattern on its back. The twospotted stink bug is a predatory species that feeds on beetle larvae such as the Colorado potato beetle.

Collecting Tips: Rough stink bugs can be collected throughout the year, but searches are best made late in the summer when populations are highest. They may be found clinging to bark or on leaves. In the latter instance, they can sometimes be dislodged by shaking or beating branches and collecting the insects on a drop cloth or beating tray.

Rearing Tips: Rough stink bugs can be reared by providing fresh leaves; in the laboratory they have been reared on bean plants. Their diet can be supplemented occasionally with small caterpillars or leaf beetles.

MORE LARGE STINK BUGS—SAY'S STINK BUG AND CONCHUELA
Chlorochroa sayi (Stäl)—Say's Stink Bug
Chlorochroa ligata (Say)—Conchuela
Chlorochroa uhleri (Stäl)

Order: Hemiptera

Family: Pentatomidae

Distribution: Generally distributed throughout the region and locally common.

Life History and Habits: *Chlorochroa* species of stink bugs spend the winter as adult bugs under debris and other protective cover. They emerge

Say's stink bug

in mid-spring and feed on growing plants; alfalfa and other legumes are particular favorites. Eggs are laid in masses on these plants, and the young nymphs emerge in about a week. The nymphs feed on flowers, fruits and leaves of various plants, becoming full grown in July.

There is probably only one generation in most of the region. In the warmer areas of the region, some of the earliest first-generation stink bugs may attempt to reproduce and repeat the cycle. However, nymphs that fail to develop by the time of killing frosts are unable to successfully survive the winter.

These stink bugs are capable of causing serious crop injury. They prefer to feed on the developing fruits or seeds of a variety of plants, and in the process kill small areas of plant tissues around where they have inserted their mouthparts. This frequently causes plants to abort the damaged fruit or seed. Fruits that remain on the plant may develop spongy or corky areas. Alfalfa grown for seed, peas, cotton and peaches are among the crops most frequently damaged.

Related Species: In addition to the rough stink bugs (see previous section) the green stink bug, *Acrosternum hilare* (Say), is a large species found in parts of Montana, Utah and Colorado, and generally resembles the *Chlorochroa* species. The green stink bug is an occasional pest of crops grown for seed, particularly legumes such as beans.

Collecting Tips: These stink bugs are commonly collected on fruiting plants in midsummer. Yucca and mullein are among the plants that should be inspected for these bugs at that time. Alternatively, using a sweep net in alfalfa is a productive method for collecting *Chlorochroa* species of stink bugs.

ORDER: THYSANOPTERA
Thrips

The thrips have several features that are unusual among the various insect orders. The name of the order is derived from the Greek *thysano*, referring to the peculiar highly fringed wings possessed by most adults. The mouthparts are a specialized sucking type that is often described as "rasping-sucking," in contrast to the "piercing-sucking" mouthparts of many other insects. In thrips, there are only three piercing stylets (one mandible, two maxillae), since the second mandible is very reduced in size and nonfunctional. The stylets are used to penetrate and break tissues. The conelike proboscis surrounding the stylets then allows the fluids to be sucked up.

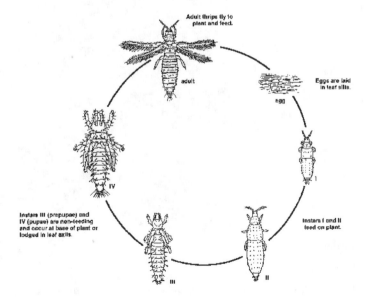

Adult thrips fly to plant and feed.

adult

Eggs are laid in leaf slits.

egg

Instars III (prepupae) and IV (pupae) are non-feeding and occur at base of plant or lodged in leaf axils.

IV

Instars I and II feed on plant.

III

II

Life cycle of the onion thrips, a typical plant-feeding thrips

The metamorphosis of the thrips is intermediate between simple and complete types. Eggs are inserted into plant tissues. This is followed by two feeding stages, usually called larvae. After the immature feeding stages have been completed, thrips undergo two or three nonfeeding stages known as prepupa and pupa.

The thrips are an extremely common group of insects but are frequently overlooked. A few species are serious plant pests, including the onion thrips, *Thrips tabaci* Lindeman, and the western flower thrips, *Frankliniella occidentalis* (Pergande). Injuries result from scarring wounds made to leaves, fruits and flowers. Thrips are also capable of transmitting tomato spotted wilt virus, a widespread problem of many vegetable and greenhouse crops grown in North America.

Largest Thrips—Bandedwing Thrips
Aeolothrips fasciatus (Linnaeus)

Bandedwing thrips; photograph courtesy of Brigham Young University

Order: Thysanoptera

Family: Aeolothripidae

Distribution: Apparently introduced from Europe, but now widely distributed throughout the region.

Life History and Habits: The bandedwing thrips are predators of various small arthropods such as mites and other species of thrips. Rarely, they also may feed on plant juices and pollen when prey are not available. The bandedwing thrips may be important for the biological control of certain greenhouse pests and are being considered for this use.

Eggs are laid by the female in plant tissue. As with most thrips, they have an unusual life cycle that has two active larval stages during which they feed, followed by two pupal stages on the ground inside a small cocoon. The bandedwing thrips overwinter in the cocoon, emerging in spring.

The female is blackish-brown with red pigmentation banding on the body, and reaches a length of 1/10 inch (2.4 mm). The male is smaller than the female and lighter in color. Both sexes have colored bands on their fringed wings. Female thrips can produce young without mating.

Related Species: A closely related species, *Aeolothrips duvali* Moulton, is also common in the region. It has often been collected on the curly cup gumweed plant. A slightly larger (1/8 inch [3 mm]) species of thrips, *Acanthothrips folsomi* (Hood) (Phlaeothripidae family), occasionally may be found, but information on its regional distribution and life cycle is lacking.

Other species of bandedwing thrips can be found where sources of prey are abundant. These include crops such as corn that is infested with spider mites or flowers that contain large populations of flower thrips.

Collecting Tips: Bandedwing thrips are most easily located while searching flowers in late spring and early summer. They are best preserved in a small vial containing 70 percent ethyl alcohol. They can be picked up easily using a small moistened paintbrush.

ORDER: NEUROPTERA/MEGALOPTERA
Lacewings, Antlions, Dobsonflies and Mantidflies

The Neuroptera are soft-bodied insects with four membranous wings in the adult stage. The wings are marked by numerous small veins, the characteristic for which the order is named (*Neuroptera* means "nerve wings"). When at rest, their wings are usually held over their back in a rooflike manner. They are weak fliers.

Larvae of all species are predators of insects or other arthropods. They usually possess a pair of curved, forward-pointing mouthparts used to suck the body fluids of their prey. One family in particular, the green lacewings (Chrysopidae), are highly beneficial as biological controls of crop pests. Pupation occurs in a silk cocoon. Neuropterans undergo complete metamorphosis.

Some collectors subdivide the Neuroptera into several orders. One common division is to separate the dobsonflies and fishflies (Megaloptera), the snakeflies (Raphidiodea) and the lacewings, mantidflies and antlions (Planipennia).

Adult Neuroptera can be displayed by pinning, although some are better preserved in alcohol. Some adult stages, such as antlions, are very long, and are best displayed by supporting the abdomen while pinning. When dry, most are quite fragile and may lose some color. Larvae should be kept in alcohol.

Hellgrammite, photograph courtesy of Brigham Young University

Largest Megalopteran—Hellgrammite
Corydalus cornutus Linnaeus

Order: Neuroptera (Megaloptera)

Family: Corydalidae

Distribution: Common in the eastern United States and parts of the southwestern United States. It has been collected in the Purgatoire River system in southeastern Colorado and the Colorado and Green rivers in Colorado and Utah.

Dobsonfly

Life History and Habits: Mating and egg laying by the adult stage, known as a type of dobsonfly, occur in early summer. Females attach eggs to objects that overhang the water and are not exposed to direct sunlight. When the eggs hatch, the larvae drop to the water. Larvae, called "hellgrammites," are fierce predators that will feed on anything that they can overpower, primarily other insects. After becoming full grown, they crawl out of the stream and pupate under rocks, in logs or in soil, often several dozen feet (meters) from the water in which they developed. Larvae require a year or more to complete their life cycle.

Adult males possess jaws that are considerably larger than those of the female. However, the jaws are much less pronounced in *Corydalus cornutus* found in Colorado than in those found eastern North America.

Collecting Tips: Adults are most easily collected by use of lights near streams in June and July. Larvae can be collected with an aquatic net or seine while overturning rocks and other debris in the water. Larvae can pinch if handled, but are not poisonous.

Largest Antlion—
Vella fallax texana (Hagen)

Vella fallax texana is the largest antlion found in the region.

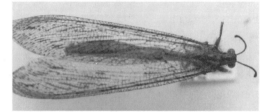

Order: Neuroptera (Planipennia)

Family: Myrmeleontidae

Distribution: Many species of antlions are found throughout the region. The largest, *V. fallax,* is limited to the western areas of the region. Smaller species of antlions (genera *Brachynemurus* and *Myremeleon*) are widespread throughout the region and can even be found at high elevations.

These pits in the soil are produced by antlion larvae.

*An antlion larva;
photograph courtesy
of USDA*

Life History and Habits: Antlions get their name from the means by which they catch their prey. Larvae construct shallow pits in loose soil and live at the base. Ants or other small arthropods that attempt to cross the pit fall to the bottom of the pit and are grabbed by the large pincer mouthparts of the antlion larvae. Antlions also may flick or throw soil to cause the prey insect to fall within reach.

The overwintering stage of the antlion is a full-grown larva in the soil pit. In spring it changes to the pupal stage. Adults emerge in late spring and early summer. There is one generation per year.

Collecting Tips: The adult stage flies in the early evening and is attracted to lights. They also can be captured while sweeping shrubbery with a sweep net.

Larvae can be dug out of their pits, which are often located under an overhang, such as a rock, bridge or eave, or in some other location protected from direct rains.

Rearing Tips: The larvae can easily be reared in a jar partially filled with sand and provided with insect prey for food.

Miscellaneous: Adult antlions superficially resemble damselflies, for which they are commonly mistaken. The easiest way to distinguish them is by their antennae: on antlions they are prominent and clubbed; on damselflies they are very small and hairlike.

Largest Mantidfly—Western Mantispid
Climaciella brunnea (Say)

Western mantispid

Order: Neuroptera (Planipennia)

Family: Mantispidae

Distribution: Generally distributed in much of North America, but usually only locally common. This species is apparently most abundant in the more southern areas of the region.

Life History and Habits: Larvae of most species of mantidflies are predators of spiders or their egg sacs. For example, larvae of *Climaciella brunnea* have been collected while feeding on wolf spiders and their egg sacs. Eggs are laid on vegetation and the larvae actively move about in search of prey.

Adults of *C. brunnea* have frequently been collected while resting on rabbitbrush and other shrubs in July and August. Other mantidflies are found resting on foliage of cottonwood trees and willow. They are thought to be predators of other insects, which they capture using their prominent grasping forelegs.

C. brunnea is an excellent mimic of other insects, particularly various species of paper wasps (Vespidae). The common form found in the region closely resembles the western paper wasp, *Mischocyttarus flavitarsis* Saussure, also discussed in this book.

Related Species: A few other species of mantidflies occur in the region, including at least four species in the genus *Mantispa*. *M. interrupta* Say rivals *C. brunnea* in size, but is less commonly collected and more restricted to southern areas in the region. All the mantidflies are thought to develop as predators of spiders or spider egg masses.

Collecting Tips: Adult mantidflies can be collected in midsummer by sweeping rabbitbrush, sunflowers, tamarisk (salt cedar) or other shrubbery with a net. They are also readily attracted to blacklight traps during the night.

LARGEST SNAKEFLY—STIGMATIC SNAKEFLY
Inocella inflata (Hagen)

The female snakefly of the Raphidia *species possesses a long ovipositor; photograph courtesy of Brigham Young University.*

Order: Neuroptera (Raphidiodea)

Family: Inocelliidae

Distribution: Generally distributed in the region in forested areas west of the Continental Divide.

Life History and Habits: Snakeflies (also called "serpentflies") are predators of other insects, their larvae developing by feeding on small insects such as aphids, bark beetle larvae and caterpillars. Most commonly they are found under bark, although they also can be found in debris on the ground. Larvae of snakeflies may closely resemble larvae of certain beetles, with which they are often confused.

Winter is spent in the pupal stage, which usually occurs in decayed wood or bark, occasionally in the soil. Exposure to very low winter temperatures is needed to allow the insect to complete its development, which limits where snakeflies may be found. If development continues, they transform to the adult stage the following spring. Females, which possess a long ovipositor, lay eggs in small masses on the bark, which hatch in early summer. Adults are also predaceous, but have relatively small mouthparts and can capture only small insects.

Related Species: Although the stigmatic snakefly is the only "giant snakefly" (genus *Inocellia*) in the region, more than a dozen smaller snakefly species in the genus *Rhaphidia* occur, and many are locally very common. Adults of both groups of snakeflies are characterized as brown to black, with clear highly veined wings that are held rooflike over their back. They have large, flattened heads and a very long, slender prothorax (neck). Snakeflies lack the prominent grasping forelegs of the mantidflies, but otherwise resemble them in many features, and are much more common.

Collecting Tips: Snakeflies are usually collected by sweeping trees, shrubs and areas of dense vegetation from April through July. Pines and junipers are particularly good spots to search for adults.

ORDER: COLEOPTERA
Beetles

The beetles are a tremendously large and diverse group of insects. Approximately 40 percent of all insect species are beetles, including almost 27,000 species in the United States. The order Coleoptera contains more species than all the plants, algae and fungi combined.

The primary characteristic of the beetles is the hardened covering of the front wing, known as the elytra (*Coleoptera* means "sheath winged"). Underneath the protective elytra is typically a membranous hind wing used by most beetles to fly. However, many beetles have very reduced wings or have an elytra that is fused together, preventing flight.

Beetles feed by chewing and have very prominent mouthparts. Feeding habits vary, however. Many beetles feed on plants, including some of our most serious agricultural pests, such as the Colorado potato beetle, cabbage flea beetle and Mexican bean beetle. Others are highly beneficial, such as the familiar lady beetles and ground beetles that prey on pest species. Many other beetles are scavengers and are important in recycling nutrients. Beetles can be found in almost any habitat.

Beetles have complete metamorphosis. Immature stages (larvae) also have chewing mouthparts. Larvae may require as few as four to as many as twelve stages to complete their development, after which they pupate. The typical life cycle of most beetles in the region is one generation per year. However, a few (such as lady beetles) can have several generations during the season, while others (many longhorned beetles) require two or more years per generation.

Beetle adults should be preserved by pinning through the upper right section of the wing cover. Larvae should be preserved in 70 percent alcohol, after boiling briefly in water.

Largest Beetles—Ponderous Borer and California Prionus
Ergates spiculatus (LeConte)—Ponderous Borer
Prionus californicus Motschulsky—California Prionus

Order: Coleoptera
Family: Cerambycidae

Adult of the ponderous borer, a very large longhorned beetle; photograph by David Leatherman

A male (left) and female (right) of the California prionus *can be distinguished by the differences in their antennae.*

Distribution: The ponderous borer occurs in forested areas of ponderosa pine and Douglas fir, its principal hosts. The California prionus is more widely distributed and more commonly encountered, developing on cottonwood, oak and other trees planted near dwellings. Both are generally distributed throughout the region, except along the eastern plains.

Life History and Habits: Both the ponderous borer and the California prionus are very large (2.5–3.5 inches [6.3–9 cm]), dark-colored beetles. The latter is slightly shorter, stouter and more uniformly dark brown than the ponderous borer. It also possesses three prominent teeth on the sides of the thorax that are lacking in the ponderous borer.

Larval stages of both species develop as wood borers, a type of roundheaded borer known to foresters as "timber worms." Those of the ponderous borer typically develop in Douglas fir

Larva of the California prionus, *a very large roundheaded borer*

The adult of the locust borer is a bright yellow and black beetle commonly collected in late summer; photograph courtesy of USDA.

or ponderosa pine that has recently been felled or killed by fire. Healthy trees are not attacked, but infestations of the larvae sometimes ruin fire-damaged wood before it can be salvaged. Larvae of the California prionus (also known as the "giant root borer") usually develop in the roots or crown area of trees such as oak, apple, cottonwood and various conifers. Deadwood is particularly used by this insect.

The adult beetles are active beginning in early summer, and may be present into September. Females lay eggs in cracks in the bark of suitable logs or stumps. The larvae tunnel into the tree; during early development, most feeding occurs in the sapwood, but later they tunnel extensively through the tree. The larval stage typically takes three to five years to complete. However, this period may be extended considerably in wood that has been milled and used in construction. Pupation of the ponderous borer takes place in a cell cut out of the wood in which the insect develops; the California prionus often leaves the roots in which it was feeding and makes a pupation chamber in the soil.

Longhorn beetles (Tetraopes species) are associated with milkweed.

Females of both species are differentiated from the males by their more slender wing covers and shorter, less developed antennae. The highly developed antennae of some species have led them to be called "tile-horned beetles" or "tile-horned prionus."

Related Species: Several dark-colored longhorned beetles in the genus *Prionus* occur in the region. Although most of these also reach fairly large size (over 1 inch [2.5 cm]), they are significantly smaller than the California prionus.

More than one thousand species of longhorned beetles occur in North America. Although most develop solely in wood that has recently been cut or killed, a few species occur as pests of forest and shade trees. Among these are the cottonwood borer (see following section), the locust borer, *Megacyllene robiniae* (Forster), and the poplar borer, *Saperda calcarata* (Say). Many longhorned beetles also develop in the stems or crowns of herbaceous plants such as sunflower and milkweed. Commonly associated with the latter are various "milkweed longhorns" (*Tetraopes* species), reddish beetles with dark spots that are about 3/4 inch (1.9 cm) in length.

Longhorned beetles are generally distinguished by their prominent long antennae, which may even exceed the length of the body in some species, such as the pine sawyers (see "Large Longhorned Beetles—Pine Sawyers"). However, one common species that differs in this feature is the pole borer, *Parandra brunnea* (Fabricius), which develops as a typical roundheaded borer in dead or dying wood of willow, maple, elm and other shade trees. The adults lack

The pole borer, sometimes known as the "aberrant wood borer," commonly tunnels into dead trunks and branches.

long antennae and have prominent jaws that may cause them to be confused with other beetles, such as stag beetles.

Collecting Tips: Adult beetles of both species are most commonly found in July and August. Areas of recent Douglas fir or ponderosa pine logging are particularly good sites to find them. Adult beetles, particularly females, can be attracted to lights. Beetles and larvae may occasionally be collected from firewood.

Miscellaneous: The mechanics of boring by the ponderous borer inspired the invention of the chain saw by an observant logger.

A LARGE LONGHORNED BEETLE—COTTONWOOD BORER
Plectrodera scalator (Fabricius)

Order: Coleoptera

Family: Cerambycidae

Distribution: Found primarily in the southeastern parts of the region where hosts (cottonwood, poplars, willow) are present.

Life History and Habits: The life cycle of this insect requires two years to complete. Adults appear in late spring or early summer.

A mating pair of cottonwood borers; photograph by David Leatherman

They chew on the leaves and bark of twigs and can cause damage to tender shoots. The eggs are laid at the base of the tree in pits chewed by the adult female. Larvae, a type of roundheaded borer, feed on the roots during their first year and tunnel in the heartwood at the base of the tree during the second year. In early spring of the following season, they form a pupal cell underneath the bark and later emerge as adults.

Collecting Tips: Search trunks of cottonwood and poplar for adults in June and July. Occasionally they can be captured at light traps. The cottonwood borer is prized by collectors because of its distinctive black and white markings.

A LARGE LONGHORNED BEETLE—CACTUS LONGHORN
Moneilema armatum LeConte

Order: Coleoptera

Family: Cerambycidae

Distribution: Restricted primarily to the southern areas of the region, along with its primary host plant, cholla or candelabra cactus.

Life History and Habits: Cactus longhorn beetles develop by feeding on various cacti in the genera *Opuntia* and *Cylindropuntia*. They survive winter within a pupal cell they construct in late summer and

*Cactus longhorn;
photograph courtesy
of R. F. Kirchner*

early fall around the base of the cactus. They transform to the pupal stage in spring, and adults emerge in late spring and early summer. Adult beetles feed at night, typically eating young cactus pads or oozing sap. After mating, the females glue eggs to the cactus pad. The young larvae attempt to tunnel into the cactus, causing the plant to ooze sap at the wound. At first they feed in this ooze and later enter the plant, feeding throughout the summer and early fall. Usually one generation is produced per year, but some of the later larvae may not emerge until the second season.

Related Species: Several species of *Moneilema* occur in the southwestern United States, all restricted to various cacti. These include *M. annulatum* Say, *M. appressum* LeConte and *M. semipunctatum* LeConte. These generally resemble the cactus longhorn, but are smaller. Darkling beetles in the genus *Eleodes* also resemble longhorn beetles in the genus *Moneilema*, but have very different habits (see "Largest Darkling Beetles—'Skunk', 'Stink' or 'Circus' Beetles").

The blue cactus borer, *Melitara dentata* (Grote), the larva of a pyralid moth, is also a common borer of *Opuntia* cacti throughout the region (see "Largest Pyralid Moth—Blue Cactus Borer").

Collecting Tips: The large black adults are conspicuous and easily collected from *Opuntia* cacti, particularly in late June and July. Although most active at night, they may be found during the day hiding around the base of the plant or in protected sites such as branch crotches. Tunnels of the larva within the cactus are often marked with dark ooze produced around the wound site.

Collectors should use a pair of long forceps to collect this insect from cactus to avoid injury by cactus spines.

Miscellaneous: The cactus longhorn was purposely introduced into Australia to aid in the biological control of prickly pear cactus, which became a serious rangeland weed in that country.

Large Longhorned Beetles—Pine Sawyers
Monochamus species

Order: Coleoptera

Family: Cerambycidae

Distribution: Found primarily in conifer forests where their hosts—dying and downed pine or spruce wood—are found. Also found throughout the region emerging from pine firewood. The two common large species are *Monochamus scutellatus* (Say) and *M. clamator* (LeConte).

Life History and Habits: The larvae of these insects, known as "pine sawyers," feed on dead and dying conifers, including pine, spruce, fir and Douglas fir. They tunnel under the bark, then later may move throughout the wood; the tunnels provide an entrance for wood-rotting fungal spores. Adults feed on needles and young twigs but seldom cause extensive damage. Eggs are laid in pits chewed in the bark. Development from egg to adult takes one to two years. Pine sawyers will not attack wood after the bark has been removed.

This group of longhorned beetles is perhaps best distinguished by their extremely long antennae, which may exceed body length.

These beetles are important in some areas of the country because of their ability to transmit the pine wood nematode, a type of roundworm that develops under the bark of certain pines and may kill the trees. Problems with pine wood nematode are as yet

The adult of a pine sawyer is a common species associated with pine logs; photograph by David Leatherman.

unknown in the region, but they do occur in some of the states just east of the High Plains.

Adult pine sawyers, and many other longhorned beetles, produce an audible squeaking sound.

Collecting Tips: The pine sawyers are most often seen during the day in late summer, particularly in areas of recent pine or spruce cutting, around log decks or new firewood piles. Look for them at places selling green firewood or other wood products with bark intact.

LARGEST PREDACEOUS DIVING BEETLES—
DYTISCUS SPECIES
Dytiscus dauricus Gebler
Dytiscus hybridus Aube
Dytiscus marginicollis LeConte

Order: Coleoptera

Family: Dytiscidae

Distribution: Generally distributed but uncommon, tending to be more abundant in the southern areas. All are associated with permanent ponds or lakes, in which they live.

Males and many related species of Dytiscus dauricus, *a large predaceous diving beetle, have smooth, shiny wing covers.*

Life History and Habits: Predaceous diving beetles are predators of insects and other small animals, including fish, found in water. The larvae, sometimes known as "water tigers," have a pair of long, sicklelike jaws that they use to catch prey. The prey is quickly paralyzed by enzymes in the saliva. After it has been partially digested, fluids are sucked up. Larvae of *Dytiscus* species must periodically return to the surface to breathe. However, several other predaceous diving beetles acquire oxygen through air trapped in plant stems or by use of gills.

Adult beetles are well adapted for swimming. Their body is smooth and oval. The hind legs are flattened and fringed to form an excellent paddle. Predaceous diving beetles can carry a bubble of air underneath their wing covers that allows them to remain submerged for long periods of time. Adult beetles can be seen resting in the water, hanging downward with the hind tip of the abdomen sticking into the air. Adult beetles have chewing mouthparts typical of many other beetles.

Related Species: Many smaller species of predaceous diving beetles are common in the region, including the genera *Agabus*, *Thermonectus*, *Laccophilus* and *Rhantus*.

Predaceous diving beetles are easily confused with the water scavenger beetles (see following section). The two groups of beetles can be distinguished by their antennae (long and threadlike in diving beetles; short and clubbed in water scavenger beetles); their means of swimming (predaceous diving beetles use their legs like oars; water scavenger beetles swim as an insects walks, moving their

Larva of a predaceous diving beetle; photograph courtesy of Brigham Young University

hind legs alternately) and by the presence or absence of a large spine running along the underside (present in water scavenger beetles; absent in predaceous diving beetles).

Smaller species of predaceous diving beetles are sometimes confused with whirligig beetles (Gyrinidae family). Whirligig beetles are most often seen gyrating on the surface of the water in small groups, feeding primarily on insects that have fallen in the water. Unlike the smaller predaceous beetles, whirligig beetles have compound eyes that are divided, allowing them to view objects both above and below them.

Collecting Tips: Adult beetles can often be seen cruising a few feet offshore in search of prey. Adults and larvae are best collected with a dip net designed to capture aquatic insects. Adult beetles, particularly of the smaller species, are often attracted to lights and can be caught in light traps.

LARGEST WATER SCAVENGER BEETLE— GIANT WATER SCAVENGER BEETLE
Hydrophilus triangularis Say

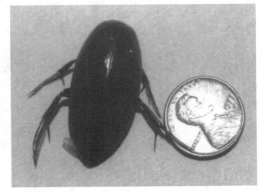

Giant water scavenger beetle

Order: Coleoptera

Family: Hydrophilidae

Distribution: Generally distributed throughout the region in association with pools of standing water. It is a strong flier and may even colonize small pools, such as livestock watering tanks.

Life History and Habits: *Hydrophilus triangularis* is a large, shiny black beetle that develops in water. The immature stage is a predator of other insects and small animals found in water. After completing its development, it pupates in a silken case attached to underwater plants.

The adult beetles are scavengers of dead plant and animal materials. They are excellent swimmers, propelling themselves by alternately moving their hind legs. Water scavenger beetles are also adapted to carry a thin film of air along their underside, which acts as a sort of aqualung, allowing them to remain under water for considerable periods.

Related Species: Many smaller species of water scavenger beetles are common in the region, including the genera *Berosus*, *Helophorus*, *Tropisternus* and *Enochrus*. Water scavenger beetles can easily be mistaken for the predaceous diving beetles (Dytiscidae) (see previous section).

Collecting Tips: Water scavenger beetles are strong fliers and are readily attracted to lights. They also fly during the day and are attracted to shiny objects, including shiny car finishes (particularly blue, green and black). Adults and larvae can be collected with dip nets or aquatic nets in the shallow water along shorelines. They often colonize livestock watering tanks.

LARGEST BLISTER BEETLES—OIL BEETLES
Meloe Species

Large oil beetles, Meloe *species, are the largest blister beetles found in the region; photograph by John Capinera.*

Order: Coleoptera

Family: Meloidae

Distribution: Generally distributed throughout the region.

Life History and Habits: Blister beetles all survive as larvae by parasitizing other insects. Those in the genus *Meloe* parasitize different species of ground-nesting bees. Winter is spent in the adult stage and, perhaps, also as a nearly full-grown larva. Adults can be seen in spring and are fairly long-lived. Females lay eggs near flowers and the newly hatched larva, known as a triangulin, is highly active and attaches itself to a visiting adult bee. The triangulin is then carried into the nest and the young blister beetle feeds on the immature, developing bees. As the blister beetle larva grows, it molts repeatedly and takes on a variety of different forms after each molt (hypermetamorphosis). It becomes full grown after a couple of months and pupates within the remnants of the bee nest. Adult beetles of *M. laevis* Leach begin to emerge in early summer and feed on a variety of plants, particularly members of the nightshade family (potatoes, tomatoes, etc.)

Black blister beetle, Epicauta pennsylvanica

The large black blister beetles in the genus *Meloe* are sometimes known as "oil beetles," because they often exude an oily substance from the joints of their legs, a defensive behavior known as "reflex bleeding." Blister beetles (Cantharidae) get their name from a compound they contain, called cantharidin, which causes an irritating blister when the beetles are handled. This toxin is particularly dangerous to horses; feeding on blister beetle–infested alfalfa hay can cause poisoning. The large *Meloe* species do not have large amounts of this toxin. Some very toxic species of blister beetles exist, however, particularly in the eastern and southeastern areas of the region.

Related Species: The largest of the oil beetles is *Meloe laevis* Leach. Approximately six additional species occur in the region, with *M. niger* Kirby and *M. impressus* Kirby being most abundant. All are large, black and generally soft-bodied.

In addition, there are dozens of other regional species of blister beetles; those in the genus *Epicauta* are very common and widespread. These species have wing covers (elytra) that cover their abdomen but are soft. Perhaps the most common regional species is the black blister beetle, *Epicauta pennsylvanica* (De Geer), a 1/2-inch-long (1.3-cm) black species that feeds on various flowers late in the summer. Other blister beetle species are striped or spotted, including those that are particularly hazardous to livestock that may eat them. The larvae of the *Epicauta* species of blister beetles feed on the egg pods of grasshoppers; their abundance often follows periods of heavy egg laying by grasshoppers.

This spotted blister beetle is a member of a toxin-producing species that can injure horses when eaten in hay; photograph by John Capinera.

Another group of larger blister beetles that attract attention are members of the genus *Lytta*. Adult beetles are fairly large, 1 inch (2.5 cm) or more in length, and many have metallic green, blue or purple wing covers. Adults are most commonly collected on leguminous plants, such as lupine or locoweed, and may occur in masses in early summer. Larvae are predators of grasshoppers.

Collecting Tips: Blister beetles in the genus *Meloe* do not fly. They can be detected by carefully examining the soil in areas where they are known to occur in spring and early summer. These beetles can also be found feeding on various weeds, such as nightshade.

Most other blister beetles do fly and periodically congregate on flowering plants. In particular, they are found, often for only brief periods, on pea family plants such as honey locust, lupines and alfalfa; one species, the caragana blister beetle, *Epicauta subglabra* (Fall), specializes in caragana foliage and flowers. Most blister beetles are particularly abundant in early summer, but the black blister beetle is present and abundant on flowers into September.

The toxin produced by blister beetles can be very irritating, particularly if it gets into the eyes. Use extra caution when handling blister beetles. Gloves are suggested for collecting the more toxic species, although most do not produce a blistering action.

Meloe blister beetles are quite soft-bodied and will shrink considerably after pinning and drying.

LARGEST CARRION BEETLE—RED AND BLACK BURYING BEETLE
Nicrophorus marginatus Fabricius

Order: Coleoptera

Family: Silphidae

Distribution: Common throughout the region around open fields, usually near animal carcasses.

Life History and Habits: Overwintering adult beetles become active in mid-spring. The adult beetles seek out small animal carcasses (such as mice), which they locate by detecting hydrogen sulfide and other gases produced by decomposition. Beetles (usually one pair) then prepare the carcass by burying it in the soil, forming a small underground chamber and later removing the hair from it. The adult beetles then mate underground and the female lays up to thirty eggs. After mating, the male beetle leaves the chamber and the female remains to feed the developing young for a few hours. The larvae develop rapidly upon the animal carcass, becoming adult beetles in about a month.

Adult beetles also feed on fungi and animal manure.

Related Species: Several other large carrion beetles in the genus *Nicrophorus* occur in the region, including *N. carolinus* (Linnaeus), *N. guttula* Motschulsky, *N. investigator* Letterstedt, *N. hybridus* Hatch and Angell and *N. obscurus* Kirby. All are fairly large beetles, from 5/8 to 1 inch (1.6–2.5 cm) in length, and most are generally dark and shiny

The red and black burying beetle

Carrion beetle (Necrophilia
americana)

with colorful markings. The wing covers of the adults are short and do not cover the tip of the abdomen.

Another common group of carrion beetles are species in the genus *Necrophilia* (=*Silpha*). These are also fairly large beetles, usually about 1/2 inch (1.3 cm) in length, with a generally oval and flattened shape. Most of these beetles are scavengers that feed on dead animal matter, but do not bury their food. However, larvae of some species feed on the leaves of vegetables and are occasionally recorded as pests.

Collecting Tips: *N. marginatus* and other carrion beetles can easily be trapped with a pitfall trap (a can filled with water) baited with a mouse, fish or chicken parts (legs, wings). These baits are particularly attractive after being "well ripened" for one or two days in a covered container. The various carrion beetles also can be collected from under animal carcasses. Collection of beetles should be done in late spring and early summer, when adult beetles are locating food.

Carrion beetles in the genus *Nicrophorus* may superficially resemble bees or wasps and may even buzz. They are harmless to humans.

LARGEST ROVE BEETLE—HAIRY ROVE BEETLE
Creophilus maxillosus Linnaeus

Hairy rove beetle

Order: Coleoptera

Family: Staphylinidae

Distribution: Generally distributed throughout North America. This species is almost cosmopolitan, having been recorded on most continents.

Life History and Habits: Adults of *Creophilus maxillosus* are usually found associated with rotting organic matter, carrion and dung. It was once assumed that they fed on these materials, but it is now known that they are predators of insects attracted to these sites, notably fly maggots.

The adults are strong fliers and lay eggs where prey is abundant. The overwintering stage is an adult, and there appear to be one or two generations per season.

This species has fully developed wings that are folded under the short leathery forewings. Beginning collectors sometimes confuse rove beetles with earwigs, since both have short wing covers. Rove beetles lack the distinctive hind cerci (pinchers) present on earwigs.

Related Species: The rove beetles are the largest family of insects in North America, with an estimated 3,200 different species. Most are predators, particularly of fly larvae, and many are highly beneficial in their habits. They can be found almost everywhere, including ant and termite nests, caves and even nests of mammals and birds. Little is known about the great majority of species, and many remain undescribed.

Many rove beetles will curl their abdomen upward when disturbed, a posture that mimics a stinging insect. However, none of them sting or are known to be harmful.

Collecting Tips: The hairy rove beetle can be collected around animal carcasses or manure that has aged a week or more and that supports large numbers of fly larvae, on which this insect develops. The larger species of rove beetles, such as *C. maxillosus*, can produce a painful pinch with their mandibles when handled carelessly.

LARGEST DERMESTID BEETLE—COMMON CARRION DERMESTID
Dermestes marmoratus Say

Common carrion dermestid

Order: Coleoptera

Family: Dermestidae

Distribution: Common throughout the region.

Life History and Habits: This species and many of the other fifteen species of *Dermestes* are associated with animal carcasses in the latter stage of decomposition. Larvae and adults feed on the dried animal material. Pupation occurs at or near the food source; the number of generations produced is variable, depending on temperature and the quality of the food supply. Larvae may survive for extended periods in the absence of food, and actually molt to a smaller stage while maintaining themselves until new food supplies are discovered.

Related Species: Dermestid beetles are very common scavengers throughout the region. Among the larger species are the larder beetle, *Dermestes lardarius* Linnaeus, and the black larder beetle, *Dermestes ater* De Geer. Dermestids feed primarily on materials of animal origin, such as animal carcasses, dried meats, fur, woolens and dead insects. Several species are important household pests, especially smaller species in the genera *Trogoderma* and *Anthrenus*, and may damage woolen fabrics, stuffed animals, furs, many kinds of stored food and insect collections. Dermestid beetles are also known as "hide beetles," "larder beetles" or "carpet beetles." The latter name is based on their former importance as a pest of wool carpeting.

The common carrion dermestid and other species of the genus *Dermestes* are often maintained by taxidermists or museums to "clean" mammal skeletons.

Collecting Tips: The adults and larvae are most easily found in dried animal carcasses. Adults can also be collected at light traps.

LARGEST CLICK BEETLE—EYED ELATOR
Alaus oculatus (**Linnaeus**)

Eyed elator

Order: Coleoptera

Family: Elateridae

Distribution: Generally distributed throughout the region and most abundant in the southern areas. They are uncommon and rarely collected.

Life History and Habits: The life cycle of the eyed elator is poorly understood. The larval stages (a large "wireworm") are predators of wood-boring insects. Adult beetles are most commonly found around rotting logs and stumps searching for egg-laying sites in midsummer. Many wireworms may require several years to become fully grown and to pupate.

Typical of other click beetles, the eyed elator adult can flip, with an audible clicking noise, when placed on its back. The adults also make a loud buzzing noise while in flight.

Related Species: Numerous species of click beetles occur in the region, but none approach the eyed elator in size. Most feed on underground parts of plants, usually grasses or grains. The larvae (wireworms) are occasional pests of seedling plants and root/tuber crops, such as potatoes.

Collecting Tips: The eyed elator is difficult to collect. Probably the best way to locate the adults is to search rotten tree stumps in early summer. They sometimes can be found resting on plants during the day in midsummer.

Other species of click beetles are readily collected with light traps throughout late spring and summer.

LARGEST FIREFLIES/LIGHTNING BUGS—
PHOTURIS SPECIES

Order: Coleoptera

Family: Lampyridae

Distribution: Members of the genus *Photuris,* which are capable of producing bright flashing light, are uncommon in the region and restricted primarily to limited areas east of the Rocky Mountains. Irrigation has produced much additional habitat, however, and some species are expanding their range. Many other fireflies that cannot produce light, or produce only weak light, are native and common throughout the region.

Life History and Habits: Fireflies develop as predators, feeding on mostly slugs and snails as well as a few insects and earthworms. They spend the winter as partially grown larvae and resume feeding in spring,

The light-producing fireflies of the Photinus *species are abundant in eastern North America but occur infrequently in the Rocky Mountain states.*

becoming full grown in late spring or early summer. Pupation occurs in the soil.

Adults are usually most abundant in late June and early July. The flashing light that is so characteristic of this group of insects is used to attract mates; different species use different flashing patterns. Indeed, fireflies in the genus *Photuris* are difficult or impossible to distinguish except by the flashing pattern of the adults.

The light produced by fireflies is achieved by a unique chemical reaction that produces an almost pure "cold" light. Two compounds, luciferin and luciferase, produce the light when combined in the presence of oxygen. By controlling the release of these chemicals and the oxygen supply, fireflies can create the pattern and intensity of the flashing.

Related Species: There are 136 species of fireflies in North America, with the great majority found in the eastern half of the country. In addition to members of the genus *Photuris*, large fireflies in the genus *Photinus* are well recognized for their ability to produce light, although none of the latter are apparently established in the region.

However, several species that produce only weak light or do not produce any light can be found throughout much of the region, particularly those in the genera *Lucidota* and *Pyropyga*. Adults of these species tend to be active during the day and are most commonly found near water (or irrigated yards) where slugs and snails occur.

Collecting Tips: Adult males of *Photuris* species are most easily collected with a net in late June and July when they are flashing at night to attract females. Females, which less commonly produce flashes and which occur on the ground, are more difficult to find.

All fireflies are most abundant near moist areas that support slugs and snails, on which the larvae primarily feed.

The nonflashing species that predominate in the region are frequently found on vegetation throughout much of the summer. They are day fliers and can be collected easily by searching plants or sweeping with a net.

A LARGE GROUND BEETLE—FIERY HUNTER
Calosoma calidium (**Fabricius**)

The fiery hunter is a large species of ground beetle; photograph courtesy of USDA.

Order: Coleoptera

Family: Carabidae

Distribution: Generally distributed throughout the region, but uncommon.

Life History and Habits: The fiery hunter and other ground beetles in the genus *Calosoma* prey on other insects as both larvae and adults. Some are known as "caterpillar hunters" because of their importance in destroying various caterpillar pests such as cutworms. The largest representative of the genus, the fiery hunter, is generally black with red or yellow pits on its back.

As larvae and adults, ground beetles are characterized by large biting mandibles or jaws. They are often found on or just below the soil surface. Adults are common under rocks, plants or litter and move quickly when disturbed. Most ground beetles are poor climbers, but the fiery hunter will sometimes climb trees and plants to capture caterpillar prey.

Related Species: Three other species of ground beetles in the genus *Calosoma* rival the fiery hunter in size: *C. calidium* Fabricius, *C. triste* LeConte and *C. lugubre* LeConte. These are limited primarily to the eastern half of the region. They lack rows of metallic dots on their wing covers, which are characteristic of the fiery hunter. An even larger species is the bright metallic green, *C. scrutator* (Fabricius), introduced during the early part of the century and since then only rarely collected. Unlike the other members of this genus, *C. scrutator* is well adapted to climbing trees.

A very large number of other ground beetles occur in the region. Almost all are considered highly beneficial predators of other insects. Because of their size and coloration, they are one of the most commonly collected group of insects. Members of the genera *Harpalus, Carabus* and *Pasimachus* (see following section) can also be are quite large and commonly collected.

Collecting Tips: *Calosoma* beetles are most easily collected under rocks or logs. They are often caught in pitfall traps. The larger species produce a mildly painful pinch with their mandibles if handled, but they rarely break the skin.

Rearing Tips: Ground beetles can be kept easily in captivity for several weeks. Small caterpillars, mealworms or other insect larvae are good food sources.

LARGE GROUND BEETLES—*PASIMACHUS* SPECIES
Pasimachus depressus LeConte
Pasimachus elongatus LeConte

Order: Coleoptera

Family: Carabidae

Distribution: Found widely at lower elevations throughout the region. The larger species (*Pasimachus depressus*) are limited to the more southern areas.

*Large ground
beetle
(Pasimachus
species)*

Life History and Habits: Like most ground beetles, both adult and
larval stages are general predators of soft-bodied insects and other
arthropods. They are active during the day and night, hiding in soil
or under rocks and other protective sites when not foraging. Larvae
feed on soft-bodied insects such as grubs, termites and maggots,
while adult stages feed on a wide range of insects including May
beetles and grasshoppers.

   The beetles have a fairly long life cycle, typically two years.
Overwintering occurs deep in the soil; they become active again in
April and May.

Related Species: Although unrelated and having greatly different
habits, ground beetles in the genus *Pasimachus* are frequently confused with stag beetles (see "Largest Stag Beetle"). Some species are
also confused with darkling beetles: both types of beetles are often
found in the same environments.

Collecting Tips: Species of *Pasimachus*, and many other ground beetles,
are most easily collected with a pitfall trap sunk into the ground in
areas used by these beetles. Where use of pitfall traps is not possible,
check under dried cow pats or under stones and logs. *Pasimachus* ground
beetles are active in the daytime, which is unusual behavior for members of this family. They can often be encountered in grassland and
shrubland areas and are easily spotted when they cross roads.

   Although the jaws of this species look fearsome, the pinch is
more startling than painful. However, they will clamp onto soft

objects with considerable strength. The beetles can also produce defensive chemicals with a strong odor.

Rearing Tips: These large ground beetles can be easily maintained in an aquarium. Because of their appetite they must be fed frequently; caterpillars, mealworms and other insect larvae are good food sources. They can be cannibalistic and should be kept alone or with other large armored insects.

Largest Tiger Beetles— *Amblycheila* Species

Largest tiger beetle,
Amblycheila
cylindriformis

Order: Coleoptera

Family: Cicindelidae

Distribution: The large tiger beetle, *Amblycheila cylindriformis* Say, can be collected from several locations in the eastern half of Colorado and New Mexico. The closely related species *A. schwarzi* Horn can be found in parts of Utah. *A. picolominii* Reiche occurs in the Four Corners area. All are fairly rare.

Life History and Habits: The life history of these insects is poorly understood, owing to their rarity. However, they appear to have a

Most tiger beetles are Cicindela *species and differ primarily in their patterning and where they are found.*

one-year life cycle, as do most other tiger beetles. The overwintering stage is larvae, which live in underground tunnels that may extend as much as 3 feet (.9 m) below the surface. At night the "grubs" lie in wait for prey near burrow entrances, capturing them with their powerful jaws. Often several larval burrows will be constructed near each other. Ants appear to be one of the most common foods of the larvae.

Adults are present from May through August. They are active at night, or occasionally during cloudy, cool periods of the day. They roam around locating their prey primarily by touch, and feed on various insects or other arthropods. During the day they hide either in burrows they have constructed or, more commonly, under cover of logs, rocks and other debris. Females lay eggs in small groups near the ground. The newly hatched larvae tunnel into the ground almost immediately after hatching.

Related Species: The great majority of tiger beetles in North America are in the genus *Cicindela*. All are highly active, brightly patterned insects that develop as predators of other insects. Among the more common and widespread species in the region are C. *punctulata* Olivier, C. *oregona* LeConte, C. *tranquebarica* Herbst and C. *repanda* Dejean. Other tiger beetles have a highly restricted habitat, such as the Idaho sand dune tiger beetle, C. *arenicola* Rumpp, and the great sand dune tiger beetle, C. *theatina* Rotger, both restricted to areas of large sand dunes.

Collecting Tips: These insects are best searched for during the night using a flashlight. They are usually found near permanent or semipermanent streams and rivers, always in areas of clay, rather than sandy, soils. Adults can also be captured in pitfall traps. Occasionally, beetles are found in the daytime under rocks or wood. Use care while searching: rattlesnakes and scorpions also frequent these sites.

The adults have powerful jaws that can pinch and occasionally break the skin. However, they do not have poisonous saliva and are easily handled without the risk of biting.

The common *Cicindela* species of tiger beetles can be a challenge to capture since they are fast fliers and can be readily disturbed. A net that allows air to flow through it easily is important in successful tiger beetle hunting; if the net is placed over the beetles on the ground, some species will fly upward into the net and can be extracted; however, other species will stay on the ground and attempt to escape through openings at the edge of the net.

Miscellaneous: The large size and rarity of this insect have made it particularly prized by insect collectors. For example, collectors and dealers could charge $12 to $20 for individual specimens in 1876; handbills describing the insect were distributed to traders visiting the region so that the beetles might be collected.

A report suggests that these beetles produce a poisonous compound to deter predators, based on the observation that toads, confined with the beetles in a jar overnight, were killed or paralyzed.

LARGEST DARKLING BEETLES—"SKUNK," "STINK" OR "CIRCUS" BEETLES
Eleodes suturalis (Say)
Eleodes spinipes ventricosus LeConte
Eleodes obscurus obscurus (Say)

Order: Coleoptera

Family: Tenebrionidae

Distribution: Found in semiarid areas throughout the region, including wheat fields. These species can be abundant in certain years.

Life History and Habits: The adults of these beetles can be recognized by their characteristic defensive posture. When disturbed,

Eleodes
suturalis, *a large*
"stink beetle"

they raise their abdomen at a 45-degree angle and emit a foul-smell-
ing compound, which gives rise to their common names: "head-
standing beetles," "circus beetles," "skunk beetles" or "stink beetles."

Larvae look like wireworms and feed underground on the roots
of grasses and other plants. The adults are scavengers, feeding on a
variety of decaying plant and animal materials. They may migrate
during the day or night, in spring and early summer, although some
individuals can be found throughout most of the year. They are
usually smooth and shiny black.

Adults are attracted to moist areas and occasionally can be a
nuisance when they enter homes or swimming pools. When disturbed, the beetles emit smelly chemicals that they use for defense.
These chemicals can be irritating and may "tan" the skin. Because of

Beetles in the genus
Eleodes *are*
sometimes called
"circus beetles"
because they stand
on their heads
when disturbed.

Stink bugs produce an odor when disturbed; however, they are not beetles.

the odor associated with these beetles, they are commonly, but incorrectly, called "stink bugs," a term that should be applied only to the common group of true bugs in the family Pentatomidae that also produce defensive odors.

A Cochiti Indian legend offers one explanation of the head-standing behavior of these insects. According to the legend, the beetle was given the responsibility of placing the stars in the sky but dropped many as it worked, forming the Milky Way. The beetle was so ashamed that to this day it hides its face when people approach.

Related Species: Although the three species mentioned are the largest of the darkling beetles, many other smaller species of *Eleodes* occur in the region. Another familiar group of darkling beetles are the mealworms (*Tenebrio* species) that are commonly reared as pet food.

Collecting Tips: These beetles are easy to catch as they walk along roadsides, particularly on cloudy days. They can also be collected in pitfall traps. Most prairie areas and particularly sand dune sites are good locations for finding these beetles. A fairly thick pin (no. 3 size or larger) may be needed to penetrate their tough wing covers.

The *Eleodes* darkling beetles are extremely resistant to insecticides or poisonous gases since they are protected by a thick body covering and can seal off their breathing openings (spiracles) when threatened. Deep-freezing is a more effective means of killing these beetles than are most killing jars.

The adult of the yellow mealworm is an insect that is commonly raised for pet food; photograph courtesy of Oregon State University.

Rearing Tips: These beetles are very long-lived and may survive for several years in captivity. They can easily be maintained on a diet of plant matter (apples, oatmeal, etc.) supplemented with fish food. Adults will lay eggs in sandy soil that is slightly moist. In a terrarium, layering some moistened sphagnum peat moss between sand layers will provide good conditions for the larvae to develop.

The darkling beetle known as the yellow mealworm, *Tenebrio molitor* Linneaus, is commonly reared for pet food. Cultures can be started by placing a few of these insects in a canister of oatmeal or wheat flakes. This should be supplemented periodically with pieces of apple or potato. All stages of the insect can be completed in the container with little additional maintenance.

LARGEST METALLIC WOOD BORER—SCULPTURED PINE BORER
Chalcophora anguilicollis (LeConte)

Order: Coleoptera

Family: Buprestidae

Distribution: Generally distributed throughout the region in association with its host plants, pine, fir and Douglas fir.

Life History and Habits: This is the largest species of metallic wood borer, almost one and 1 1/2 inches (3.8 cm) long, shiny gray-black with a bronzy luster. The surface of the wing covers have a wrinkly or sculptured texture, which gives the insect its name.

Eggs are laid in July and August around scars or crevices of bark on newly felled logs or stumps. The larvae are a type of

Bagging Big Bugs

Sculptured pine borer

flatheaded borer that feed under the bark of dead and dying trees, producing sawdust-packed tunnels in the wood. Development requires one year to complete, and they pupate in chambers cut into the wood. Sculptured pine borer adults are quite noisy when they take flight, sounding like a small airplane.

Related Species: One group of metallic wood borers that rivals the sculptured pine borer in size are members of the genus *Dicerca*. Some of these beetles are almost 1 inch (2.5 cm) long, and most are a lustrous dark gray color with slightly sculptured wing covers. In addition to differences in size, they can be distinguished from the sculptured pine borer by the pointed tips of their wing covers. Species of *Dicerca* develop in dead wood of various hardwoods as well as conifers.

Other large metallic wood borers include *Hippomelas sphenica* (LeConte) and *H. obliterata* (LeConte). These beetles are dark green and reach a size of 1 inch (2.5 cm). They are reported to develop in willow but are most often collected while the adults rest on saltbush or mesquite in midsummer. These beetles are found in western Colorado, Utah and New Mexico.

Collecting Tips: As with the pine-feeding longhorned beetles (pine sawyers, *Monochamus* species), the sculptured pine borer is most

A flathead borer; photograph courtesy of Oregon State University

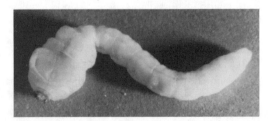

commonly collected in midsummer in areas of recently felled Douglas fir and pine trees. They can also be found at locations that sell fresh wood products such as firewood or wooden fencing with the bark intact and poles.

LARGE METALLIC WOOD BORERS— *BUPRESTIS* SPECIES

The golden buprestid, Buprestis aurulenta

Order: Coleoptera

Family: Buprestidae

Distribution: Found in wooded areas throughout the region.

Life History and Habits: Adult beetles in the genus *Buprestis* are often a striking green or bronze with a metallic and reflective body. One of the more attractive species is the golden buprestid, *B. aurulenta* Linnaeus, which has metallic green or blue-green wing covers with gold flecks and with copper edges. Approximately a dozen species of *Buprestis* occur in the region.

Females lay eggs in masses wedged under the bark of dead or dying trees. The larvae of these insects (flatheaded borers) are legless, elongate, pale-colored insects with a flattened area behind the head. They develop under the bark of dead and dying trees, feeding primarily in the cambium area just under the bark and producing characteristic meandering tunnels. Most do not damage healthy trees, but a few species, notably the golden buprestid, may help kill trees suffering from wounds or stress. The tunneling by the larvae occasionally causes damage to buildings and finished wood products. Adults feed on needles and tender bark. In the forest, the life cycle typically requires two or three years to complete. If development occurs in finished wood, egg to adult development may take up to sixty years, making these one of the longest-lived insects.

Most *Buprestis* beetles develop in conifers such as ponderosa pine, lodgepole pine, grand fir and Douglas fir. However, one common metallic green species, *B. confluenta* Say, develops in cottonwood and aspen.

Related Species: Several other species of metallic wood borers occur in the region, but most are only about 1/2 inch (1.3 cm) or less in length. In particular, members of the genus *Agrilus* are common in stressed or dying trees, the larvae creating meandering tunnels under the bark. The bronze birch borer, *Agrilus anxius* Gory, commonly kills birch trees in the region, and the rose stem girdler, *A. aurichalceus* Redtenbacher, girdles stems of rose, currant and raspberry.

Collecting Tips: *Buprestis* beetles are active throughout the first half of the summer. They are most commonly seen as they visit flowers or rest on tree trunks. Areas where logging or fires have recently occurred are good sites for these beetles, which develop in recently killed trees.

Largest Weevil—Clay-colored Billbug
Sphenophorus aequalis Gyllenhall

Order: Coleoptera

Family: Curculionidae

Distribution: Probably found throughout most of the region in areas that support the wetland plants on which the insect feeds.

Clay-colored billbug

Life History and Habits: Little is known about the biology of this species. The clay-colored billbug develops primarily on rushes, sedges and reeds that grow along streams and in other wetland sites. The overwintering stage is probably the adult, hidden under cover of plant debris. It becomes active in late April and May. In late spring and early summer, the females chew small pits in the base of food plants to insert their eggs. The grublike larvae develop within the base of the plant, sometimes causing it to wilt and die. They become full grown after two to three months of feeding and pupate within the plant. Adults emerge in late summer, feed a little on plants while weather permits, then move to winter shelter.

This insect has been reported to occasionally damage crops, such as wheat, corn and millet, planted in or near wet areas.

Related Species: "Billbug" is the name given to several grass-feeding weevils, usually in the genus *Sphenophorus*. Two species of billbugs, the bluegrass billbug (*S. parvulus* Gyllenhal) and the "Denver billbug" (*S. cicatristriatus* Fabraeus), develop on the roots and crown area of grass and are common pests of lawns and sod farms in much of the region.

Larvae of the Denver billbug

A group of large weevils that rivals the clay-colored billbug in size belong to the genus *Ophryastes; O. tuberosus* LeConte is particularly large, about 5/8 inch (1.7 cm) in length. These weevils are generally gray and striped and can be found feeding on various rangeland shrubs. The larvae are reported to feed on the roots and lower trunk of sagebrush.

Weevils are generally considered to be the most diverse family of animal life in the world. More than 50,000 species are estimated to occur worldwide, with at least 2,600 in North America—far more than all the species of vertebrates (mammals, fish, birds, reptiles, etc.) combined.

Collecting Tips: Adults are usually most abundant and active in late May and June and can be found at the base of wetland plants at this time. Some can also be captured with a sweep net at these sites. Larvae may be found in summer by examining the base of plants that show wilting due to tunneling by the insect.

A Large Weevil—Poplar-and-Willow Borer
Cryptorhynchus lapathi (Linnaeus)

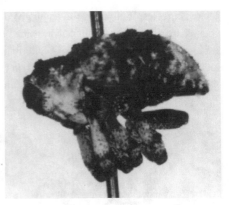

Poplar-and-willow borer

Order: Coleoptera

Family: Curculionidae

Distribution: This introduced species has spread to many areas of the United States. It is found in association with willow stands.

Life History and Habits: The larvae of this species mine beneath the bark and into the wood, causing the stem to break. Willow is preferred, but poplar, alder and birch are also attacked. The larvae push sawdust through holes in the stem, and the large piles that form are a clue to their presence.

The development from egg to adult requires one year. However, some adults can live up to three years, so many overlapping generations occur and all stages may be present during the summer. Eggs are laid in slits in the bark; the new adults appear in mid-June.

Collecting Tips: Poplar-and-willow borers are most commonly found in willow thickets along streams. Adults can easily be collected from branches infested with nearly full-grown larvae. Fresh wood shavings indicate the presence of an actively developing larva.

A LARGE WEEVIL—BLACK VINE WEEVIL
Otiorhynchus sulcatus (Fabricius)

Black vine weevil; photograph by John Capinera

Order: Coleoptera

Family: Curculionidae

Distribution: Probably now found throughout much of the region, it is a recently introduced species that is steadily spreading in range.

Life History and Habits: The black vine weevil usually spends the winter as a larva in the soil around the root zone of plants on which it feeds. Adults may survive winters if they find the shelter of homes. Black vine weevils are occasionally nuisance invaders of homes in the fall. Larvae resume feeding in spring and can extensively damage roots during May and June. After becoming full grown, they pupate in the soil, and adult weevils begin to emerge in mid-June. Black vine weevil adults feed on the leaves of various plants during the night and cause characteristic notching wounds that may resemble grasshopper injury. After about two weeks, the females begin to lay eggs around the base of plants. Eggs begin to hatch in midsummer; the legless larvae feed on plant roots until cold weather temporarily stops development. One generation is produced per year.

The black vine weevil is a very serious pest of landscape plants and nurseries in many areas of the United States. In the Rocky Mountain region, it is most commonly associated with euonymus. Strawberry, *Taxus*, clematis, cotoneaster and rhododendron are among the many other plants that may be damaged.

Related Species: Several other root weevils are very common, most notably the strawberry root weevil, *Otiorhynchus ovatus* (Linnaeus), which commonly invades homes in midsummer and can be a serious nuisance in some areas. It is most frequently found at higher elevations.

Collecting Tips: Since black vine weevils hide during the day, they can be difficult to capture. One of the best places to find them is on plants (such as euonymus) that show evidence of feeding damage. The weevils can be collected from these plants at night by shaking the bush over a sheet. They may also be found within folded burlap laid at the base of plants. Like most weevils, black vine weevils drop readily when disturbed.

LARGEST PLEASING FUNGUS BEETLE—
CYPHEROTYLUS CALIFORNICUS LACORDAIRE

Order: Coleoptera

Family: Erotylidae

Distribution: Common throughout the region in forests and mountainous areas.

Life History and Habits: This pleasing fungus beetle feeds on soft conk fungi that develop on aspen, ponderosa pine and other logs. The biology of these insects is largely unknown. Some apparently spend the winter in the adult stage and lay eggs in spring; others

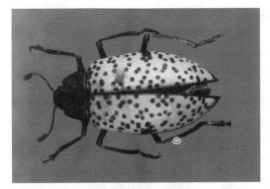

Pleasing fungus beetle

survive as larvae within the fungus. The larvae feed on the fungus in late spring and early summer, consuming large quantities. When full grown, the larva hangs from the underside of the logs and transforms to a pupa, often in groups of several dozen. This habit causes the pupal stage to resemble a bat. After about a week, the adults emerge and are present through the summer and early fall. There is one generation per year.

Collecting Tips: The beetles are often encountered crawling over the ground in the woods. They are more readily found under rotting logs and under loose bark of fallen trees. Typically the adults hang upside-down under the wood, sometimes suspended by only a few legs. Collections of pupae or old pupal skins may be found under rotten wood.

Pleasing fungus beetles are usually metallic blue or purple. However, they lose much of their color after they die.

LARGEST SCARAB BEETLE—TENLINED JUNE BEETLE
Polyphylla decemlineata (Say)

Order: Coleoptera

Family: Scarabaeidae

Distribution: Found throughout the region, but most common at lower elevation.

Life History and Habits: This beetle is very large and has greenish-brown or silvery-white stripes. It is a type of "May" or "June beetle" that is active at night in late spring and early summer. Occasionally it draws attention when it bangs into screens, attracted to light. The adult beetles feed on leaves of various trees and shrubs.

Eggs are laid in the ground by the adult females in midsummer. Larvae develop as a type of white grub, feeding on the roots of various trees and shrubs. Occasionally they cause serious injury to young trees. The life cycle from egg to adult is assumed to take three years.

Tenlined June beetle

The tenlined June beetle can make a squeaking sound to startle predators.

Related Species: *Polyphylla hammondi* LeConte and *P. arguta* Casey are two closely related species that rival the tenlined June beetle in size but lack the distinctive striping of the wing covers. (Both species have variable striping.) *P. hammondi* is an occasional turf pest in southeastern Colorado. Other large scarab beetles include the goldsmith beetles, *Cotalpa* species (see next section) and several members of the genus *Phyllophaga* (the May/June beetles). This latter group of beetles are serious pests of lawns and rangeland in the plains areas of the region east of the Continental Divide.

A scarab beetle that rivals the tenlined June beetle in size, but is very rare in the region, is the spotted Pelidnota, *Pelidnota punctata* (Linnaeus). Adults reportedly feed on grape, spinach and related plants. The larvae are found in decaying wood. They have been collected in southeastern Colorado and New Mexico.

The family of scarab beetles (Scarabaeidae) is very large, containing approximately 1,400 species in North America. Adults of most species are dark colored, oval and heavy-bodied. The larvae

White grub larva of the tenlined June beetle

are known as "white grubs"; most develop as scavengers of animal manure, decaying plant matter and carrion. White grubs are the most important insects involved in the breakdown of cattle manure, which allows nutrients to be recycled.

Collecting Tips: Tenlined June beetles are most easily collected with light traps during the peak flight period, late May through July.

LARGE SCARAB BEETLES—GOLDSMITH BEETLES
Cotalpa subcribrata Wickham
Cotalpa lanigera (Linnaeus)
Cotalpa consobrina Horn

Order: Coleoptera

Family: Scarabaeidae

Distribution: *C. subcribrata* is fairly common in the eastern plains areas of the region. *C. consobrina* may be found in the Four Corners area of Utah, Colorado, New Mexico and Arizona. *C. lanigera* is rarely collected and is restricted to the extreme southeastern areas of the region.

Life History and Habits: The larvae of goldsmith beetles are white grubs most commonly found in sandier soils. They reportedly feed on the roots of grasses and occasionally other plants such as strawberries and corn. Goldsmith beetle larvae may cause some damage

A goldsmith beetle (left) is compared with the spotted Pelidnota (right).

to these crops in the more eastern areas of the region, although they occur so infrequently that they are not considered to be serious pests. The life cycle probably requires two years to complete under the weather conditions of the region. Adults are most abundant in June and July.

The adult beetles of these species closely resemble the true goldsmith beetle, *C. lanigera,* differing slightly in coloration and size, the latter having more metallic coloration. Adults are primarily nocturnal but sometimes fly during the late afternoon. They feed on the leaves of trees, especially elm, aspen, poplar, willow and cottonwood. Swarms of adult beetles have been reported to occur on corn, but cause little injury.

Collecting Tips: Goldsmith beetles can be most easily collected at lights on midsummer nights. They can also be found by shaking trees, on which the adult beetles feed.

Largest Stag Beetle—
Pseudolucanus mazama (Le Conte)

Order: Coleoptera

Family: Lucanidae

Distribution: Found in wooded areas with decaying wood. They are most abundant west of the Continental Divide.

Life History and Habits: The stag beetles are sometimes called "pinching bugs" because of the large pair of mandibles found on the

Female stag beetle

males. (Females have much smaller mouthparts.) Despite their appearance, stag beetles are not aggressive and feed on decaying wood. Larvae develop as grubs in decaying wood, living on the juices.

Related Species: Several other species of stag beetles occur in the region, but only *P. mazama* is large, with some individuals close to 2 inches (5 cm) in length. The genera *Platycerus* and *Ceruchus* also occur, but these are much smaller and are rarely collected, usually found by searching rotting logs. The giant stag beetle, *Lucanus elaphus* (Fabricius), is often featured in entomology books but is primarily an eastern species, ranging into Oklahoma. This beetle is often offered for sale in entomology publications for as much as $50 per pair.

Stag beetles are commonly confused with ground beetles in the genus *Pasimachus* (see "Large Ground Beetles—*Pasimachus* species").

Collecting Tips: Adults can be attracted to lights at night near wooded areas. Adults and larvae also can be found by examining decaying logs.

A LARGE LADY BEETLE—SEVENSPOTTED LADY BEETLE (C-7)
Coccinella septempunctata Linnaeus

Order: Coleoptera

Family: Coccinellidae

Distribution: Purposely introduced by various state and federal agencies, beginning in the late 1970s, as a potential biological control of

Four species of lady beetles: convergent lady beetle (top left); sevenspotted lady beetle (top right); variegated lady beetle (bottom left); P-14 lady beetle (bottom right); photograph by Frank Peairs

plant pests. It has since become very well established and is common throughout the region.

Life History and Habits: The sevenspotted lady beetle (C-7) is primarily a predator of aphids, occasionally feeding on other soft-bodied insects, such as small caterpillars or beetle larvae. It spends the winter in the adult stage under cover of sheltering debris or in other protected sites. The adults start to become active in mid-May and feed on aphids. After a few weeks, the females lay masses of eggs, usually on leaves near food for the developing young.

The eggs hatch in about five days, and the larvae roam plants in search of insect prey. They have a voracious appetite and will feed on several hundred aphids before the larvae have completed development. They then transform to the pupal stage, which is attached to leaves, twigs or other objects. Approximately one week later, the adults emerge and repeat the cycle. Probably at least three generations are produced during a season, with adults during the last generation becoming dormant and moving to winter shelters.

Related Species: Two species of lady beetles collected in the region are actually bigger than the sevenspotted lady beetle. *Anatis* *lecontei* Casey reaches a length of about 2/5 inch (1 cm). It is most commonly found in forested areas in the foothills and at higher elevations. *Anatis labiculata* (Say), a species found mostly in the eastern United States, has also been collected in Colorado. However, both *Anatis* species are relatively uncommon and infrequently collected.

There are scores of lady beetle species throughout the region. With the exception of the Mexican bean beetle, all develop as predators of arthropods such as aphids, scales, spider mites and thrips; many are very beneficial. "Ladybirds" and "ladybugs" are common names for this family of insects.

Collecting Tips: This insect is now widespread and easily collected by searching foliage. Sweep net sampling of crops infested with aphids will usually produce some adults as well as other lady beetle species. Adults can also be collected when they visit plants that provide nectar and pollen for them to feed on.

This lady beetle larva feeds on an aphid colony; photograph courtesy of USDA.

Insects and Biological Control

Insects can be used to help control pest species. Many kinds of insects feed on and destroy pests that damage crops, injure livestock or otherwise cause harm. Much of this occurs without human intervention, representing an important type of natural control. In addition, however, these insects can be purposefully enlisted for biological control of pests as predators, parasites and diseases.

Biological control can take many forms. The most important form is recognizing and working with existing natural enemies of pest insects. This can be accomplished with techniques that protect the "good bugs" from damaging practices, such as the use of certain pesticides. Some types of beneficial insects can also be reared or collected and moved to areas to be used for managing pests. This is a very common practice in the production of many greenhouse crops, involving insects such as green lacewings and parasitic wasps.

"Classic biological control" is another way to use pests' natural enemies. This involves introducing beneficial insects into a region to control specific pest species. This technique has great potential because many of our pest insects (and weeds) were introduced into the region without the natural controls that exist in their native countries. The advantages of this method are numerous, including low cost (if successful), permanence and avoidance of more harmful pest-control methods such as insecticides and herbicides.

Major efforts to introduce beneficial insects have been undertaken for decades under the coordination of such organizations as the U.S. Department of Agriculture (USDA) and state departments of agriculture. Several major programs are under way in the region to promote biological control of weeds such as leafy spurge and insects such as the Russian wheat aphid. However, several insects have already been introduced into the region to control insect pests and weeds. Among these are the following:

Sevenspotted lady beetle (C-7)	A general predator that is particularly effective against aphids. Recently introduced but already widespread.

Rhinocyllus conicus	A weevil that develops in the heads of musk thistle, a common weed of pastureland. Destruction of the seed head greatly reduces reseeding and spread of this weed.
Bathyplectes curculionis	A parasite of alfalfa weevil larvae, an important pest of alfalfa. The developing wasp larvae typically kill over 25 percent of the alfalfa weevil larvae, reducing the need to control them with insecticides.
Diaeretiella rapae	A tiny braconid wasp that develops as a parasite of many species of aphids, including cabbage aphid and Russian wheat aphid.

A LARGE LADY BEETLE—MEXICAN BEAN BEETLE
Epilachna varivestis Mulsant

Order: Coleoptera

Family: Coccinellidae

Distribution: Found throughout the lower elevations of the region, in association with areas where beans are grown.

Life History and Habits: Unlike all other regional lady beetles, which are important predators of pest species, the Mexican bean beetle feeds on plants. It can be a serious pest of pole beans in gardens and occasionally damages other beans as well.

Mexican bean beetles pass the winter in the adult stage, hidden in protective locations. In late spring they emerge from overwintering areas, seek beans to feed on and lay eggs. The eggs hatch in about a week and the spiny yellow larvae (grubs) feed on the bean foliage.

Adult of the Mexican bean beetle; photograph by John Capinera

Initial feeding is of the skeletonizing type, by which the tissues between larger veins are selectively fed on. As the larvae develop, they feed more extensively. Larger larvae also may feed on developing pods.

When full grown, the larvae shed their skin and transform to a yellow pupa, which is attached to the underside of undamaged leaves on the plant. The adult stage subsequently emerges in about ten days and repeats the cycle. In the region, two or three generations are produced during the growing season.

Collecting Tips: The Mexican bean beetle is a common and occasionally serious pest of field and garden beans. It is best collected on these host plants in midsummer.

Bean beetle larvae; photograph by John Capinera

Largest Leaf Beetle—Colorado Potato Beetle
Leptinotarsa decemlineata (Say)

Colorado potato beetle

Order: Coleoptera

Family: Chrysomelidae

Distribution: Found in the eastern portions of Colorado and Wyoming and in southern Idaho. It has spread across the United States to the Atlantic Ocean and was accidentally introduced into Europe, where it is now a major pest.

Life History and Habits: Colorado potato beetles overwinter as adults in protected locations under debris near their food plants. In late spring the adults emerge and seek out various solanaceous (nightshade family) plants, on which they feed. Garden plants such as eggplant, potato and tomato are common food plants; the Colorado potato beetle can cause serious damage to these plants. Several nightshade weeds are also fed on. Bright orange eggs are laid in groups of five to twenty-five on the underside of leaves. These eggs may superficially resemble those of the ladybird beetles, but are generally larger in size and more orange in color.

The immature stage of the Colorado potato beetle is a bright

Larva of the Colorado potato beetle

orange-red grub that feeds on plant leaves. After completing development, it drops to the soil and pupates underground. A second generation of beetles typically occurs, but is often smaller, since many beetles lay fewer eggs and beetle predators become abundant.

Related Species: The Colorado potato beetle is commonly confused with the sunflower beetle,

Zygogramma exclamationis (Fabricius). The sunflower beetle is slightly smaller than the Colorado potato beetle and confines its feeding to sunflowers.

Sunflower beetle, photograph by Frank Peairs

Collecting Tips: Colorado potato beetles can be readily collected by searching of nightshade-family weeds and susceptible garden plants such as potato and eggplant.

Miscellaneous: Colorado has been attached to the name of this very important pest because the first description of this insect—feeding on buffalo burr—was thought to have originated in Colorado. More recent evidence indicates that a previous description from Iowa actually existed.

LARGEST BARK BEETLE—RED TURPENTINE BEETLE
Dendroctonus valens LeConte

Order: Coleoptera

Family: Scolytidae

Distribution: Found throughout the region in forested areas containing pines. It is most common in the southern areas of the region.

Red turpentine beetle

Life History and Habits: Turpentine beetles favor large, declining or injured pine trees in which to develop. Trees injured by fire, damaged by construction equipment or recently transplanted are particularly common targets of infestation by the red turpentine beetle.

Adult beetles bore into the lower trunks of trees and construct tunnels under the bark (egg gallery) in which the eggs are laid. Generally a mass of pitch forms at this entry site. The young bark beetles feed in groups and develop underneath the bark. The adults transmit

Typical galleries produced by engraver beetles (Ips); photograph by David Leatherman

blue stain fungi while tunneling in the trees, and larval galleries are surrounded by this fungus. Two or three generations are completed during a season.

Related Species: The genus *Dendroctonus* contains several very serious pests of trees. The mountain pine beetle, *D. ponderosae* Hopkins, and the Douglas fir beetle, *D. pseudotsugae* Hopkins, are the most damaging bark beetles in Rocky Mountain forests. Red turpentine beetles are larger (about 3/8 inch [.9 cm]) and wine red in color, distinguishing them from these other species.

Many other bark beetles occur throughout the region. One of the largest groups is the engraver beetles (*Ips* species), which tunnel under the bark of recently killed or weakened pines and spruce. Perhaps the most notorious bark beetle is the European elm bark beetle, *Scolytus multistriatus* (Marsham), which transmits the fungus causing Dutch elm disease.

Collecting Tips: Red turpentine beetles are most abundant in outbreak areas of pine forests where recent logging or fires have occurred. Adult beetles can be collected from underneath the entry pitch masses or as they emerge from infested logs.

The smaller European elm bark beetle is the insect that transmits Dutch elm disease.

Order: SIPHONAPTERA
Fleas

Fleas are unusual insects that develop as parasites of mammals or birds. Adults feed on the blood of their hosts and are adapted to life as a parasite. Alone among the insects with complete metamorphosis, all members of this order are wingless. The name of the order is derived from the Greek *siphon*, relating to their sucking mouthparts, and *aptera*, meaning "wingless." They are flattened in form, shaped to live on their host and highly resistant to crushing. Adult fleas can jump distances many times their body height, a useful ability when trying to locate a host animal.

Flea larvae differ greatly in habit and form from the adults and are rarely observed. They are wormlike and generally pale, undergoing three instars before they complete development. Most are found in the nests of animal hosts feeding on hair, skin flakes, dried blood and other organic matter. Pupation occurs in a small silken cocoon hidden in cracks around the nest site.

Most of the species of fleas that cause serious biting and nuisance problems to humans and pets require fairly high-humidity conditions and are poorly adapted to arid regions of the West. Despite this, the greatest number of flea species exist in the western states, approximately 230, compared to 55 in the eastern states. Most of these occur in nests of small mammals, often underground, sites that have the humidity fleas require.

Fleas are important pests in the west because they can transmit human diseases, notably bubonic plague, which wiped out over a quarter of the population of Europe during the Middle Ages. Typically there are several cases of plague in the Rocky Mountain region each summer, some of which are fatal. This disease also causes mass die-offs of rock squirrels, prairie dogs and other susceptible rodents.

Fleas are best preserved in vials of alcohol.

Largest Flea—
Diamanus montanus (Baker)

Order: Siphonaptera

Family: Ceratophyllidae

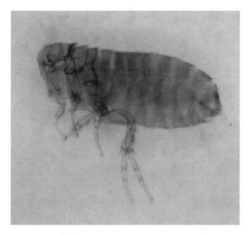

The flea Diamanus montanus

Distribution: Generally distributed throughout western North America, in association with the nests of ground squirrels red squirrels and gray squirrels, which are its hosts.

Life History and Habits: *Diamanus montanus* is a parasite of various rodents, particularly the ground squirrel, *Spermophilus variegatus*. Larvae develop on nest debris, including dried blood and the hair of the host, as well as some plant material. Adults are parasites of rodents, feeding on their blood. Populations of this flea are highest in June and July, in contrast to those of many other fleas. Like other fleas, it requires fairly high humidity to thrive, and populations are therefore almost entirely restricted to the underground nests of rodent hosts.

Related Species: Approximately one hundred species of fleas are recorded in the region, although few are highly abundant. The most commonly encountered species is the human flea, *Pulex irritans* Linnaeus. Despite its name, the human flea usually breeds in nests of raccoons, skunks and foxes, and feeds on humans only incidentally. Household invasions and human bites occur where these animal hosts nest around dwellings and then abandon the nest.

Collecting Tips: Because of the potential hazard of plague transmission by fleas, inexperienced collectors should avoid collecting them. This is particularly true for species that are most commonly associated with the disease, including *D. montanus*.

Miscellaneous: In the region, *D. montanus* is one of the most important vectors of the potentially lethal disease bubonic plague, caused by the bacteria *Yersinia pestis*, which annually claims a few victims in the Rocky Mountain region.

After feeding on host animals infected with plague, the flea can become a vector, capable of transmitting the bacteria during feeding. *D. montanus* is not a highly efficient vector, however, since it cannot transmit the disease until about six to seven weeks after infection. The bacteria is also lethal to the flea, so most fleas die before they are able to spread it. The bacteria can also be spread in the feces of the flea.

The state departments of health monitor the incidence of plague in rodent populations and treat for fleas in outbreak areas. Suspected plague outbreaks, as evidenced by die-offs of rock squirrels, ground squirrels, prairie dogs or other rodent carriers of the disease, should be reported immediately to public health authorities. Usually these areas are put off-limits until the plague outbreak has subsided.

ORDER: DIPTERA
Flies, Mosquitoes and Midges

Members of the order Diptera have only one pair of wings during the adult stage. The second pair of wings is reduced to a small, knobbed structure known as the halteres. The name of the order is derived from the Greek *di*, meaning "two" and *ptera*, or "winged."

Few animals approach the flies in diversity of appearance, habits and activities. Mouthparts of adult flies vary: some, like the houseflies', are adapted for sponging fluids; others have mouthparts designed to pierce skin and suck blood. Many immature Diptera, known as "maggots," lack a distinct head. The mouthparts of these flies are small hooks sunken within a fold of the body. Insects in the order Diptera undergo complete metamorphosis.

Diptera have very diverse habits and often occur in extremely large numbers. Many feed on fungi or algae, causing little damage to humans and serving as an important part of the natural food chain. Flies contribute to decomposition and recycling of plant and animal material, often surpassing the bacteria and fungi in this ecological role. Many species also are important predators or parasites of insect pests.

Other Diptera, such as mosquitoes, horseflies and biting midges, are very important as pests of animals and plants, feeding on animal and human blood. Several of these also spread diseases, including malaria, equine encephalitis and tularemia; it is estimated that one-third to one-half of the world's population suffers from diseases spread by members of this order. Diptera that occur as plant pests include the gall midges and leafmining flies.

Adult Diptera should be preserved by pinning through the thorax or by gluing to a card point. Larvae should be preserved in alcohol.

LARGEST CRANE FLY—
TIPULA SPECIES

Order: Diptera

Family: Tipulidae

Distribution: Common throughout the region near streams and rivers below 10,000 feet (3,040 m).

Life History and Habits: Adult crane flies lay eggs in or along the edges of streams and rivers. The larvae feed on decaying organic matter and are most often found feeding on leaf packets and silt deposited in slow-moving parts of streams and rivers. The feeding activities of crane flies break down organic matter in water.

*A mating pair of craneflies (*Tipula species*)*

The usual overwintering stage is a full-grown larva; pupation occurs in spring along the water's edge, in debris or moss. Adults emerge throughout the spring and early summer in the late hours of the morning. Adult crane flies live for only a couple of weeks. There is one generation per year for most species.

Adult crane flies, although they resemble large mosquitoes, do not have biting mouthparts and are harmless to humans. They are sometimes referred to as "mosquito hawks," a term more appropriately applied to dragonflies, which actually eat mosquitoes.

Related Species: There are about 1,525 species of crane flies in North America, many of which are quite large. Almost all crane flies are thought to develop in moist areas high in organic matter. Most feed on this organic debris; a few are predators of other arthropods.

Collecting Tips: Adult crane flies are most easily collected near streams and rivers. Adults may be found among streamside vegetation or in protected areas near breeding sites. The legs of crane flies are very delicate and break off easily in display cases. In museum collections, crane flies are maintained in clear envelopes to help avoid this problem.

LARGEST MOSQUITO—
CULISETA INORNATA (WILLISTON)

Order: Diptera

Family: Culicidae

Distribution: Common throughout the region, primarily in association with livestock.

Life History and Habits: *Culiseta inornata* spend the winter in the adult stage, becoming active with the return of warm weather in spring. They may even be present when snow is on the ground and thus are sometimes known as "snow mosquitoes." After taking a blood meal, the female lays a mass of eggs in a raft on still, cool water. Temporary pools of water, such as roadside ditches, clogged streams, rain pools and irrigated pastures, are preferred sites for egg laying. The eggs hatch after a few days and the larval mosquitoes, called "wrigglers," emerge and develop by feeding on microscopic plants

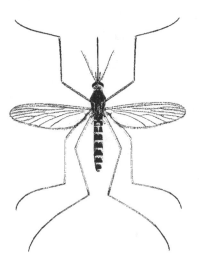

Culiseta inornata, *female*

and organic debris in the pool. Pupation occurs in the water. Several generations can be produced per season.

As with other mosquitoes, only the females bite and feed on blood, using the protein of the blood meal to mature the eggs. Male mosquitoes feed on nectar and survive on a high carbohydrate diet.

Although it is one of the most common mosquitoes in the region, *C. inornata* does not frequently bite humans. It is, however, a serious pest of livestock in certain ranges. *C. inornata* has been found infected with western equine encephalitis, but is not considered an important vector of this disease to humans.

Related Species: The most common mosquitoes in the region are various *Aedes* species, including *A. dorsalis* (Meigen) and *A. melanimon*

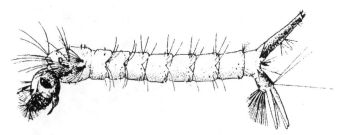

Mosquito larva

Dyar. These are known as "floodwater mosquitoes" because they lay eggs around the edge of receding water and the eggs hatch with the onset of flooding water (rainfall, snowmelt, irrigation) that covers them. They often have several generations per season and can be seriously annoying pests.

Culex tarsalis Coquillett is generally the mosquito species of greatest local health concern, since it is a vector of several encephalitis viruses. This is the species whose wings make an annoying high pitched whine as it flies.

Collecting Tips: These mosquitoes can be collected easily in midsummer as they attack cattle and horses. They also visit light traps.

LARGEST HORSEFLY— *TABANUS ATRATUS* FABRICIUS

Order: Diptera

Family: Tabanidae

Distribution: Generally found at lower elevations, near ponds or other water. It is most common in the southern areas of the region.

Life History and Habits: *Tabanus atratus* usually spend the winter in the larval stage. They develop in moist areas at the edges of ponds, irrigation ditches or seepages. Immature stages burrow in mud and debris, where they feed on worms, snails and other insects. They may also swim and have been found in mats of algae. In form the larva is a fairly typical maggot—rather cylindrical and tapered at

Largest horsefly,
Tabanus atratus

Western horsefly,
Tabanus punctifer

the end. It is greenish-white with some dark markings and can reach over 2 inches (5 cm) in length.

When full grown, the larvae migrate above water to pupate. Pupation usually occurs around mid-spring and adults begin to emerge in early June. Adults are most common in early summer, at which time the females lay masses of white eggs on vegetation in muddy breeding sites.

The large, dark-colored adult flies emerge, and the females feed on the blood of various mammals, occasionally interfering noticeably with feeding by cattle. Males do not bite, but instead feed on nectar or other sweet liquids. *Tabanus atratus* can have a highly variable life cycle. Typically there is one generation per year; however, some may take two seasons, and there is some evidence that others complete development in a single summer, emerging as adults in early fall.

Related Species: There are many other regional species of horsefly and the closely related deerflies. One of these, known as the western horsefly, *Tabanus punctifer* Osten Sacken, is nearly as large as *Tabanus atratus*. *Tabanus punctifer* has a gray thorax and is found throughout most of the region.

Collecting Tips: Adult horseflies are strong fliers that can range far from their immature-stage habitats. They tend to be most common in areas of sunlight, warmth and high moisture. They are attracted to moving objects and are best collected with an aerial sweep net. Adult flies commonly rest on small branches and twigs near breeding areas in summer. Carbon dioxide baits are also attractive to horseflies.

Largest Botflies—Rabbit/Rodent Bots
Cuterebra tenebrosa Coquillett
Cuterebra lepusculi Townsend

Adult rabbit bot

Order: Diptera

Family: Cuterebridae

Distribution: Generally distributed in the region and locally common near the habitat of its hosts. Adults are rarely collected, however.

Life History and Habits: Flies in the genus *Cuterebra* develop as internal parasites of rodents or lagomorphs (rabbits, jackrabbits). Of the two largest species, *C. lepusculi* is associated primarily with cottontail rabbits (*Sylvilagus* species), and *C. tenebrosa* parasitizes wood rats (*Neotoma* species).

Winter is spent in the pupal stage in the soil. The adult flies emerge in late June or early July. Female flies mate about two days after emergence and begin laying eggs within the week. Eggs are laid near the habitat of their host; *C. tenebrosa* lay eggs near dark crevices in rocky areas and *C. lepusculi* oviposit near rabbit runs.

The eggs hatch in a few days. The larvae enter the host mammal through natural openings, such as the nose, then migrate through the body of the animal, ultimately lodging under the skin. They form a breathing pore to the outside and live within a tumorlike "warble," feeding on the fluids of the host. Heavily infested animals may be under considerable stress and occasionally die.

The grubs become full grown in about one month, exiting the host and immediately burrowing into the soil. They transform to the pupal stage in approximately six days, then go into a form of hibernation (diapause). There is one generation per year.

Related Species: Several other *Cuterebra* species that are slightly smaller occur in the region, including *C. polita* (Coquillett), a parasite of pocket gophers; *C. jellisoni* Curran, a parasite of rabbits; *C. approximata* Walker, a parasite of white-footed mice (*Peromyscus* species); and *C. americana* (Fabricius), a parasite of wood rats.

Collecting Tips: Adult flies are rarely collected and live for only a few days. Males of *C. tenebrosa* aggregate on vertical cliff surfaces in midsummer. Larvae may be found in road-killed hosts, particularly in late August through September.

LARGE BOTFLIES—CATTLE GRUBS
Hypoderma bovis (**Linnaeus**)—**Northern Cattle Grub**
Hypoderma lineatum (**Villers**)—**Common Cattle Grub**

Adult of the northern cattle grub; photograph courtesy of Oregon State University

Order: Diptera

Family: Oestridae

Distribution: Generally distributed throughout the southern areas of the region. In the north it is largely replaced by the northern cattle grub.

Life History and Habits: Cattle grubs develop as internal parasites of cattle and bison. Adults of the common cattle grub, known as the "heel fly," are hairy, heavy-bodied flies that resemble bumble-bees. The females glue eggs on hairs of the cattle, usually landing in the shadow of the animal and approaching it along the ground to lay eggs on its heels. The activity of the northern cattle grub, or "bomb fly," is more dramatic as the insects dart into the flanks or underside of the animal. The buzzing and activity of the flies can be very unsettling to cattle, which may run wildly to escape them.

Eggs hatch within a week; the young maggots bore into the skin near the base of the hair, which causes considerable irritation to the animal. They then migrate through the host, ultimately locating themselves on the back of the animal, usually by early winter. There they form cysts, or "warbles," in which they live, with a tube through the skin of the animal for air. The maggots live on the secretions of the animal host, which are produced in response to the spines of the maggot larvae within the cyst. During spring, over a period of several months, the mature larvae wriggle through the skin of the animal host and pupate in the soil. Adult flies emerge about a month later. Where both species occur, the adults of the common cattle grub are present about one month earlier than the northern cattle grub.

Cattle grubs can be extremely serious pests of cattle, although most herds are now treated to prevent infestations. In addition to the injuries caused by the developing larvae, the buzzing of the adult flies may terrorize and cause cattle to stampede. This behavior is known as "gadding." "Gadfly" is therefore a common name for adult cattle grubs.

Related Species: The nose bot of deer, *Cephenemyia jellisoni* Townsend, infects the head sinuses and throat of mule deer. It is an extremely fast flier and is very difficult to collect. Males are sometimes seen darting over hilltops or other prominent objects.

Oestrus ovis Linneaus, known as the "sheep botfly," is an introduced species found in parts of the region. It flies in early summer and deposits maggots in the noses of sheep, goats and deer. The maggots work their way into the head sinuses, causing disorientation ("staggers") and occasionally death.

The common horse bot or "nit fly," *Gasterophilus intestinalis* (De Geer), and the nose botfly, *G. haemorrhoidalis* (Linneaus), also occur throughout the region. (These insects are sometimes placed in a different family: Gasterophilidae.) The female flies usually lay eggs on the back of the foreknees of horses; the eggs hatch in response to moisture and rubbing, which occurs when the horse licks itself. The larvae enter through the mouth, then attach to the wall of the stomach until they become full grown in late spring. At this time they release themselves from the animal and pass out of the body through the intestines. They pupate within the manure about one month. The adult fly lives only briefly, approximately one week.

Collecting Tips: The larval stages of these insects are perhaps the most easily collected. The cysts or warbles in which they develop in winter form prominent lumps on the backs of cattle. Larvae can be expelled from these cysts by pressure, although care must be taken not to crush them—the animal may experience shock. Butchered animals are also a ready source of larvae.

LARGEST TACHINID FLIES—
PARADEJEANIA RUTILIOIDES (JAENNICKE) AND *ADEJEANIA VEXATRIX* (OSTEN SACKEN)

Order: Diptera

Family: Tachinidae

Distribution: *Adejeania vexatrix* is generally distributed in the region, associated primarily with hilly terrain in foothill areas. *Paradejeania rutilioides* is restricted to the southern areas of the region.

A tachinid fly, Adejeania vexatrix, feeds at a flower. A small longhorned beetle is also visiting the flower.

Life History and Habits: The biology of the two largest tachinid flies is not well understood. Larvae reportedly develop as parasites of various caterpillars. The overwintering stage is likely to be a pupa, with adults emerging in late spring. Adult flies feed on nectar. The females glue eggs to caterpillar hosts; the newly hatched larvae tunnel into the caterpillar and feed within it over the course of a couple weeks, ultimately killing it.

Related Species: Tachinid flies are one of the most beneficial groups of insects, being important natural enemies of many pest species. Several dozen species occur in the region, attacking such important pest insects as tent caterpillars, squash bugs and Colorado potato beetles. All are internal parasites of other insects, the larval stage feeding within the host insect, which is ultimately killed.

Tachinid flies can be difficult to distinguish from many other more common types of flies, such as blow flies (Calliphoridae) and flesh flies (Sarcophagidae). The most obvious feature of tachinid flies is the stout spines on its abdomen.

Collecting Tips: Adults are most commonly collected as they feed on flowers such as rabbitbrush and Canada thistle in late summer. The presence of larvae is most easily determined by examining caterpillars or other host insects for tachinid fly eggs glued to the body, usually near the head. Such insects are very likely infested with developing tachinid fly larvae that will transform to the adult fly form after killing the host.

Tachinid fly eggs laid near the head of hornworms; photograph by John Capinera

LARGEST SYRPHID FLIES—RATTAILED MAGGOTS/DRONE FLIES
Eristalis bardus (Say)
Eristalis latifrons Loew
Eristalis tenax (Linneaus) and Others

Drone fly

Order: Diptera

Family: Syrphidae

Distribution: Commonly found throughout North America, with the rattailed maggot *Eristalis tenax* being an intorduced species from Europe.

Life History and Habits: Larvae of the genus *Eristalis* are known as rattailed maggots because they have a very long breathing tube on their hind end. They develop in polluted, organic matter–rich water, often partially buried in the mud. Occasionally they are associated with carrion. Their elongate posterior breathing tube allows them to live in environments most oxygen-breathing insects cannot tolerate. Development requires about six weeks to two months to complete. Overwintering occurs in the adult stage.

Adults are large flies marked with orange-yellow and black that superficially resemble honeybees, particularly male bees (drones). They feed on nectar.

Related Species: The family Syrphidae is large, with diverse habits. Another species of rattailed maggot with apparently similar habits is *Mallota bautias* (Walker), which has been found feeding in pockets of water decay in trees. Perhaps the most unusual large species are in the genus *Microdon*, which develop as parasites of ant colonies. Larvae of this group are so unusual in appearance that they have sometimes been mistaken for mollusks.

Most species of syrphid flies have very beneficial habits, the larvae being important predators of aphids. The adults are common

The narcissus bulb fly, a pest species of syrphid fly, develops in flower bulbs.

garden inhabitants. They are marked with bright yellow or orange and black, resembling bees. They are nectar feeders, frequently on plants with fairly shallow flowers. Eggs are laid singly, usually near colonies of aphids, and the larvae may feed on scores of aphids during their development. Unlike many other predatory insects, such as lady beetles, they can enter curled leaves where aphids occur, and are not often bothered by ants that protect aphids. One particularly large species of predaceous syrphid is *Spilomyia interrupta* Williston, most commonly found in the western areas of the region.

Some significant pest species also occur within this family. The narcissus bulb fly, *Merodon equestris* (Fabricius), may be very damaging to daffodils and hyacinths, rotting the base of the bulbs with their tunneling. The lesser bulb fly, *Eumerus strigatus* (Fallen) occasionally damages onions, potatoes and various other bulbs, although it usually invades only after the plant has been wounded.

Collecting Tips: Adult drone flies feed on nectar, particularly of aster family plants (Asteraceae), and are most easily collected at flowers from late spring through early autumn. Populations are likely to be highest near breeding areas used by the larvae, such as small pools of foul water.

Bees, Wasps or Flies?
Syrphid Flies and Insect Mimicry

Growing up as an insect is a tough life. Infant mortality runs very high, and the developing insects frequently suffer from starvation, adverse weather, diseases and predators. As a result, usually only a small fraction (usually less than 5 percent) of any insect species makes it to adulthood.

Adult insects are subject to attack by many organisms—birds, lizards and other insects, to name a few. However, many insects have a variety of strategies to thwart or confuse these potential natural enemies.

Use of chemical defenses is widespread among insects as a means of deterring predators. Many insects can sting or produce noxious compounds that will usually prevent attack, such as the unpleasant sprays emitted by a stink beetle or stink bug when they are disturbed. Other insects feed on plants that contain toxic compounds that the insect then maintains in its body and uses for defense.

The monarch butterfly is a good example of the latter. The caterpillars of this insect feed on milkweed, a plant that is usually rich in a toxic compound known as cardiac glycosides. These compounds remain in the adult monarch and, as a result, birds that feed on the adult butterflies have a very distasteful experience when they try to feed on them. Most birds will vomit and few will attempt to feed on the monarch a second time.

The bold orange and black markings of monarch butterflies are a warning to birds of their distastefulness. Many other insects that lack this defense mimic the monarch. One of the most well known is the viceroy, which very closely resembles the monarch in the adult stage. (Recent evidence

The viceroy (right) closely mimics the monarch.

indicates that the viceroy is somewhat distasteful to predators on its own.) Indeed, red or orange and black are common warning colors that usually advertise that the insect has some chemical defenses—or is mimicking insects that do.

Yellow and black are also warning colors, widely found among stinging insects such as honeybees, yellow jackets and other wasps. These colors and even the body form are used by numerous insects, including several whole families such as the syrphid flies and robber flies. Essentially all of the syrphid flies are excellent mimics of bees and wasps, sometimes even capable of buzzing, although they are completely harmless.

A typical syrphid fly resting on a leaf

Largest Blowflies—
Calliphora vomitoria (Linneaus)
Calliphora vicina Robineau-Desvoidy
Phormia regina (Meigen)—Black Blowfly

Order: Diptera

Family: Calliphoridae

Distribution: Widely distributed and common throughout the region. Blowflies are sometimes described as the "houseflies of the West."

Life History and Habits: Adults of this ubiquitous family are usually metallic green or blue and are commonly observed resting on walls or visiting sources of food (nectar, dung, freshly dead animals). The

Calliphora vicina is among the largest blowflies in the region.

maggots breed mostly in carrion, animal manure or rotting organic matter, including wet garbage.

Blowflies are capable of extremely rapid development. Adult flies that locate potential sources of food for their young lay clusters of eggs that hatch within days; the developing larvae become full grown in as little as one week. After they have finished feeding, they scatter and may crawl several yards from the food source in search of a place to pupate.

Blowflies are important from a medical and veterinary standpoint. The most common species can transmit disease organisms, particularly bacteria associated with food poisoning, through their habits of visiting and breeding in garbage and manure. Some species, notably the notorious screwworm, *Cochliomyia hominivorax* (Coquerel), feed as parasites in the living tissues of wounded animals in Central America and occasionally parts of the southern United States.

Related Species: One of the most common flies found in homes of the region are the cluster flies, *Pollenia pseudorudis* Rogues and *P. rudis* (Fabricius). These develop as parasites of earthworms during the growing season. In late summer, the adult flies seek winter shelter and often move into homes, particularly upper stories. Once inside, they may cluster together in large groups in wall voids, lending them the name "cluster flies." Toward late winter and early spring, increasing numbers of the flies wake from their winter dormancy and fly lazily around the rooms. Many will die indoors, but others find their way outdoors the following season and continue the cycle.

Collecting Tips: Blowflies are common and easily captured with a net or jar. Large numbers of them may be attracted to decaying meat, which can be used to bait traps for these insects.

Insects and Forensic Studies

Use of insects as forensic indicators in criminal and medical cases is garnering increased attention. Many insects are scavengers, including some that develop on animal carcasses—or human bodies. The presence of certain insects as well as their life stage can be very useful for determining the time of death, a critical fact in murder investigations, for example. Entomology has been used in forensic science in China since the thirteenth century; in recent years it has become a field of science itself, known as forensic entomology.

Animal carcasses in the wild are visited by a succession of insects, often as many as thirty species. First to come are blowflies and the flesh flies, usually within a couple of hours after death. The adult flies feed on fluids and lay eggs—or living maggots, in the case of flesh flies.

The primary contribution made by the forensic entomologist is in determining how long a corpse has been exposed to the environment. Being cold-blooded, insects develop at a rate that is dependent on temperature, and have distinct periods of activity during the year. In crime scene investigations important information can be deduced by determining the species of insects present, their life stage and their location. This information, combined with local climate records, can help to pinpoint the victim's time of death.

During the course of decomposition, other waves of insects will subsequently visit the carcass. After a few days, various predators and parasites of fly larvae, such as rove beetles and parasitic wasps, will arrive. Weeks later, as the carcass starts to dry, carrion beetles, histerid beetles and dermestid beetles will feed on the remaining tissues.

Although this process of decay may not be very pleasant to contemplate, it is an essential natural process. Decay and decomposition allow for recycling of nutrients, which, in turn, allow for new plant growth and supports new life. Scavenging insects are one of the original recyclers, and their efforts are critical to maintaining the ecosystems we all depend on.

LARGEST ROBBER FLY—
PROCTOCANTHUS MICANS SCHINER

A robber fly, Proctocanthus micans, *feeds on a smaller species of robber fly.*

Order: Diptera

Family: Asilidae

Distribution: Widely distributed in grassland areas of the region. Other large robber flies are also found throughout the region.

Life History and Habits: Adult *Proctocanthus micans* are predators of flying insects. They wait on either the soil or low-growing plants for these insect prey to pass. Robber flies have very good vision and can capture insects 6 to 12 feet (1.8–3.7 m) from the rest area. The robber fly grabs and injects the prey with a paralyzing toxin through its strong mouthparts. Almost any large insect may be prey, including moths, wasps, grasshoppers, flies and even other robber flies.

Females lay eggs in the soil of shaded areas surrounding shrubs. The larval habits of robber flies are not well studied. They occur in the soil and are presumed to be predators of soil arthropods. The larval stage may take one to three years to complete, while adult flies typically live less than a month.

Related Species: Robber flies are abundant in the arid areas of the western North America, and more than two hundred species occur in the region. All feed on other insects and are usually the most conspicuous and important aerial predators of the grasslands and shrublands. Many species are excellent mimics of bees and wasps.

Other species of *Proctocanthus* can be abundant, including *P. hinei* Bromley, *P. milbertii* Macquart and *P. nearno* Martin. Several species of *Proctocanthus* are restricted to sand dune habitats of the region. In addition, the genera *Efferia*, *Diogmites* and *Promachus* contain species that are particularly large and common. One of these, *Diogmites grossus* Bromley, is known as the "green-eyed monster" and is often seen lumbering about in helicopterlike flight among vegetation of canyon streams. Several species of *Promachus* are known as "bee killers" both because of the high-pitched buzz they make in flight and their use of honeybees as prey.

The largest robber fly in North America (1 3/4 inches [4.4 cm]), *Microstylum morosum* Loew, occurs in the extreme southeastern part of the region, but is rare. This species reportedly feeds on medium-sized cicadas and large grasshoppers.

Collecting Tips: *Proctocanthus micans* can be collected throughout July and August. All robber flies are fast fliers and can be difficult to collect with a sweep net. However, those feeding on prey or mating are more easily collected since these fly more slowly. In addition, flies may return to favored perches after being disturbed. When you are walking through rangeland areas they may follow or fly ahead for short distances, apparently seeking grasshoppers and other insects disturbed by your movements.

Larger species of robber flies can bite if handled carelessly.

ORDER: LEPIDOPTERA
Butterflies, Moths, Skippers

The order Lepidoptera is characterized by scale-covered wings in the adult stage. The scales (the "dust" that is easily rubbed off when handling) are often marked in bright colors or distinctive patterns, making the Lepidoptera a favorite to collect. Adult stages usually feed on fluids, such as nectar, which they suck through a mouthpart formed like a small tube. Adults of the butterflies and skippers are active during the day. Most moths tend to be active at night and are readily collected at lights.

Larvae of the Lepidoptera are known as caterpillars, which feed by chewing on plants. After becoming full grown, the caterpillars wander away from the plant on which they were feeding and pupate. Caterpillars have silk glands, and the pupal stage of most moths occurs withing a silken cocoon. Butterfly larvae form a chrysalis, which is a pupal state not covered by silk.

*A typical butterfly
(top), moth (left)
and skipper (right)*

Larvae of some Lepidoptera are serious plant pests, including the various cutworms, tent caterpillars, clearwing borers, hornworms and cabbageworms. However, most cause little serious injury to plants. Butterflies are appreciated because of their beauty and are actively encouraged by gardeners.

Adult Lepidoptera are preserved by pinning. Wings should be displayed by carefully moving them so they are fully spread when dry. A spreading board is very useful for displaying Lepidoptera properly. Caterpillars should be preserved in alcohol; to preserve their color they should be briefly boiled beforehand.

LARGEST MOTH—THE BLACK WITCH
Ascalapha odorata (**Linnaeus**)

Order: Lepidoptera

Family: Noctuidae

Distribution: The black witch is a tropical species of moth that infrequently strays into the region and has been found as far north as Alaska. It is native and common in Florida and warmer areas of the Gulf states, and ranges south through South America.

Life History and Habits: The black witch is the largest North American moth and is a member of the cutworm family Noctuidae. In appearance, however, it resembles a giant silk moth (see "A Large Silkworm Moth—Cecropia Moth" and "Polyphemus Moth"),

The black witch is a very large moth that infrequently flies into the region.

complete with eyespots on the wings and a heavy, hairy body. The wingspan of the adult black witch is approximately 4 inches (10.2 cm).

The larvae are large (up to 3 inches [7.6 cm]), grayish caterpillars that feed on the leaves of various leguminous trees such as catclaw (*Acacia decurrens*), *Cassia* species and Kentucky coffeetree. Breeding areas move northward during the summer; most moths that reach the region probably originate in northern Mexico. Breeding does not occur in the Rocky Mountain region.

The black witch is sometimes called the "giant noctuid." It is considered to be the largest moth that occurs in the region based on its wingspan, which can range up to 6 inches (15.2 cm). Some of the silk moths and sphinx moths nearly equal the black witch in wingspan but are more heavy-bodied.

Related Species: The family Noctuidae is very large, containing such insects as the armyworms, cutworms and various "loopers" (for example, cabbage looper, alfalfa looper). Perhaps the most well known of these is the army cutworm, *Euxoa auxiliaris* (Grote), better known as the "miller moth." Larvae of this insect typically overwinter in fields of alfalfa or winter wheat, occasionally damaging these crops in spring. They transform to the adult moth in late spring, and the miller moths survive the entire summer. During this time they feed on nectar and seek out cool sites for rest, a habit that leads them to migrate to higher elevations. It is during these migrations that tremendous numbers can be observed, particularly as populations concentrate along the Front Range of Colorado. In late summer, the adults migrate back to lower elevations and lay eggs.

Aside from the black witch, the largest members of the family are the "underwings," a large group of moths in the genus *Catocala.* These have brightly colored hind wings that are usually obscured by gray or brown forewings; wingspan may be as much as 3 inches (7.6 cm). The underwings are discussed in the following section.

Collecting Tips: The black witch is infrequently found in the region because it is dependent on chance migrations aided by winds from its southern breeding areas. It is most frequently collected near lights at night.

LARGE NOCTUID MOTHS—UNDERWINGS
Catocala Species

An underwing moth

Order: Lepidoptera

Family: Noctuidae

Distribution: This is an extremely abundant group of moths containing more than one hundred North American species. More than two dozen of these occur in the Rocky Mountain region, and many are common.

Life History and Habits: The underwing moths are so named because they have a brightly patterned hind wing obscured when at rest by the dull gray forewing. Predominant hind wing colors are reddish, pink, orange and white with dark patterns.

Larvae of the moths feed on the foliage of various trees and shrubs. Eggs are laid in late summer and the caterpillars emerge in spring to feed on leaves. Food plants of most of the larger species are willow and poplar, while other species feed on oak, honey locust, walnut and other plants. Most underwing caterpillars are grayish with some light striping along the body. Pupation occurs within a cocoon on or around the host plant. Adults may emerge by early summer but are most common in August and September.

Collecting Tips: The gray forewing is cryptically colored, allowing the adult moths to blend in well while resting against bark or similar surfaces and making them difficult to detect. Adult moths are highly attracted to light, however, and can be caught visiting lights or in light traps. Peak periods of flight are in late summer.

Larvae are similarly difficult to detect, but, careful searches of poplar or willow in late spring or early summer may uncover them.

Rearing Tips: The caterpillars can be reared on leaves and allowed to transform to the adult stage.

A Large Silkworm Moth—Cecropia Moth
Hyalophora cecropia (Linnaeus)

Cecropia moth

Order: Lepidoptera

Family: Saturniidae

Distribution: Found throughout most of the eastern United States. In the Rocky Mountain region it is limited to areas east of the Rockies. The closely related Glover's silk moth also occurs and is generally distributed at higher elevations of the Rocky Mountains.

Cecropia moth caterpillar; photograph by David Leatherman

Life History and Habits: This is a well-known representative of the family known as the silk moths. A distinctive feature of this group is the tightly woven silk cocoon that the larvae spin and in which they pupate. The insect overwinters as a pupa inside the cocoon fastened lengthwise to the branches of host trees.

From April through June these large moths emerge and lay eggs. They are slow, ponderous fliers and sometimes can be observed flying in the early morning. Eggs are laid on a variety of trees and shrubs including viburnum, lilac, dogwood, walnut, willows, cherries, apple, ash and poplar. The larvae are very distinctively colored: bright green with rows of blue, yellow and red tubercles or "knobs" along their back. They are about 4 inches (10.2 cm) long when full grown. Some people describe them as "big green hotdogs." Larvae can be found on the host tree from June through October. Only one generation occurs per year. They are often parasitized by tachinid flies and are susceptible to diseases that may result in a low adult population the following year.

Related Species: The Glover's silk moth, *Hyalophora gloveri* (Strecker), is common at higher elevations in the region and much more common west of the Continental Divide. It has marks similar to those of the cecropia moth, but has reddish-brown coloring along the

Cecropia moth (left) and the Glover's silk moth (right) are two closely related silk moths.

interior of the wing as opposed to the gray areas of the cecropia moth. Larvae of the Glover's silk moth have yellow tubercules rather than reddish ones like the cecropia. Caterpillars feed primarily on leaves of native sumac *Rhus trilobata*, but maple, willow, chokecherry, alder and wild currant are among their other hosts. Although the Glover's silk moth is considered to be a species distinct from the cecropia, they occasionally interbreed.

Collecting Tips: Adults will readily fly to lights at night. Cocoons containing pupae are visible on bare branches.

Rearing Tips: Pupae collected during the winter can be stored in a garage area or brought indoors. The adults will emerge after approximately one month at room temperature. Pupae collected in early fall will not emerge until they are exposed to a period of cold temperature.

A LARGE SILKWORM MOTH—POLYPHEMUS MOTH
Antheraea polyphemus (**Cramer**)

Order: Lepidoptera

Family: Saturniidae

Distribution: Generally distributed throughout North America.

Life History and Habits: This insect, one of the largest moths found in the region, gets its name from its distinctive clear and blue eyespots on the wings of the adults, Adults emerge in late spring and early summer and lay biscuit-shaped brown eggs on the leaves of host plants.

Polyphemus moth

Larva of the polyphemus moth; photograph by David Leatherman

Larvae feed throughout the summer on a wide variety of deciduous hosts, including viburnum, weeping birch, plum, dogwood and hawthorn. The fully developed larvae are large and green with raised white, diagonal lines on the sides of the body and orange-golden tufted tubercles on each segment. They become full grown in late summer, wander into the vicinity of their host plant and spin silken cocoons.

Related Species: The silk moth family Saturniidae contains many of the largest and most brightly patterned moths in the region. Among these are the Nevada buck moth, *Hemileuca nevadensis* Stretch, which occasionally occurs in outbreak numbers and defoliates stands of cottonwood and poplar in forested areas. The pandora moth, *Coloradia pandora* Blake, feeds on the older growth of lodgepole and ponderosa pines.

The brightly colored caterpillars of the Io moth possess spines that sting when touched.

One of the more unusual of the silk moths is the Io moth, *Automeris io* (Fabricius). The brightly colored larvae of this insect possess stinging hairs that produce a burning rash on contact with either the caterpillars or the pupal cocoons. The Io moth is restricted largely to the southern areas of the region.

Collecting Tips: As with the cecropia moth, these moths readily fly to lights at night. Pupae can be collected on the ground around the base of the plants.

Rearing Tips: If the pupae have been exposed to a period of cold temperature, they can be forced to emerge prematurely indoors.

LARGEST SPHINX MOTHS—WESTERN POPLAR SPHINX AND LARGE POPLAR SPHINX
Pachysphinx occidentalis (Hy. Edwards)—**Western Poplar Sphinx**
Pachysphinx modesta (Harris)—**Large Poplar Sphinx**

Western poplar sphinx

Order: Lepidoptera

Family: Sphingidae

Distribution: Both the western poplar sphinx and the large poplar sphinx occur throughout western North America in association with their primary host plants, cottonwood and poplars.

Life History and Habits: The overwintering stage of the poplar sphinx is a very large (2–3 inches [5–7.6 cm]) pupa in the soil near the base of host plants on which the caterpillar stage fed. Adults emerge in late spring and fly to poplars and cottonwoods, on which eggs are laid.

The developing caterpillars (larvae) are a type of hornworm, generally green and white with light stripes. They feed heavily on tree leaves but are almost never abundant enough to cause injury to the tree. There are usually two generations per season, with adults from the second generation present in July and August.

The poplar sphinx are members of the family of moths (Sphingidae) known as "sphinx moths," sometimes also called

The large poplar sphinx

"hummingbird moths" or "hawk moths." These moths are active at dusk and have very long tongues that allow them to reach nectar at the base of long, tubular flowers. Larvae are known as "hornworms" because they have a conspicuous spine on their hind end.

Related Species: There are many other large species of sphinx moths/hornworms in the region. In vegetable gardens the tobacco hornworm, *Manduca sexta* (Linnaeus), and, much less commonly, the tomato hornworm, *M. quinquemaculata* (Haworth), are garden pests of tomatoes and related plants. Several other hornworms develop on trees and shrubs. Among those most frequently encountered are the giant ash sphinx, *Sphinx chersis* (Hübner), and the wildcherry sphinx, *Sphinx drupiferarum* J. E. Smith. Another common species is the Achemon sphinx, *Eumorpha achemon* (Drury), a "hornless hornworm" that develops on grape plants and Virginia creeper.

The whitelined sphinx, *Hyles lineata* (Fabricius), is the most common sphinx moth in the region, but is smaller and marked with conspicuous white stripes on the forewings. The larvae feed on purslane, primrose and other wild plants. They occasionally become extremely abundant and may be observed migrating across highways.

Collecting Tips: Sphinx moths are readily attracted to lights at night. Hummingbird moths also may be collected with a net at dusk near deep-lobed, dark flowers such as petunia, nasturtium and nicotiana.

Rearing Tips: Larvae can be reared on leaves of food plants, but some soil or sand should be placed in the rearing container to allow them to pupate.

Large Hornworms—Tomato Hornworm and Tobacco Hornworm
Manduca quinquemaculata (Haworth)—
Tomato Hornworm/Five-spotted Sphinx
Manduca sexta (Linnaeus)—
Tobacco Hornworm/Carolina Sphinx

*Adult of the tobacco
hornworm*

Order: Lepidoptera

Family: Sphingidae

Distribution: Both can occur throughout the region where their host plants are found.

Life History and Habits: The tomato and tobacco hornworms overwinter as pupae in the soil in the vicinity of gardens. Unlike many moths, they do not spin a cocoon; the naked pupa may be encountered when spading the garden during spring. The adult moths (a type of "sphinx," "hawk" or "hummingbird" moth) emerge in late May and June. They are strong fliers that may fly long distances, and appear after dusk.

Female moths lay large pearl-colored eggs on the upper surface of leaves. The young caterpillars hatch and feed on the plant for a month or more. They have tremendous appetites and consume large amounts as they grow older and larger. After feeding, they wander away from the plant and pupate in the soil. In most areas of the region, a second generation appears to occur, with caterpillars present in late July and August.

Larva of the tobacco hornworm

Both the tobacco hornworm and the tomato hornworm are pests in vegetable gardens. The caterpillars chew leaves, and plants can be defoliated rapidly. Fruits may also be chewed. Tomatoes are particularly susceptible to injury, but other related plants, such as peppers and potatoes, are occasionally infested.

The tobacco hornworm is usually more common in regional vegetable gardens than the tomato hornworm, but both may be found together, and they have similar habits. The tomato hornworm has a green "horn" with black sides, while that of the tobacco hornworm is red. The caterpillars also are differentiated by the pattern of white striping along their sides: a series of Vs on the tomato hornworm, and diagonal dashes on the tobacco hornworm.

Occasional dark forms of the tomato hornworm larvae occur. The caterpillars of these are much darker than the normal green, although the adult moths differ little in appearance.

The adult moths can be distinguished by examining the hind wing: on the tomato hornworm there are two separate wavy bands close to the wing border; on the tobacco hornworm the bands are fused. Also, the white marks on the abdomen of the tomato hornworm are more angular.

Collecting Tips: Adult moths are attracted to lights and can be collected from late May through August. Caterpillars are most often found on tomatoes or other nightshade family plants (Solanaceae).

Rearing Tips: The caterpillars can be reared by feeding them leaves of their host plants, although they can eat an impressive amount when they are nearly full grown. Several inches of soil should be kept in the container to allow them to pupate. Larvae collected late in the season will require a few months of exposure to cold temperatures before they will transform to the adult stage.

LARGE CLEARWING BORER—AMERICAN HORNET MOTH
Sesia tibialis (Harris)

*American hornet
moth*

Order: Lepidoptera

Family: Sesiidae

Distribution: Locally abundant and found throughout much of the western United States, in association with cottonwood, poplar and willow.

Life History and Habits: Winter is spent as a partially grown larva within the lower trunks and exposed roots of cottonwood, aspen, poplar or willow. The larvae resume feeding with the return of warm weather and during mid-spring transform to the pupal stage. Adults emerge in June, often pulling the pupal skin out of the soil. The adult moths are active through July. Eggs are laid in cracks on the base of the trunk of cottonwoods at this time. Trees under stress or recently injured areas of the tree are favored spots for egg laying. The larvae feed on the bark and later tunnel into the cambium of the tree. There is one generation per season.

The adult superficially resembles a yellow jacket wasp, having similar black and yellow banding. As with the other clearwing borers, they are day-fliers. The larvae are pale-colored borers with very reduced prolegs, found tunneling within the wood of various trees. Sometimes the larvae are known as "cottonwood crown borers." (These are not to be confused with another large borer found in the trunk of cottonwoods, the cottonwood borer, a type of longhorned beetle also discussed in this book.)

A male peach tree borer

Related Species: In the southern part of the region, two other species of clearwing borers occur that are actually larger than the American hornet moth. *Melittia gloriosa* (Hy. Edwards) and *Melittia grandis* (Strecker) are large gray moths with orange legs that develop within buffalo gourds, a wild perennial squash.

The clearwing borers also include several economically important species. Larvae of the peach tree borer, *Synanthedon exitiosa* (Say), chew the lower trunk and roots of peach, plum and other *Prunus* species of plants throughout the region. Ash and lilac are commonly attacked by the ash borer, *Podosesia syringae* (Harris). The raspberry crown borer, *Pennisetia marginata* (Harris), can be a local problem on raspberry, tunneling the crown area of the plant and killing it.

The clearwing borers are one of the only groups of moths that are active during the day. This is apparently due to their resemblance to stinging insects, such as yellowjackets and bees. Another common family of moths that mimic wasps and are active in the daytime are the ctenuchid moths (Arctiidae family). Adults of these insects can be observed visiting flowers in midsummer. The caterpillars develop on grasses and other plants in meadow areas.

Collecting Tips: This is a difficult species to collect because the adults are not attracted to light and the larvae tunnel in trunks of large trees. They are most easily collected with pheromone traps, being occasionally attracted to the chemical found in the standard "clearwing borer" lure (Z,Z-3-13-octadecadien-1-ol acetate) used for monitoring flights of peach tree borer and ash borer.

LARGEST CARPENTERWORM—CARPENTERWORM
Prionoxystus robiniae (Peck)

Carpenterworm adult

Order: Lepidoptera

Family: Cossidae

Distribution: Generally distributed in the region, except at higher elevations, but particularly common in prairie areas east of the Rocky Mountains.

Life History and Habits: Carpenterworms develop as wood borers and spend the winter as larvae in tunnels in tree trunks, particularly elm, ash and cottonwood. They pupate in spring and the adult moths emerge around late May, leaving their large purplish pupal cases sticking out of the exit hole.

After mating, the females lay eggs in clusters around crevices or wounds in the bark. When the eggs hatch, the young larvae bore directly to the inner bark and feed. When about half-grown, the larvae bore into sapwood, tunneling upward into sapwood and heartwood and pushing sawdust as they go. Completion of feeding typically takes two to three years, during which time the caterpillars may produce a 1/2-inch (1/3-cm) wide tunnel winding nearly 10 inches (25.4 cm) through the tree.

Carpenterworms can damage trees by their tunneling activities, and are particularly common on shelterbelts on the eastern plains. Trees infested over many years become gnarled and misshapen as well as more susceptible to breakage by wind and snows.

Related Species: Several other species of carpenterworms occur in the region. *Acossus undosus* Lintner, found west of the Continental Divide, rivals the carpenterworm in size. *Acossus centerensis* (Lintner) and the pine carpenterworm, *Givira lotta* Barnes and McDunnough, are other large species in the region.

Collecting Tips: The adult moths are best trapped at lights set out in late May or June. The moths are large and heavy-bodied, resembling hornworms.

Largest Pyralid Moth—Blue Cactus Borer
Melitara dentata (Grote)

Blue cactus borer, adult

Order: Lepidoptera

Family: Pyralidae

Distribution: Found throughout Colorado and adjacent states up to elevations of about 7,000 feet (2,133 m), in association with prickly pear cactus (*Opuntia*).

Life History and Habits: Adult female moths lay eggs in an unusual "eggstick" mass along the spines of prickly pear cactus in midsummer. After the eggs hatch, the larvae tunnel into the cactus pad at the needle base. They spend the winter as partially grown larvae and continue to feed with the return of warm weather in spring. As the larvae increase in size, the group scatters throughout the plant, attacking adjacent pads. Occasionally they are abundant enough to kill the pads of the cactus or even the entire plant. They are an unusual blue color, which gives them their common name.

When full grown, in late June or July, the larvae leave the pad, wander a considerable distance from the plant and pupate within a

Blue cactus borer larva; photograph by John Capinera

cocoon under debris. Adults typically begin to emerge in mid-July and can be found through August. After adults mate, the eggstick masses are laid on the spines. There is one generation per season.

Increased populations have been associated with periods of moist weather that stimulates growth of grasses around the cactus. Tachinid flies and parasitic wasps are natural enemies, emerging during the pupal stage of the blue cactus borer.

Related Species: The Pyralidae family is very large and includes a great number of species that develop into small to moderate-sized moths. Among the more common pyralid species are the various "sod webworms," which develop on lawn grasses; the European corn borer, *Ostrinia nubilalis* (Hübner), an important pest of field corn east of the Rockies; and the alfalfa webworm, *Loxostege cerealis* (Zeller).

Collecting Tips: Larvae can be found by searching low-growing prickly pear cactus. Evidence of their tunneling is collections of frass oozing from openings in the cactus pad. Larvae are most easily located as they become nearly full grown in late spring.

Adults may be collected at light traps placed near infested sites in mid-July and August. They are heavy-bodied moths with slightly mottled gray wings and a wingspan of up to 2 inches (5 cm). They are most common in properly grazed pastures, and are less abundant in overgrazed areas or following periods of drought.

Rearing Tips: Larvae collected from cactus pads can be reared to the adult stage.

Largest Woollybear—Saltmarsh Caterpillar/Acrea Moth
Estigmene acrea (Drury)

Adults of some of the common woollybears. Female and male of the saltmarsh caterpillar (Acrea moth) (top), adult of the yellow woollybear (Virginia moth) (bottom left), adult of the banded woollybear (Isabella moth) (bottom right)

Order: Lepidoptera

Family: Arctiidae

Distribution: Common throughout the region and occasionally a pest species.

Life History and Habits: The saltmarsh caterpillar survives winter as a pupa within a cocoon, hidden in protective cover. The adult moths typically emerge in June; females lay eggs in masses on the underside of leaves. When the eggs hatch, the young larvae as a group usually first feed on the leaves, skeletonizing the leaf surface. As they get older, they disperse but continue to feed for about one month. Saltmarsh caterpillars are initially dark brown, but later turn different colors, including yellowish-brown and black.

When full grown, the caterpillars wander away from their host plant and find a protected site in which they spin a cocoon. The cocoon is composed of the silk but also includes the hairs of the

*Saltmarsh caterpillar
larva; photograph by
John Capinera*

caterpillar. After two to three days they transform to a pupa. In summer, the adults emerge two weeks later and a second generation occurs. Larvae produced during this latter generation become dormant after pupation and prepare for winter.

Saltmarsh caterpillars eat a very wide variety of garden plants and have been known to occur in numbers that damage crops. Their name is derived from their damage to gardens of New England settlers that were located in saltmarsh areas.

Related Species: The name "woollybear" is generally applied to any caterpillar in the family Arctiidae that is densely covered with hair. Within the region there are at least two additional species considered to be woollybears: the yellow woollybear, *Spilosoma virginica* (Fabricius), and the banded woollybear, *Pyrrharctia isabella* (J. E. Smith). Their life history is similar to that of the saltmarsh caterpillar, although the banded woollybear survives winters as a full-grown larva and again feeds for a brief time in spring before pupating.

Moths of many members of the family are commonly known as "tiger moths." For example, the adult of the banded woollybear is

*Silver-spotted
tiger moth*

This tent was produced by a colony of the fall webworm.

sometimes known as the "Isabella tiger moth," and the adult of the yellow woollybear may be called the "Virginia tiger moth." The term "tiger moth" refers to the strongly banded patterns of many of these moths, which typically include pink or orange patterned underwings.

Some tiger moths, including species in the genus *Halysidota*, have attractive silvery spots on their wings. Caterpillars of these "silver-spotted tiger moths" develop on piñon, juniper, ponderosa and lodgepole pine. They are one of the few insects that continue to feed throughout the winter, as weather permits, and characteristically construct a tent of webbing on the tops of infested trees.

Perhaps the most conspicuous member of this insect family is the fall webworm, *Hyphantria cunea* (Drury), which creates large, loose tents of silk in cottonwood, chokecherry and many other trees

Adult fall webworm

during the summer. The adult moths, like the saltmarsh caterpillar, are generally white, attractive moths that are most easily captured at lights in June and early July. Although it is one of the most common tent-making caterpillars, the fall webworm is not a true tent caterpillar. Tent caterpillars (*Malacosoma* species in the family Lasiocampidae) produce tight tents in the crotches of branches during spring.

Collecting Tips: Adult moths are most easily collected at night around lights, from late May through mid-August.

Larvae are commonly seen migrating across roads in late summer. They are often attacked by parasitic flies and wasps.

Rearing Tips: The full-grown caterpillars (larvae) can be reared to the adult stage. However, after they pupate in fall, they require a few months of cold weather before they will transform to the adult stage. A somewhat protected location, such as the corner of a garage, is a good place to store the pupae during the winter. When brought out, the emerging moths will need a stick or other perch to allow them to spread their wings.

LARGEST BUTTERFLIES—TWO-TAILED SWALLOWTAIL AND WESTERN TIGER SWALLOWTAIL

Papilio multicaudatus Kirby—Two-tailed Swallowtail
Papilio rutulus Linnaeus—Western Tiger Swallowtail

Order: Lepidoptera

Family: Papilionidae

Distribution: Tiger swallowtails are found throughout the region. The two-tailed swallowtail predominates in the eastern areas, while the western tiger swallowtail occurs primarily in the western areas.

Life History and Habits: The overwintering stage of swallowtails is a pupa, a grayish chrysalis that becomes the color of, and camouflages with, the background on which it forms. Adults emerge in May and June, mate and lay eggs on the plants fed on by the caterpillar stage. Green ash and chokecherry are host plants of the caterpillar stage of the two-tailed swallowtail; willow, cottonwood and chokecherry are fed on by the western tiger swallowtail.

Adult of the two-tailed swallowtail; photograph by Paul Opler

Young swallowtail larvae often resemble bird droppings. Older larvae of the two-tailed swallowtail turn a more orange-brown color and have striking "eyespot" markings; older larvae of the western tiger swallowtail are green. All swallowtail larvae can extrude a pair of smelly "horns" (osmeteria) when disturbed. Adult butterflies feed on nectar. There is one generation per season.

Related Species: The black swallowtail (also known as the "eastern black swallowtail"), *Papilio polyxenes asterius* Stoll, is commonly found east of the Continental Divide. The larvae, called "parsleyworms," feed on dill, parsley, carrot, fennel and related plants in the family Umbelliferae. The caterpillars have distinctive yellow and black stripes. The adults are present from May through August. In the southern areas of the region, the closely related anise swallowtail, *Papilio*

A tiger swallowtail caterpillar; photograph by Frank Peairs

zelicaon nitra Edwards, develops on yellow mountain parsley in the larval stage.

Several other swallowtails may drift into the region but cannot establish permanent breeding populations, such as the pipevine swallowtail, *Battus philenor philenor* (Linnaeus), and the pale swallowtail, *Papilio eurymedon* Lucas.

Collecting Tips: The adults of these species are common city inhabitants during flight periods. They are attracted to a

This black swallowtail rests on a zinnia flower.

variety of flowering plants, such as zinnia, milkweed, thistle and butterfly bush, and are most easily collected at these sites. Flights typically occur in June and July.

Larvae are often encountered wandering across lawns late in the summer, as they are searching for a place to pupate and are no longer feeding.

Rearing Tips: Swallowtail caterpillars can be easily reared by providing fresh leaves of their host plants. When full grown they will need a support, such as a twig, on which they can change to the chrysalis stage. They require exposure to cold for several months before they will transform to the adult stage. They are best stored during the winter in a cool area protected from extreme cold.

The parsleyworm is the larva of the black swallowtail.

LARGEST PIERID BUTTERFLY—QUEEN ALEXANDRA'S SULPHUR
Colias alexandra alexandra Edwards

Queen Alexandra's sulphur

Order: Lepidoptera

Family: Pieridae

Distribution: Generally distributed throughout most of western North America and locally common.

Life History and Habits: This butterfly varies in color from pure lemon-yellow to orange. Pure white females may make up about 5 percent or less of various populations. Winter is spent as a green chrysalis attached to plants or in protected sites. Adults emerge in late June, and after mating, females lay eggs on various leguminous plants, including clover, golden banner, vetch and locoweed. The larvae hatch from the eggs in about one week and feed on the plants, developing into a dark green caterpillar with white and orange stripes along the sides. The body of the caterpillar is covered in short hairs with small black points. Usually only one generation is produced annually in mountain areas, but at least two generations can occur at lower elevations.

Related Species: Butterflies in the family Pieridae are known as "whites," "sulphurs," "dog-faces" or "orange-tips" depending on their coloration and patterning. They are moderately large, with a typical wingspan of about 1 inch (2.5 cm), and include some of the most frequently encountered butterflies in the region. Two of the most common species

*Pine butterfly, photograph
by David Leatherman*

are the alfalfa butterfly or orange sulfur, *Colias eurytheme* Boisduval, and
the common or clouded sulphur, *Colias philodice* Godart. These slightly
smaller butterflies resemble Queen Alexandra's sulphur and similarly
develop on legumes.

Even more common in most areas is the cabbage butterfly/cab-
bage white, also known as the "imported cabbageworm," *Pieris rapae*
(Linnaeus). This white butterfly develops as a slightly fuzzy, green
caterpillar feeding on cabbage, broccoli and other plants in the
mustard family, and is an important pest of these crops. A white
butterfly with similar habits and appearance is the southern cabbageworm or checkered white, *Pontia protodice* Boisduval and
LeConte, found most frequently in the southern areas of the region. In ponderosa pine forests, the larvae of the pine white butterfly, *Neophasia menapia* (Felder and Felder), feed on the needles, and
the adult butterflies can be observed swarming around the trees in
mid-August.

A few species of sulphur butterflies that are larger than the Queen
Alexandra's sulphur occur in the region, but are more rarely collected.
Colias gigantea Strecker, known as the "giant sulphur," develops on willow in boggy areas from the Rocky Mountains of Wyoming northward into Alaska. Several species in the genus *Phoebis* sometimes stray
into the eastern plains from their breeding sites along the Gulf Coast
and Mexico. These include the orange-barred sulphur, *P. philea*

(Johansson), the cloudless orange sulphur, *P. agarithe* (Boisduval), and the cloudless sulphur, *P. sennae* (Linnaeus), all of which may have a wingspan approaching 3 inches (7.6 cm).

Collecting Tips: Queen Alexandra's sulphur is most commonly collected while visiting flowers in meadows from late June through early August.

Alfalfa fields are particularly good areas to collect the alfalfa butterfly and common sulfur, while the cabbage butterfly is found in almost any garden where cabbage family plants are raised.

Rearing Tips: The caterpillars are easily reared by feeding them foliage of their host plants every few days. As with other species of butterflies, they will need a surface on which to produce the chrysalis that also provides enough space for them to spread their wings when they emerge. The majority of caterpillars are parasitized by wasps or tachinid flies.

Largest Brushfooted Butterfly—The Mourning Cloak/Spiny Elm Caterpillar
Nymphalis antiopa (Linnaeus)

Mourning cloak butterfly

Order: Lepidoptera

Family: Nymphalidae

Distribution: Found throughout the region and often common.

Life History and Habits: The adult butterfly, known as the "mourning cloak," is one of the few butterflies that spend the winter in the

A spiny elm caterpillar, larva of the mourning cloak; photograph by David Leatherman

adult stage. They hide in protected sites, such as flaps of bark, and may emerge periodically during warm days in late winter and early spring.

The butterflies lay eggs shortly after new leaves start to emerge in April and May. The eggs are laid in masses around small twigs and branches of several trees, including aspen, willow, elm, hackberry, cottonwood and poplar. The newly hatched larvae are often the first caterpillars found on trees in spring; they feed in groups, stripping leaves from branches. As they get older, the caterpillars turn velvety-black, covered with several rows of fleshy spines. They sometimes cause localized defoliation of branches, but are so abundant that they can also cause serious tree damage. After completing development, mature larvae migrate from the tree and pupate within a silvery chrysalis. They emerge as adults in late July or August and lay eggs for the next generation, which produce the overwintering adults.

Related Species: The family Nymphalidae contains scores of species, many of which are easily observed or collected. These have such names as "admirals," "fritillaries," "crescentspots," "anglewings," "checkerspots" and "tortoiseshells." Among the larger brushfooted

Painted lady butterfly

butterflies are the Weidemeyer's Admiral, *Limenitis weidemeyerii* Edwards, and the viceroy, *L. archippus* (Cramer). The larvae of both species develop on willow; aspen and cottonwood are additional hosts of the Weidemeyer's Admiral. Another slightly smaller species that can be locally common is the hackberry butterfly, *Asterocampa celtis* (Boisduval), the caterpillars of which develop on hackberry trees.

The most common brushfooted butterfly is the painted lady, *Vanessa cardui* (Linnaeus), an annual migrant into the region in late spring; migrations sometimes occur in spectacular numbers. The larvae, known as "thistle caterpillars," feed on various thistles, lupines and some crop plants. Unlike the other famous migratory butterfly, the monarch, the painted lady continues to feed and breed throughout the year. In warm months it may be found as far north as Canada. In late summer and early fall, migrations are made to the south to areas where food plants remain.

Collecting Tips: Adult mourning cloak butterflies can easily be collected with a sweep net. They tend to be most common in areas where host plants used by the caterpillars are abundant and where there are wooded sites to provide cover. The adults rarely feed on nectar but will visit sap flowing from trees and rotting fruit. During migrations the butterflies often follow river systems or shorelines.

Rearing Tips: The larvae can be reared by providing fresh leaves of their food plants. After they have pupated, they should be kept in a container that both provides a perch on which the emerging butterflies can hang and sufficient room to allow their wings to fully expand.

Insect Migrants of the Rocky Mountain Region

The story of the annual migrations of the monarch butterfly is well known to most bug-watchers. However, they may be surprised to learn that many other familiar insects also cannot survive the winter conditions of the region and therefore spend the winter in more southern areas, annually dispersing northward each spring with the assistance of winds. The list of annual migrants includes many of our most important insect pests as well as some of the familiar butterflies. Among the seasonal migrants into the region are the following:

Armyworm	An important regional caterpillar pest of wheat, barley and other small grains.
Greenbug	An aphid that damages corn, wheat and sorghum.
Potato/tomato psyllid	The most important pest of tomatoes and potatoes in much of the region; plants are damaged by toxic saliva it introduces while feeding.
Corn earworm	The common "worm" that infests the ear tips of sweet corn as well as tomato and pepper fruits.
Painted lady	A very common butterfly that makes annual migrations into the area in late spring, then returns to more southerly areas in late summer.
Variegated fritillary	An attractive orange and black butterfly that develops on pansies and other garden flowers.

The Big Bugs of the Rockies

Blue darner	One of the largest dragonflies in the region, it makes annual northward migrations in the spring.

Other insects make different migrations. East-west (plains-to-mountain) migrations are made by some butterflies and moths. The best example of this is the army cutworm, **Euxoa auxiliaris** (Grote), more commonly known as the "miller moth" in eastern Colorado, Wyoming and Montana. This insect survives the winter as a partially grown caterpillar in wheat fields, alfalfa fields, lawns and gardens. After completing development and transforming to the adult stage, the moths migrate to the mountains, where cool temperatures and abundant nectar sources allow them to survive the hot summers. Late in the season they return to the plains to lay eggs. The butterfly known as the "Milbert's tortoise shell," **Nymphalis milberti** Godart, makes similar plains-to-mountain migrations in parts of the region.

Largest Satyrid Butterfly—Wood Nymph
Cercyonis pegala (Fabricius)

Order: Lepidoptera

Family: Satyridae (or the subfamily Satyrinae of the Nymphalidae)

Distribution: Generally distributed throughout the United States and southern Canada.

Wood nymph

Life History and Habits: The larvae of the wood nymph develop on various grasses and occasionally sedges. Winter is spent in hibernation as tiny, first-instar larvae that resume development the following spring. After about three months they become full grown, turning into a dull green caterpillar with white and yellow stripes. Pupation within a chrysalis occurs in clumps of grasses, and the adults emerge in early summer.

Adult males are often seen while cruising their territories, typically along the edges of wooded areas.

Related Species: The dark wood nymph, *Cercyonis oetus* (Boisduval), is common throughout the region in grassland and scrubland areas at elevations above 5,000 feet (1,522 m), often supplanting the wood nymph. Boisduval's wood nymph, *Cercyonis sthenele* (Boisduval), occurs in moist canyons in the western part of the region. Mead's wood nymph, *Cercyonis meadii* (Edwards), occurs in similar habitats in the eastern areas. All are generally dark butterflies with prominent eyespots on the wings.

Collecting Tips: Adult butterflies are present from mid-July into September. Occasionally they visit late-blooming flowers such as rabbitbrush, where they can easily be collected.

These butterflies often use and return to the same perch sites for extended periods. Butterflies that are disturbed into flight may shortly return.

Largest Milkweed Butterfly—Monarch Butterfly
Danaus plexippus (Linnaeus)

Order: Lepidoptera

Family: Danaidae (or the subfamily Danainae of the Nymphalidae)

Distribution: Generally distributed wherever milkweeds (*Asclepias*) grow.

Life History and Habits: Monarch butterflies are unusual in that they make annual north-south migrations. They cannot survive winters in the Rocky Mountain region, and most migrate in late summer to overwintering sites in Mexico. There they congregate in incredible numbers, often covering trees. In spring the survivors

Comparison of the monarch butterfly (top) and the queen butterfly (bottom), two milkweed butterflies found in the region

migrate north, laying eggs on milkweed. Eventually progeny of the overwintered butterflies reach areas into southern Canada.

The adult butterflies lay eggs on milkweed. The larva is a very attractive, black, yellow and white "zebra-striped" caterpillar and is very conspicuous on the milkweed plant. Both larvae and adults obtain a toxic chemical from the milkweed that in turn makes them toxic and distasteful to birds. When full grown, the larva moves to a protected area and forms a beautiful pale green pupa, or chrysalis ("house with the golden nails") decorated with a band of gold dots. Pupae collected in the field will emerge in a short time in the orange, black and white butterfly stage.

Monarch butterflies have two or three generations a year and are conspicuous on milkweed plants. The adults feed on nectar and can be attracted to yards with flower plantings. At the end of the summer, the butterflies migrate back to their overwintering areas in Mexico, which provide protection and adequate humidity so that the they can remain inactive and conserve their energy during the dormant season. There is great concern about the future of this species because these winter refuges are being destroyed by logging.

Monarch caterpillar

Parallel migrations of monarch butterflies occur among populations in the Pacific states. These butterflies migrate for winter protection to forested areas around Pacific Grove, California. It is thought that at least some of the butterflies from Utah and Idaho move to these overwintering sites, although this has not been confirmed.

Related Species: The large orange butterfly known as the "queen," *Danaus gilippus* (Cramer), also develops on milkweed. However, this insect is primarily subtropical and is very rare in the region, occurring only as an occasional migrant.

The viceroy, *Limenitis archippus* (Cramer), resembles the monarch. Slightly smaller and with different markings, the viceroy is thought to mimic the monarch butterfly to fool birds and other predators that have learned not to feed on the more common monarch because it contains distasteful chemicals. The viceroy is a species of brushfooted butterfly in the family Nymphalidae.

Collecting Tips: The larval stage is found on milkweed plants. Adults can be collected at a variety of flowers from June through early October.

Rearing Tips: The larvae can be reared easily if fed milkweed and given enough space for newly emerged adults to spread their wings.

Miscellaneous: Because the monarch butterfly is a native insect found throughout the United States, the Entomological Society of America is acting to have it declared the national insect. It is now the state insect of Illinois and Vermont.

LARGEST SKIPPER—STRECKER'S YUCCA SKIPPER
Megathymus streckeri (Skinner)

Order: Lepidoptera

Family: Hesperiidae

Distribution: Generally distributed in the region from eastern Montana southwest into northern New Mexico and Utah. It is restricted to the lower elevations, usually in desert or semidesert areas.

Life History and Habits: The larva of Strecker's yucca skipper develops as a borer in the root stalk of the yucca known as "Spanish

Strecker's yucca skipper

bayonet," *Yucca glauca* Nuttall. Winter is spent in the form of a nearly full grown larva within the plant; it tunnels into the base of the plant to form a pupation chamber the following spring. Adults may begin to emerge in late spring, and flights extend into early summer.

The adult females lay eggs on the underside of leaves. After hatching, the larvae tunnel into the stalk at the base of the leaves. As they feed, they also construct a protective silken tent over the tunnel entrance. There is one generation per year.

Related Species: A closely related species is the yucca skipper, *Megathymus yuccae* (Boisduval and LeConte). This species, restricted to more southerly areas in the region, also develops on species of yucca. Both of these skippers are large, with a wingspan of up to 1 1/2 inches (3.8 cm). Typical of other skippers, they are heavy-bodied but lack a hook at the end of the antennae, instead having clubbed antennae like the butterflies.

Collecting Tips: The adults can be found from May into July near stands of yucca. Colonies are reported to occur most often on sloping ground. Adults do not feed on nectar but may drink at damp patches of sand or soil. The adults are strong fliers and can be difficult to capture.

Rearing Tips: Larvae found on infested plants can be reared. Look for the tent they have formed at the base of the leaves.

ORDER: TRICHOPTERA
Caddisflies

Caddisflies develop as aquatic insects, living in streams, rivers, ponds, lakes and marshes; many are restricted to habitats of cool running water. Many species produce a silken case, in which the larvae live, made out of sand, small pebbles, leaf fragments or twigs. These cases are quite distinctive for each species of caddisfly. The larvae carry the case with them as they search the beds of waterways for food. Other caddisflies do not produce cases but may construct nets to snare small insects or other food. Some caddisflies develop within silken tubes constructed at the bottom of streams or in debris, while a few free-living species move around and hunt without constructing any special structure.

Trichoptera means "hair wings," a reference to the fine hairs that cover their wings. Many caddisfly adults superficially resemble small moths, but lack the wing scales of the order Lepidoptera and have very long antennae. The wings of caddisflies are held rooflike over their abdomen. They are fairly weak fliers.

Caddisflies undergo complete metamorphosis, with the egg, larval and pupal stages occurring in or immediately adjacent to water. The larvae are easily collected using a dip net or strainer while searching streams. The adults are attracted to lights. They are best preserved by pinning through the thorax and spreading, as with moths and butterflies. Adults of smaller species and larvae should be stored in alcohol.

Caddisfly larva with case; drawing from An Illustrated Guide to the Mountain Stream Insects of Colorado

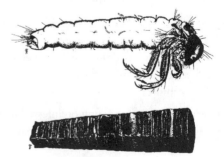

LARGEST CADDISFLY—
DICOSMOECUS ATRIPES (HAGEN)

The caddisfly Dicosmoecus atripes

Order: Trichoptera

Family: Limnephilidae

Distribution: Common near high mountain streams.

Life History and Habits: Larvae of *Dicosmoecus atripes* develop in mountain streams, living within a case made of small pebbles. They reportedly feed on both vascular plant matter and small aquatic insects.

Winter is spent as larvae, sealed within their case and attached to rocks. They resume feeding in spring; the full-grown larvae pupate in late spring and early summer. Adults emerge from late July through September and are most active in the morning. The peak flight period is late August. Females lay eggs in gelatinous masses, fastened to rocks or vegetation at the waterline. The larvae generally feed in fall and throughout the warmer months of the following season. The entire life cycle requires two years to complete.

Related Species: More than two hundred species of caddisflies occur in the region. Among the genera that contain the largest caddisflies are *Hesperophylax, Limnephilus, Onocosmoecus* and *Psychoglypha.*

Collecting Tips: Adults are best collected by sweeping vegetation near streams in late summer. They can also be attracted to lights at night. Larvae are usually found attached to rocks among small stones in slower areas of fast-moving streams.

ORDER: HYMENOPTERA
Wasps, Bees and Ants

Insects in the order Hymenoptera are extremely diverse in habits and form. They are generally characterized as having chewing or chewing-lapping mouthparts in the adult stage, two pairs of wings that often function as a single pair by being hooked together and complete metamorphosis. With the exception of the plant-feeding horntails and sawflies, the Hymenoptera also have a distinct constriction between the thorax and abdomen ("wasp-waist").

Immature stages of most Hymenoptera are relatively inactive "grubs" that are fed by the females. Sawflies and horntails again are the exception, being active plant feeders in their immature stages. Many Hymenoptera, such as ants and many bees and wasps, are also social insects that form colonies and have a distinct caste structure with queens, males and workers.

Members of this order are among the most beneficial to human activity. Pollination of many crops in the United States is dependent on foraging by various bees, such as the leafcutter bees, the bumblebees and the introduced honeybee. In addition, honey, beeswax and other commodities are produced by honeybees. Perhaps most important are the activities of parasitic wasps and hunting wasps in control of pest species of insects.

Relatively few Hymenoptera have damaging habits. Sawflies occasionally damage plants by feeding on foliage; some seed chalcid wasps adversely affect crops such as alfalfa. The defensive stinging habit of certain Hymenoptera, particularly social bees and wasps, is perhaps the injury most widely recognized with this group of insects.

Adult Hymenoptera are best preserved by pinning through the upper right thorax. Larvae should be preserved in 70 percent alcohol.

LARGEST HUNTING WASP—CICADA KILLER
Sphecius grandis (Say)

Order: Hymenoptera

Family: Sphecidae

Distribution: Within the region, this wasp has been collected in New Mexico, Colorado and Utah in association with its prey, dog-day

Cicada killer with dog-day cicada prey; photograph by Howard Evans

cicadas. Another species, *Sphecius speciosus* (Drury) is known in eastern Colorado.

Life History and Habits: Adult cicada killers are most abundant in late July and August, at which time they search for adult cicadas and prepare nests. Nests are located in loose sandy soils that are exposed to the sun and dug to a depth of 1 foot (30.4 cm) or more. Several chambers are excavated in each nest; the young are reared individually in these chambers. After nest construction the female wasps search for cicada prey; once captured, the prey is immobilized with a paralyzing sting, then carried back to the nest in a series of short flights. Usually only the larger, egg-filled female cicadas are used by the cicada killer. Because the prey weighs more than the wasp, it is often dragged up trees or buildings to allow the adult wasp to make short gliding flights back to the nest. The cicada is then pulled into the nest hole and an egg is laid on it.

Two cicadas are used when the wasp rears a female; one is sufficient for the food needs of the smaller male wasps. The young wasps feed on the paralyzed cicada, becoming full grown in a few weeks. The overwintering stage of the wasp is a diapausing larva within a cocoon. There is one generation per year.

Related Species: The Sphecidae family is very large, containing some 1,100 species in North America, several hundred of which occur in the Rocky Mountain region. All are hunting wasps that variously specialize in collecting prey such as leafhoppers, aphids, caterpillars, weevils or spiders, which they use to provision their nest cells. With some species, nesting occurs in holes dug into the soil, while others use natural cavities, such as hollows in wood or the center of pithy plants, or create mud nests.

Several other large species of sphecid wasps are common throughout the region, including the steel-blue cricket hunter, *Chlorion aeraerium* Patton. This is a shiny, blue-black wasp that may exceed 1 inch (2.5 cm) in length and hunts field crickets. Nests are dug in sandy soils and may contain several cells, each provisioned with paralyzed crickets for the developing wasps to feed on. Also locally common is the great golden digger, *Sphex ichneumoneus* (Linnaeus), which uses katydids and other longhorned grasshoppers ("meadow grasshoppers") as prey. This species has long been a favorite of insect behaviorists, who have made numerous studies of their highly stylized nesting behavior. Other large sphecid wasps occur in the genera *Bembix*, *Chalybion* and *Ammophila* (see following section).

Collecting Tips: Adult cicada killers are most easily found while they search for cicada prey or while feeding. The nectar of certain flowers, particularly milkweed, is used by the wasps, as is the ooze caused by bacterial wetwood in cottonwood and other trees. Cottonwood is also the most common tree on which cicadas lay eggs and immature cicadas develop (see "Largest Homopteran––Dog Day Cicada").

Nests produced by the cicada killer and many other hunting wasps can be detected by the large mounds of sandy soil around the entrance.

LARGEST THREADWAISTED WASPS—*AMMOPHILA* SPECIES
Ammophila macra Cresson
Ammophila procera Dahlbom

Order: Hymenoptera

Family: Sphecidae

Distribution: *Ammophila procera* is very widely distributed across America. The closely related species *A. macra* is restricted to the Rocky Mountain West. Both are very similar in appearance and habit and are considered by some experts to be strains of the same species.

*A large hunting wasp
(*Ammophila *species) with
cherry sphinx prey*

Life History and Habits: These large (up to 1 1/2 inches [3.8 cm]),
slender-bodied wasps are hunters of large caterpillars, particularly
hornworms. Before capturing prey, the females dig a nest cell in the
soil, with a vertical central tunnel ending in a chamber for rearing
young. Great care is taken to spread the soil removed during the exca-
vation to disguise the entrance, unlike the habit of many other hunting wasps to leave mounds near the nest. When the nest cell is finished, the female leaves it, carefully covers the opening and searches
for prey. The search may take a couple of days, but she remembers the
location of the nest by using landmarks around the nest.

When a suitable caterpillar is located, it is stung and paralyzed.
The wasp then carries it back to the nest, slung underneath her
body. After opening the nest entrance, she drags the caterpillar into
the nest cell and lays an egg on it. As the female leaves the cell, she
carefully covers the entrance with small pebbles and then soil, tamp-
ing it down with her head or with the aid of tools such as twigs or
pebbles. The young wasp feeds on the paralyzed caterpillar and
spends the winter in the nest cell. Pupation occurs in the spring,
and adult wasps emerge in late spring.

During the night these and other wasps will rest on plants,
sometimes in small groups. Upright branched plants are used, particularly those that provide some shelter from winds yet allow exposure to the sun during morning and late afternoon. While resting, they grasp the twig with their jaws and position their abdomen
horizontal to the plant.

The common mud dauber,
Sceliphron caementarium,
*makes nests of mud and packs
the cells with paralyzed spiders
it has captured.*

Related Species: The genus *Ammophila* is one of the most common and widespread of the hunting wasp groups in the region, with approximately two dozen species. All hunt various species of caterpillars or occasionally the larvae of sawflies. They dig cells in the soil, and most create several nest cells at a single site.

Many other "threadwaisted" wasps are common in the region. One of the larger and more conspicuous is the black and yellow mud dauber, *Sceliphron caementarium* (Drury). Females of this wasp construct parallel nesting cells of mud on walls, in overhangs of cliffs or under eaves, which they provision with paralyzed spiders.

Collecting Tips: These wasps are found in areas that provide caterpillar prey and have the proper soil conditions for nest building. Firm but light-textured soils are favored for nests. Males and some females can sometimes be collected late in the day while resting on vegetation. The wasps are active throughout most of the summer.

The larger hunting wasps can sting, although the pain does not persist for long.

LARGEST SPIDER WASPS—TARANTULA HAWKS
Pepsis thisbe **Lucas**
Pepsis formosa formosa (**Say**)
Pepsis pallidolimbata **Lucas**
Pepsis mildei **Stäl**

Order: Hymenoptera

Family: Pompilidae

The tarantula hawk, a large dark-colored wasp with orange wings, preys on tarantulas.

Distribution: Limited to areas where their prey, the tarantula, is found. This restricts them to the more southern areas of the region. Occasionally tarantula hawks may be blown into other areas but do not breed there.

Life History and Habits: Tarantula hawks are hunting wasps that develop solely on tarantulas. The females capture the spiders with a paralyzing sting and then prepare a nesting burrow. Burrows are often dug in open areas, and may reach a depth of about 6 inches (15.2 cm) in dry, gravelly soils. Sometimes the burrow of the tarantula prey is used.

After dragging the prey into the nest, the female wasp lays an egg on the spider and seals the burrow. The young wasp that hatches feeds on the tarantula and becomes full grown in several weeks. The overwintering stage is a diapausing larva within a cocoon in the nest burrow. Tarantula hawks have one generation per year.

Related Species: The members of the family of spider wasps are quite common, with more than one hundred species in the region. All hunt large spiders (such as crab spiders, wolf spiders and nursery web spiders) and use a single spider to provision nests. Several other genera of spider wasps (*Hemipepsis, Entypus, Cryptocheilus*) have the same general coloration as the tarantula hawks: a blue-black body and orange wings. However, the great majority of spider wasps are blue-black with shiny wings.

Spider wasps can be difficult to distinguish from the sphecid wasps. Some hunting wasps (*Chalybion* species) have similar blue-black coloration, and several species hunt small spiders. Most of the sphecid wasps can be distinguished by the raised "collar" behind their head, which spider wasps lack.

Collecting Tips: Adult wasps are most active in August. Female wasps are usually more active in the early evening, while male wasps fly throughout the day. Male tarantula hawks feed on nectar and are particularly abundant on plants such as milkweed, sunflower and tamarisk (salt cedar).

If handled, females of the tarantula hawks, and most large spider wasps, can produce a very painful sting. Males do not sting.

Largest Parasitic Wasp—Giant Ichneumon Wasp
Megarhyssa macrurus (Linnaeus)

Order: Hymenoptera

Family: Ichneumonidae

Distribution: Throughout the region wherever there are hardwood trees, in which its host, the pigeon tremex horntail, develops. Elms are particularly common hosts for the pigeon tremex and for its associated parasite, the giant ichneumon wasp.

Life History and Habits: Adult wasps are present in midsummer. Female wasps, distinguished by their extremely long ovipositor ("stinger"), spend much of their time carefully examining dead hardwood branches and trunks. Upon locating a horntail larva within

The giant ichneumon wasp (top) develops as a parasite of larvae of the pigeon tremex (bottom), a type of wood borer.

the wood, the female drills a hole up to several inches (centimeters) deep into the wood, paralyzes the young horntail "grub" and then deposits an egg on it. The egg hatches and the larva of the giant ichneumon wasp feeds on the horntail, consuming it completely. The wasp then pupates within the tunnel of the horntail, emerging as the full-grown wasp in early summer.

Related Species: Both *Megarhyssa atrata* (Fabricius) and *Megarhyssa nortoni* Cresson have been collected in the region. These species are also parasites of horntail larvae but are slightly smaller.

The ichneumon wasps (Ichneumonidae family) and the closely related braconid wasps (Braconidae family) are one of the largest groups of insects, with more than four thousand species in North America. Almost all develop as parasites of other insects, so this group is of tremendous importance in the biological control of pest insects.

Collecting Tips: Look for the wasps in midsummer around older deciduous trees in declining condition, particularly those that already show evidence of horntail infestation. Giant ichneumon wasps look fearsome but are not capable of stinging humans.

LARGEST BUMBLEBEE—NEVADA BUMBLEBEE
Bombus nevadensis **Cresson**

Order: Hymenoptera

Family: Apidae

A large bumblebee

Distribution: Widely distributed throughout the region and found almost up to timberline. It is less common at lower elevations, where other species of bumblebees displace it.

Life History and Habits: The life cycle of *Bombus nevadensis* is similar to that of most other bumblebees. The overwintering stage is a fertilized female (queen) that uses protected sites for shelter. As spring temperatures warm, the female bees emerge and seek nesting sites. Rodent burrows in the ground are the most common nest site. During the establishment of the colony, the female conducts all the colony work, including foraging for nectar and pollen, constructing wax cells, laying eggs and rearing young.

Within a few weeks after colony initiation, the first worker bees emerge and begin to assist with colony maintenance. These workers are quite small owing to a reduced diet. The colony continues to increase in size throughout the summer. Toward the end of the season, fully developed females are produced that will be queens the following year; some male bumblebees are also produced, which mate with the queens. By early fall the colony dies out.

Bumblebees tend to visit flowers that have fairly deep sources of nectar, such as legumes. Many of these plants cannot be pollinated by smaller bees, such as the honeybee.

Related Species: More than twenty species of bumblebees occur in the region, several of which rival the Nevada bumblebee in size. One particularly large species, *Bombus fraternus* Smith, largely displaces *B. nevadensis* in the eastern plains. Other particularly large species are *B. morrisoni* Cresson and *B. pennsylvanicus* Degeer, both of which can be very abundant.

Collecting Tips: Bumblebees are easily collected during the day as they visit flowers for nectar and pollen. The larger bumblebees (fertile queens) are usually collected either early in the season or in late summer, remaining in colonies to produce eggs and rear young during the spring and summer.

LARGEST PAPER WASP—BALDFACED HORNET
Dolichovespula maculata (**Linnaeus**)

Baldfaced hornet

Order: Hymenoptera

Family: Vespidae

Distribution: Common throughout the region.

Life History and Habits: The overwintering stage is a fertilized female wasp that seeks protected locations for shelter. In spring the queens become active and seek sites to initiate colony nests. Trees and shrubs are common nesting areas. Nests are constructed of paperlike materials produced from ground bark and wood mixed with the wasp's saliva; they have the coloration of the wood used for construction and are often strikingly banded in colors ranging from light gray to reddish-brown.

In spring, the overwintered queen produces a few cells and rears her young on a diet of various insects, such as caterpillars, that she collects. The first wasps produced are small and infertile females, which assist with further colony development and food collection; subsequently reared wasps are fed improved diets because of better food collection; wasps produced late in the season are full-sized and fertile. Colony and nest size grow continually, becoming football-sized or larger by the end of summer. At the end of the season, some male wasps are also produced and mating occurs.

The old queen, males and early worker wasps die at the end of the season. Fertilized queens disperse for overwintering sites. The colonies are abandoned and not reused.

This paper nest, built by aerial yellowjackets, is common to several species of wasps.

Related Species: Another hornet that similarly nests in trees and shrubs is the aerial yellowjacket, *Dolichovespula arenaria* (Fabricius). These wasps are smaller than baldfaced hornets, and are marked with yellow and black rather than white and black. In most areas of the region, the aerial yellowjacket is much more common than the baldfaced hornet.

Various yellowjacket wasps (*Vespula* species) occur throughout the region, most commonly the western yellowjacket, *Vespula pennsylvanica* (Saussure), which produces paper nests, usually underground in abandoned rodent burrows. Occasionally nests are constructed in wall voids, crawl spaces and shrubs. Because the nests are inconspicuous, people are frequently stung by these insects. Without a doubt, the great majority of stings actually result from yellowjackets, rather than the highly beneficial honeybee, *Apis mellifera* Linnaeus.

Collecting Tips: Baldfaced hornets sting readily if nests are disturbed. Adult wasps are best collected as they search plants for insect prey; they become more common as the summer progresses. Old paper nests can be safely collected a month after the first killing frosts, by which time they should be completely abandoned.

A Large Paper Wasp—Western Paper Wasp
Mischocyttarus flavitarsis (Saussure)

Order: Hymenoptera

Family: Vespidae

Distribution: Found throughout the region.

Life History and Habits: The life history of the western paper wasp is similar to that of other social wasps, such as the hornets (species of *Dolichovespula*) and the yellow jackets (species of *Vespula*). Over-wintered queens become active in mid- to late April and begin to construct nests under rocks and boards, in shrubs or on buildings, occasionally expanding nests that were used the previous season. Nests are constructed from chewed wood that the queens make into a series of papery cells in which to rear the larval wasps. However, unlike the yellow jackets and hornets, the colony is not enclosed within a papery envelope.

Foraging wasps capture various small insects that they chew into a paste and later feed to the developing larvae. The foragers may also bring water to the colony during hot weather to cool the hive. All the chores of foraging and nest construction are first done by the overwintered queen, or foundress. The first young wasps are rather small workers that assist in expanding the colony. In late summer, large female reproductive forms of the wasps emerge that will later become the overwintering queens. Some male wasps are also produced at this time.

Western paper wasp

The new queens and males abandon the colony in early fall and mate outside the colony. The queens then search for overwintering shelter, and may enter homes. Occasionally large aggregations of queens occur. Other members of the colony die at the end of the season.

Related Species: The western paper wasp sometimes replaces the common paper wasps of eastern North America, species of *Polistes.* (However, the species *Polistes fuscatus centralis* Hayward occurs locally in the region, particularly in the southern areas.) Superficially they resemble each other, and both types of wasps construct a similar umbrellalike nest. Other species of *Mischocyttarus* are found in more tropical regions.

The western mantispid, a very close mimic of the western paper wasp, often occurs in the same habitats with it (see "Largest Mantidfly—Western Mantispid").

Collecting Tips: Adult wasps are often found in homes in the fall when they move in for overwintering shelter, and again in spring as they become active. They can also be seen foraging for insects in spring and summer. Colonies are difficult to find, since they usually are constructed in obscure sites; dark corners of sheds or other outbuildings are good places to look. They must be collected with care because the wasps can sting.

LARGEST ANT—CARPENTER ANT
Camponotus herculeanus (Linnaeus)
Camponotus pennsylvanicus modoc Wheeler

Order: Hymenoptera

Family: Formicidae

Distribution: Various species of carpenter ants are found throughout the region. However, the largest species are typically found above 6,500 feet (1,978 m) in mountainous, forested areas.

Life History and Habits: Typical carpenter ants form nests inside rotting wood, although the species most common in the eastern plains areas will nest in the soil. Unlike with termites, the wood is not eaten and sawdust piles will be dumped at colony entrances.

Carpenter ant worker; photograph courtesy of USDA

Worker ants (incompletely developed and infertile females) collect food such as insects and honeydew and return it to the colony. A large carpenter ant colony may contain several hundred ants. Fully developed and fertile female "queens" are occasionally produced; these are winged and emerge and periodically fly from colonies, usually in late June or July. The smaller winged males produced by the colony also fly at this time and mate with the females. A new colony is then started by each mated queen. Shortly after finding a suitable site for the a colony, the female sheds her wings.

Collecting Tips: Colonies of carpenter ants are most easily found in forested areas. They are usually formed in logs that have fallen fairly recently and are not yet in an advanced state of decay. Sawdust piles near the colony entrances are good indicators of an active colony. Individual worker ants can be collected as they forage for food.

LARGEST VELVET ANTS—COW KILLERS
Dasymutilla occidentalis commanche (**Linnaeus**)
Dasymutilla magnifica **Mickel**
Dasymutilla klugii **Gray**

The female velvet ant is sometimes called a "cow killer" because of its painful sting; photograph courtesy of USDA.

Order: Hymenoptera

Family: Mutillidae

Distribution: Larger velvet ants are locally common in southern areas of the region; other species occur throughout the region.

Life History and Habits: Despite their name, velvet ants are a type of wasp rather than a true ant. As with other velvet ants, the "cow killer" develops as a parasite of ground-nesting bees. Adult females crawl over the soil searching for burrows of bee nests. When the adult bees are absent from the nest, the cow killer enters and lays eggs on the pupae of the developing bees. The larvae of the cow killer develop by feeding on the bees.

The velvet ants spend the winter in the pupal stage within the tunnels of the bees on which they have fed. The adult wasps emerge in late spring. The males can be seen flying lazily above the ground, usually around small rises or other features in the landscape. The wingless females spend most of their time crawling over the ground searching for nesting bees. There is one generation per year.

Both the adult males and females make a squeaking noise.

A male velvet ant visits a flower.

Related Species: Dozens of species of velvet ants are concentrated in the more arid areas of the western and southwestern United States. Most are in the genus *Dasymutilla,* and many species have not yet been described. Females are hairy, wingless and usually have a reddish or orange-red abdomen. Males tend to be darker and are winged.

Collecting Tips: Normally, velvet ants are not particularly numerous but occasionally can be found in large numbers in areas previously used by ground-nesting bees. Adults are most easily collected in dry areas of sandy soil used by the bee prey. The adult female is active during the day and can be found crawling across the soil. The winged males can be observed cruising above the ground looking for females to mate with or feeding on nectar-rich plants.

Female cow killers, which are wingless, have an extremely painful sting. The winged males do not sting but possess a "pseudostinger" that cannot penetrate the skin.

LARGEST HORNTAIL—PIGEON TREMEX
Tremex columba (**Linnaeus**)

Order: Hymenoptera

Family: Siricidae

Distribution: Generally distributed throughout North America. They are most common at lower elevations in the region.

As this pigeon tremex oviposits in wood, it introduces a fungus that aids in larval development.

Life History and Habits: The pigeon tremex is the only species of horntail that does not develop in conifers. Eggs are laid deeply into trunks and branches of various hardwoods by the female in midsummer. Dead branches or logs of ash, elm and maple are particularly common places for egg laying. The larval stage develops as a wood borer that tunnels through the wood.

Wherever larvae feed, a wood-decaying fungus, introduced by the horntail during egg laying, is present also. This fungus is very important in allowing the pigeon tremex larva to develop. The tunneling and fungus can weaken the wood and cause increased susceptibility to wind breakage.

Pigeon tremex larvae become full grown and pupate in a chamber just underneath the bark. The adult wasps chew a circular hole through which they emerge. (In fact, horntails are the only kind of wood borers that regularly produce a truly circular emergence hole.) There is one generation per year.

Horntail larvae can continue to develop in wood after it has been cut. As a result they are sometimes found emerging in new homes a couple of years after construction. However, they cannot reinfest milled lumber.

A common parasite of the pigeon tremex is the giant ichneumon wasp (*Megarhyssa* species) (see "Largest Parasitic Wasp—Giant Ichneumon Wasp").

Related Species: Other very large species of horntails in the region are the dusky horntails, *Urocerus gigas flavicornis* (Fabricius) and *U. californicus* Norton. These develop in the wood of Douglas fir as well as some pines and spruce. They are much less commonly collected than the pigeon tremex.

In addition, several other species of smaller blue-black hornta-ils are common in western forests, notably species of *Sirex*. These develop within the wood of various conifers. Foresters frequently observe them laying eggs into tree trunks shortly after forest fires.

Collecting Tips: Adults can be collected as they search for sites to lay eggs, usually dead and dying hardwood logs and branches. Elm, maple and linden are particularly common hosts. Look for females on the sides of trunks in late summer; occasionally dead ones, which were unable to remove their ovipositor following egg laying, will be attached to the tree. They can also be collected as they emerge from infested wood in summer. Horntails do not sting.

A Large Sawfly—Bull Pine Sawfly
Zadiprion townsendi (**Cockerell**)

Order: Hymenoptera

Family: Diprionidae

Distribution: Generally distributed throughout the region in asso-ciation with its host, the ponderosa pine (bull pine).

Life History and Habits: The bull pine sawfly is one of the few insects that remains on the trees and may feed throughout the win-ter months, weather permitting. Like most sawflies, the larvae re-semble caterpillars (larvae of Lepidoptera), but have six or more pairs of legs rather than two to five pairs. Larvae of the bull pine

Adult bull pine sawfly

A colony of bull pine sawfly feeds on ponderosa pine.

sawfly typically feed in groups of several dozen individuals, chewing the needles of ponderosa pine. The larvae have the unusual habit of curling outward from the needle and snapping back, a behavior they may at times engage in almost continuously. This is thought to be a defensive action for avoiding attack by parasites and other natural enemies.

By the onset of winter, the bull pine sawfly larvae are about half-grown. They remain semidormant through the cold months, clustering at the base of the needles, but occasionally feed. Feeding resumes in spring, and they become full grown in May and June, at which time they drop to the ground, tunnel 1 inch (2.5 cm) or so into the soil and spin a silk cocoon. Some of the larvae then transform to the pupal stage, while others may not pupate until late in the summer or even the following season. Adults emerge a few weeks after pupation, cutting through the cocoon. The females are considerably larger than the males; both are heavy-bodied wasps with distinctive yellow and brown banding. The adult sawflies do not live long. Mated females insert their eggs into the pine needles with a sawlike ovipositor, concentrating on the upper part of the tree. Eggs hatch from July through early fall, and the larvae feed throughout this period. The entire life cycle may take one to two years to complete.

Related Species: The largest species of sawfly in the region is the elm sawfly, *Cimbex americana* Leach. It is quite uncommon, but is occasionally collected around willow groves.

A more common species of large sawfly that rivals the bull pine sawfly in size is *Zaraea americana* Cresson, which feeds on the leaves of honeysuckle.

Several species of sawflies in the region cause economic injury to trees and shrubs. Among these are various species of conifer sawflies in the genus *Neodiprion:* the imported currantworm, *Nematus ribesii* (Scopoli), a pest of currants and gooseberries, and the recently introduced brownheaded ash sawfly, *Tomostethus multicinctus* (Rohwer). Also, there are some unusual species of "slug sawflies" that resemble bird droppings and feed on the upper leaf surface of the plant. Of these, the pear sawfly or pear slug, *Caliroa cerasi* (Linnaeus), is a serious pest of cherry, ornamental plum, cotoneaster and other related plants.

Collecting Tips: Larvae of the bull pine sawfly can be found most easily during searches of ponderosa pine branches in spring. They may also be dislodged by shaking branches vigorously over a sheet.

Rearing Tips: Adults are very difficult to collect because of their short lifespan, but some can be reared from larvae collected in the field.

Large Noninsect Arthropods

Several arthropods that are not insects reach an impressive size and commonly attract attention. Most are in the class of animals known as arachnids—spiders, ticks, mites, scorpions and related species. The Rocky Mountain region also hosts a very large species of centipede, the giant desert centipede.

CLASS: ARACHNIDA
Spiders, Ticks and Scorpions

LARGEST SPIDERS—TARANTULAS
Aphonopelma Species

Class: Arachnida

Order: Araneida

Family: Theraphosidae

Distribution: There are several species of tarantulas in the region, concentrated in New Mexico and the southern areas of Colorado and Utah. *Aphonopelma* (=*Rhechosticta*) *chalcodes* Chamberlin is the most widely distributed and common species. At least two other species occur in the region, but most species of tarantulas resemble each other and are difficult to distinguish.

Life History and Habits: Tarantulas are large, hairy and long-lived spiders. Colorado species are smaller than the Mexican red-legged

Tarantula

tarantula and other species found in pet stores, averaging 1 to 2 inches (2.5–5 cm) in length. The females are slightly larger than the males. Females can live up to thirty-five years; males usually live no more than ten to fifteen years, dying shortly after they become mature and migrate to mate.

As they grow, tarantulas molt their old skin—a process that takes at least a day to complete. The stages of a developing tarantula may be very different. For example, a brown tarantula may be bluish-black after it has molted.

Like other spiders, tarantulas feed on insects and other arthropods that they kill with a venom injected through their "fangs" (chelicerae). Beetles, grasshoppers, caterpillars, crickets and other ground-dwelling insects are common prey.

Tarantulas spend much of their time within a burrow in the ground. Usually they use abandoned rodent or reptile holes, but they can also dig. The burrows are often lined with webbing. It is not uncommon to find "colonies" of tarantulas because when the young walk away from the burrows of the mother, they often settle in nearby holes. The tarantulas move out of the holes to search for prey in the vicinity, usually at night. In late summer, mature (eight- to ten-year-old) males migrate in search of females for mating. The mated females later spin a silk sheet "sandwich" in which they lay eggs.

The mortality of young tarantulas is very high because of their numerous natural enemies. One of the most important natural enemies of older tarantulas is the spider hunting wasp, known as the "tarantula hawk" see "Largest Spider Wasps").

Collecting Tips: Tarantulas are usually observed and collected in late July and August when the males, sometimes in large numbers, are migrating across roads.

Tarantulas can also be collected under rocks, where their burrows are usually constructed, as well as from the burrows themselves, which have a large opening, about the size of a quarter, and are lined with silk. Underground the burrows may extend for about 2 feet (61 cm), making an elbow bend 6 to 10 inches (15.2–25.4 cm) from the surface. By "fishing" for the tarantulas with a grasshopper or other insect on a wire, collectors can bring them up from the hole, although they rarely come out completely. They can then be dug out carefully with a shovel.

Great care should be used when searching for tarantulas under rocks, since rattlesnakes and scorpions may also be present. In addition, tarantulas can be collected at night using lights. Gloves should be worn when collecting them. Although tarantulas are often regarded as dangerously or even fatally poisonous, their venom is virtually harmless to humans. They rarely bite but can if provoked or mishandled.

Rearing Tips: Tarantulas can be kept in an aquarium. A sandy bottom with a sheltering stone will provide the cover it needs. Moistened toweling will provide moisture. They should be fed several grasshoppers or crickets at least every other week. Because they can run fast and jump, the aquarium should be covered with screening. Several publications related to tarantula rearing are available in pet stores.

Miscellaneous: The name *tarantula* is actually best applied to a species of wolf spider found in southern Europe. Legend has it that an epidemic of "tarantism" occurred around the town of Tarantum (now

Taranto), characterized by an irresistible desire to dance to exhaustion followed by periods of melancholy. This behavior was allegedly the result of a bite by a large wolf spider, *Lycosa tarantula*, the true tarantula.

LARGEST ORB-WEAVING SPIDER—
BANDED GARDEN SPIDER
Argiope trifasciata (Forskal)

Class: Arachnida

Order: Araneida

Family: Araneidae

Distribution: Common throughout the region.

Life History and Habits: The *Argiope* spiders, including the banded garden spiders, are the common "garden spiders" that produce large conspicuous webs on vegetation. The overwintering stage is eggs in the large sac produced by the female at the end of the summer. In spring the eggs hatch, and the young "spiderlings" produce silken threads and are blown about on winds (ballooning). Upon settling on an appropriate site, they begin to make their characteristic webs between sticks, grass or other upright vegetation. Flying insects that become caught in the webbing are quickly paralyzed by the bite of

Banded garden spider

*Monkey-face or
cat-face spider*

the spider and then are wrapped in a sheet of webbing. After feeding, the spiders usually cut the dead insects out of the web and allow them to drop to the ground. While tending the web, the female typically remains in the center both day and night, repairing it when it gets torn.

The spiders grow throughout the summer, reaching full size in late August and September. The males, which are much smaller than the females and do not produce webs, roam around on vegetation and mate with the females in late summer. The female then lays one or more egg sacs, which resemble a small kettle drum with a tough papery cover and may contain one thousand eggs each. The spiders die after frost. There is only one generation per year.

The garden spiders produce a characteristic zigzag band of webbing in the center of the web. This band, called a stabilimentum, is less prominent in webs produced by the banded garden spider than that of other *Argiope* species. The function of this webbing band is not known, but it may help to scare off birds that commonly feed on spiders. When disturbed, such as when the band is lightly shaken with a stick, the spider will shake the web, thereby vibrating the band.

Related Species: Another very large orb-weaver is *Araneus gemma* (McCook), sometimes called the "cat-face," "monkey-face" or "hump-back" spider because of the facelike pattern of dark markings and raised areas on its back. Females of this spider are generally rounded with angular "shoulders" and can reach the size of a quarter. They make webs in undisturbed corners, and are often found in late August and September around the eaves of houses. Unlike the banded garden spider, *A. gemma* hides in dark corners at the edge of the web during the day. It remains in contact with the web via a "trapline" thread that signals when insects have been ensnared. Webs are not repaired, but instead are regularly torn down and reconstructed.

Collecting Tips: The banded garden spiders are most easily collected late in the summer when they become large and more visible. Often the female spider is found in the center of the web, but also may be resting off to one side. Webs can be more easily observed in early morning when dew is still present.

Spiders should be preserved and displayed in alcohol.

Rearing Tips: Orb-weaving spiders of all types, including the large *Argiope* species, are easily kept in captivity and can be fascinating to watch. They need a large container in which to spin a web, and should be provided with flies or other small insects to ensnare in their web. The females, if collected late in the season after mating, will often produce two or more egg sacs if well provided with food. These will hatch, following exposure to cold, the following spring.

Some supplemental water should be provided; misting the web once a week should be sufficient. For young spiders, a capful of water should be kept in the container, with small pebbles or other objects in the water to prevent drowning.

Since most spiders are cannibalistic, they should be reared in individual containers.

LARGEST COMBFOOTED SPIDERS—WIDOW SPIDERS
Latrodectus mactans (Fabricius)—Black Widow
Latrodectus hesperus Chamberlin and Ivie—Western Widow

Class: Arachnida

Order: Araneida

Family: Theridiidae

Distribution: Common in many areas of the region. They appear to thrive under environmental conditions produced by human habitation. The region is a transition area where both the black widow and the western widow occur. (A third species, *Latrodectus variolus* (Walckenaer), has been reported in southern areas of the region, but is rare.) The black widow predominates in eastern areas, and the western widow is the dominant species west of the Continental Divide.

Life History and Habits: Eggs hatch in the egg sac, about two weeks after they are laid. The spiderlings remain in the sac for several days and may molt several times. After they have sufficiently matured, they leave the sac, cutting an opening with their fangs (chelicerae) and probably digesting the silk with enzymes. The spiderlings disperse after leaving the egg sac, often "ballooning" by releasing small silk strands that allow them to catch wind currents and be carried in the air.

Black widow spider; photograph courtesy of USDA

If the young spiders find a suitable spot, they begin to produce a web. Widow spiders build loose and irregular, mesh-type webs, often on plants, in loose stone or wood piles or in the corners of rooms, garages or outbuildings. They do not produce the symmetrical web typical of orb-weaving spiders (Araneidae) or the distinctive funnel-pattern web of the funnel-weaver spiders (Agelenidae). They then feed on insects that become trapped in the web.

Adult male widow spiders and the young of both sexes may have many red, red-orange or yellow spots and stripes on the top of their abdomen. Immature females can be gray or pale brown, with numerous banding patterns. Darker coloration increases as they get older. An hourglass pattern is visible on the underside of the abdomen throughout their development.

Male widow spiders are much smaller, about one-fourth the size of the females. They are not usually black in overall color, instead appearing light brown or gray and banded. Male widows may have an hourglass pattern, but coloration is often more orange and sometimes yellow. When mature, they have large knoblike structures *(pedipalps)* originating from the head. They are similar in appearance to immature females.

Widow spiders feed and grow throughout the warmer months, molting many times. Females typically become mature in about four to six months; development of the males is more rapid. Developmental rates are greatly influenced by temperature and the availability of food. In laboratory conditions, females can live up to a year after becoming mature. Males typically live only a few weeks. As occurs with many spiders, males may be eaten during mating.

Black widows survive winter in a mature or an immature form. During cold weather, spider development outdoors ceases and the spiders seek refuge under stones or other cover. Black widows can develop year-round indoors, and many move into homes by autumn for winter protection.

Collecting Tips: Widow spiders prefer to nest near the ground in dark, undisturbed areas. Nest sites are usually near holes produced by small animals or around construction openings and wood piles. Low shrubs are also common sites for widows.

Indoors, widows live in dark, undisturbed sites such as behind furniture or under desks. Undisturbed basement areas and crawl spaces of homes are used by nesting widow spiders.

Female widow spiders inject a toxin that affects the nervous system (neurotoxin). In humans, reactions to bites typically involve muscle and chest pain or tightness. Pain may also spread to the abdomen, producing stomach cramps and nausea. Other symptoms include restlessness, anxiety, breathing and speech difficulty and sweating. Swelling may be noticed in extremities and eyelids, but rarely at the bite site. Often there is a general sense of discomfort shortly after the bite; acute symptoms increase in severity during the first day after the bite. Symptoms usually decline after two to three days, but some mild symptoms may continue for several weeks after recovery. Prompt medical treatment can greatly reduce the effects caused by widow bites and in recent years has reduced fatalities to extremely low rates.

Spiders are best preserved in alcohol.

Rearing Tips: Widow spiders can be reared easily if provided with food and additional water. Obviously, considerable care needs to be taken when rearing these species to prevent bites.

Largest Wolf Spider—Giant Wolf Spider
Lycosa carolinensis Walckenaer

Giant wolf spider

Class: Arachnida

Order: Araneida

Family: Lycosidae

Distribution: Extremely common throughout the region. Along with the jumping spiders (Salticidae family), they make up a great portion of the spiders found at higher elevations.

Life History and Habits: The giant wolf spiders in the genus *Lycosa* are long-lived, typically surviving at least two seasons. For the most part they are free-roaming hunters that capture their prey while "on the hoof" rather than ensnaring them in webs. Wolf spiders are active spiders that can readily climb plants and run quickly when disturbed. They have keen vision, which allows them to look in all directions and detect the motion of potential prey. Giant wolf spiders hunt during the day as well as at night.

The giant wolf spider is more sedentary than most wolf spiders and constructs a silk-lined retreat that it uses during some periods in its life. It is usually a shallow depression excavated under a rock and lined with silk. Other wolf spiders make more elaborate tunnels, and some even build little turrets of sticks and grass that they use as a lookout. These tunnels involve a tremendous amount of labor; the spiders dig slowly, carrying soil out with their jaws (chelicerae). Tunneling behavior is even further developed among the burrowing wolf spiders (*Geolycosa*).

One of the most unusual habits of wolf spiders is the maternal care they give to the spiderlings. The female lays her eggs in a

*Burrowing wolf spider (*Geolycosa species*)*

Nursery-web spider carrying egg sac

round, tough sac lined with several layers of silk, made of two halves with a seam around the middle. She carries the egg sac on her spinnerets. When the eggs are about to hatch, she opens the sac and the newly emerged spiderlings crawl onto her back. These "babies on board" ride around on the mother for about a week until the next molt occurs. During this time the mother spider continues to hunt, apparently paying little attention to her young. They may leave the mother for short periods, to drink water for example, but often return quickly. They usually leave the mother after about a week to forage on their own.

Related Species: Aside from *L. carolinensis*, other large species of *Lycosa* have been collected in Colorado and Wyoming. In addition, a group of wolf spiders that rival *Lycosa* species in size are the burrowing wolf spiders, or "earth wolves," in the genus *Geolycosa*, which construct deep tunnels that typically drop vertically for 2 to 3 feet (.6–1 m). They spend most of their time within this burrow, but sometimes venture out at night. *Geolycosa missouriensis* Banks, one of the more common burrowing wolf spiders, is only slightly smaller than the giant wolf spider and can be distinguished by its dark olive-green color, as opposed to the generally gray or gray-brown color of most species of *Lycosa*.

Another family of large spiders that carry a large egg sac are the nursery-web spiders (Pisauridae family). These closely resemble wolf spiders, but the females carry the egg sac in their jaws rather than on their spinnerets. Just before the eggs hatch, the female constructs a "nursery web" in the top of a shrub or other vegetation and guards the newly hatched spiderlings until they disperse on their own.

Collecting Tips: Wolf spiders are easily collected with pitfall traps, into which the hunting spiders drop while foraging. Larger species can be captured at night by aid of lights. Night-hunting wolf spiders have eyes that reflect the light and appear to glow.

Burrowing species of wolf spiders can be dug out of their tunnels. However, this can be a tedious task since tunnels of some of the larger species may extend 3 feet (.9 m) in depth.

Wolf spiders have powerful jaws. The larger species can give a painful bite that breaks the skin.

Rearing Tips: Wolf spiders can make good pets that may survive for a year or longer in captivity. They must be regularly provided with water as well as insect prey.

COMMON LARGE DADDY LONGLEGS/HARVESTMEN
LEIOBUNUM SPECIES
Phalangium opilio Linnaeus

Class: Arachnida

Order: Opiliones

Family: Phalangiidae

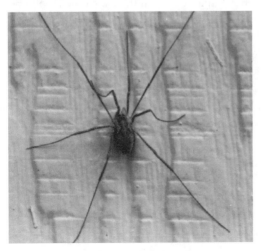

Daddy longlegs

Distribution: Several species are widely distributed and common throughout the region.

Life History and Habits: The daddy longlegs are familiar arachnids whose habits have been relatively little studied. Most are scavengers that feed on other arthropods (including other daddy longlegs) that are dead or dying. Some may be predators, although daddy longlegs possess weak jaws that limit them to small, soft-bodied prey such as aphids or mites. They also feed on plant juices and honeydew. Most activity occurs at night; they tend to hide in rocky areas or where there is plant debris during the day.

Winter is spent as eggs, laid in the soil in late summer. The young daddy longlegs develop throughout late spring and early summer, becoming full grown late in the growing season. Because some species become extremely common and noticeable late in the season, the name "harvestmen" has also been given to this group of arachnids. Adults may live two years.

There are persistent legends about the toxicity of the venom produced by daddy longlegs. These rumors are entirely false, as daddy longlegs do not even possess poison glands. Furthermore, their jaws are so weak they are capable of biting only the most feeble and soft-bodied of insects. They pose no threats to humans, who would merely feel a mild pinch if bitten.

Related Species: Throughout the world there are estimated to be approximately five thousand species of daddy longlegs, most undescribed. Within the region there are about two dozen species, including many European species that have accidently been introduced by human activities.

One group of true spiders that resembles the daddy longlegs are the daddy longlegs spiders (Pholcidae family), which commonly create webs and nests in the corners of darkened basements throughout the region. When disturbed, they bounce vigorously on the web.

Collecting Tips: Daddy longlegs are extremely common and are observed crawling on exterior walls, garden plants and many other sites throughout much of the growing season.

They are best preserved in alcohol.

LARGEST TICK—BROWN DOG TICK
Rhipicephalus sanguineus (Latreille)

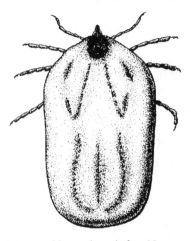

An engorged brown dog tick, from Venomous Animals of Arizona

Class: Arachnida

Order: Acarina

Family: Ixodidae

Distribution: Generally distributed in the region but uncommon. They are found indoors in association with dogs.

Life History and Habits: Brown dog ticks are the most common ticks found indoors in Colorado. Unlike the more common "wood ticks" (*Dermacentor* species) often encountered on hikes, the brown dog tick can reproduce indoors and increase in numbers. Since it is originally a subtropical or tropical species, it cannot overwinter outdoors in most of the region.

Dogs usually become infested by direct contact with other infested dogs or during warmer months as they travel through areas previously frequented by an infested dog. Kennels are also an important site of brown dog tick spread. The egg stage of the brown dog tick occurs within a large mass that usually includes several hundred eggs. Eggs hatch in about two weeks and the small, six-legged "seed ticks" move about to find dogs or rodents on which to feed.

After feeding on the blood of the host animal for a few days the young ticks drop off and hide in cracks or similar protected areas, usually near where the dog rests. They then shed their skin (molt), this time appearing as a slightly larger, eight-legged form. Another feeding cycle is completed and the third, adult stage appears. Depending on the temperature, the life cycle may take from two to twelve months to complete.

Collecting Tips: Adult brown dog ticks typically feed between the toes or near the ears of the dog. During this final blood feeding, they become engorged and may become almost 1/3 inch (.8 cm) in size and bloated. Full-grown ticks often show a strong tendency to climb and are often found on walls or hidden in cracks of ceilings and kennel roofs.

Although brown dog ticks rarely bite humans, several other ticks in the region are important in transmitting diseases.

Ticks are best preserved in alcohol.

Largest Scorpion—Giant Desert Hairy Scorpion
Hadrurus spadix Stahnke

Class: Arachnida

Order: Scorpiones

Family: Iuridae

Distribution: Uncommon in the region, and usually found in southwestern Colorado, southern Utah and New Mexico. They are most abundant in and around canyons in association with sagebrush and mixed plants. However, several other species of scorpions are present throughout much of the region.

Life History and Habits: Scorpions are a distinctive and well-recognized group of arachnids. They are most easily distinguished by their lobsterlike appearance, but particularly by their fleshy "tail" that terminates in a bulbous sac and prominent stinger. The larger front pincers (actually a modified part of the mouth) are used to capture and hold prey while feeding; the stinger is used to subdue prey and for defense. The giant desert hairy scorpion is by far the largest scorpion in Colorado, reaching a length of up to 5 inches (12.7 cm).

Scorpions have a life cycle of two to five years. They do not lay eggs; the female bears live young seven to twelve months after mating. A female may produce litters of about fourteen to as many as one hundred, and carry the young on her back until they have molted. Immature scorpions then leave the mother and become mature in about one year.

The giant desert hairy scorpion

Scorpions spend the day under cover or in burrows in the ground. At night they emerge to defend their territory and to feed. Since scorpions have poor eyesight, they do not stalk their prey, but instead lie in wait for them. Insects, spiders, millipedes and small vertebrates are common prey.

Scorpions are most commonly encountered around rocks or debris, their daytime hiding areas. They may also enter homes, apparently attracted to moisture sources.

Related Species: At least a dozen species of scorpions are known in the region, primarily those in the genera *Vejovis* and *Centruroides*. These are considerably smaller than the giant desert hairy scorpion, rarely more than 2 1/2 inches (6.3 cm) in length. However, they are much more widespread and commonly collected.

Another common arachnid found in the region that resembles the scorpion is the tiny pseudoscorpion of the order Pseudoscorpiones. These also have a prominent pair of pincers and carry the young on the mother's back. However, they lack a stinger and are much smaller than scorpions, never exceeding 1/4 inch (.6 cm). Pseudoscorpions are harmless to humans.

Collecting Tips: Scorpions can be collected by searching harborage areas, such as stone piles. However, this should be done with extreme care since rattlesnakes—as well as the poisonous scorpions themselves—are dangerous. Be sure to check the underside of rocks, to which many scorpions cling.

Scorpions fluoresce brightly when exposed to ultraviolet (black) lighting. During nighttime searches using this technique, they can be easily spotted from several yards away. Scorpions are most active in the evening when temperatures exceed 75°F.

The scorpions found in the region can produce a painful sting when handled or accidentally disturbed. Fortunately, no regional species are considered to be highly poisonous.

Rearing Tips: Scorpions can easily be kept as pets. Although they are well adapted to dry conditions, they occasionally require some free water to drink.

Largest Solpugids—Sunspiders/Windscorpions
Eremobates Species

Class: Arachnida

Order: Solpugida

Family: Eremobatidae

Distribution: Generally distributed throughout the southern areas of the region.

Life History and Habits: The sunspiders are predators of small insects and other arthropods, which they crush with their large jaws. Most sunspiders are active chiefly at night, but may also be observed during the day. They hunt primarily by means of touch, using their

Sunspider or windscorpion; photograph by Frank Peairs

long, leglike pedipalps, which also have small hooks that allow them to climb even smooth, vertical surfaces.

Eggs of the sunspiders are laid under rocks and similar covered areas in burrows constructed by the mother. Some silk is used to line these protective burrows. The mother guards the eggs and even captures prey to feed the young spiders. Sunspiders usually live one or two years, but the adults that are often encountered survive less than a single season.

Because of their fearsome and unusual appearance, sunspiders often cause alarm when they are discovered. This is particularly true when they wander into homes, where they may be found trapped in sinks. Invasions of homes can be quite common in July and early August. Sunspiders can run quickly; their common name "windscorpion" is derived from their ability to "run like the wind."

The sunspiders can bite if handled and may break the skin. No poison glands have been found associated with their mouthparts, but wounds may become infected.

Related Species: At least fifteen species of sunspiders occur in the region, concentrated in the southern half. Certain members in the genus *Eremobates* may reach 1 inch (2.5 cm) in length. Males are usually smaller than the females.

Collecting Tips: Because of their nocturnal habits, sunspiders are most easily collected using pitfall traps sunk in the ground. Placing a board loosely over the trap will increase captures as the spiders move under the boards for cover. Sunspiders can also be found under rocks and cow chips in summer.

Because they can bite, sunspiders should be collected with care.

Rearing Tips: Sunspiders make interesting and unusual pets. Terrariums should have a sand base with a few rocks or other materials for cover. The sand should be slightly moistened to allow tunneling and to provide humidity. Cages must be covered since sunspiders are excellent climbers. They will eat a variety of small soft-bodied insects.

Class: CRUSTACEA
Land Crustaceans

Largest Land Crustacean—Pillbug/"Roly-poly"
Armadillium vulgare (Latreille)

A pillbug, or "roly-poly," is capable of curling into a defensive position.

Class: Crustacea

Order: Isopoda

Family: Armadillidiidae

Distribution: This introduced species is now very common and widely distributed throughout the region.

Life History and Habits: Pillbugs spend the winter in the adult stage, protected under boards or other sheltering debris. In spring they become active, mate and the female produces eggs that she carries in a special pouch known as a marsupium. The eggs hatch in the pouch and the newly hatched young remain in it for several weeks.

By early summer the young pillbugs leave the pouch to forage and develop on their own. The young stages closely resemble those of the adults but are smaller in size and lighter in color. After several molts they reach the adult stage by the end of the season. Adult pillbugs are relatively long-lived and can live two or three years.

Pillbugs are scavengers, feeding primarily on moist, decaying plant matter. They sometimes feed on tender garden seedlings, but rarely cause any significant injury and are considered to be minor pests of regional gardens. Moreover, in some settings they are very useful for recycling plant nutrients by shredding dead plant material so that it will break down. Feeding usually occurs at night. Pillbugs tend to spend the day under cover, but can be seen in the daytime, particularly after rains.

Periodically pillbugs wander into homes, usually in spring and fall following periods of wet weather. However, because the humidity in homes is low, they rarely survive for more than a day or two.

Because of their ability to roll into a tight ball, pillbugs are commonly known as "roly-polys." In some areas they are also known as "potato bugs," although they have no special association with potatoes.

Related Species: The closely related sowbugs, *Porcellio* species, are also very common in the region. They have habits very similar to those of the pillbugs but are less heavily armored and cannot coil into such a tight ball when disturbed. Sowbugs are less adapted to dry conditions but can be very common in moist forested areas. They are sometimes known as "wood lice."

Most crustaceans live in aquatic environments; the pillbugs and sowbugs are the only members of this group that are adapted to living on land. Crayfish are the largest crustaceans found in regional waters.

Collecting Tips: Pillbugs and sowbugs are very easily collected in yards and gardens throughout the region. Searches under logs or rocks may yield several.

Rearing Tips: Pillbugs and sowbugs can be maintained for extended periods and will even reproduce well in captivity. Their basic environmental needs are sufficient moisture and appropriate food.

Rearing containers should have a base of moist soil or sand, covered with a layer of decaying leaves or old bark. The soil should be kept moist, but not waterlogged, as these animals are very sensitive to dry conditions. Flakes of fish food and pieces of vegetables or fruit (potato, carrot, apple) are good choices for foods, but need to be cleaned out frequently to prevent molds.

Class: CHILOPODA
Centipedes

Largest Centipede—Giant Desert Centipede
Scolopendra polymorpha Wood

Class: Chilopoda

Order: Scolopendromorpha

Family: Scolopendridae

Distribution: Found throughout the lower elevations in the southern areas of the region. They are most common in drier environments.

Life History and Habits: All centipedes are predators, feeding primarily on any arthropods that are small enough to be captured. Occasionally, the very large species of centipedes capture and kill small reptiles or mammals. The centipedes actively move and hunt during the night, but stay in protected areas under rocks during the day. Prey is captured by a pair of curved mandibles and killed and stunned with a pair of specialized front legs (gnathopods) equipped with a poison gland.

Eggs are laid in cavities hollowed out of decayed wood or cactus. After egg laying, the female winds around the eggs until the young have hatched, and continues to guard them until they have molted repeatedly and dispersed. Centipedes may live for four years or more.

The hind end of the giant desert centipedes forms a "pseudohead" that closely resembles the true head. It is thought that this pseudohead helps to protect it from attacks by larger reptiles, mammals and birds that prey upon it. The hind pair of legs, which are sensory only, are longer than the other legs.

Related Species: Most centipedes in the region are rather small, typically less than 1 inch (2.5 cm) in length. All are predators of other arthropods and few are capable of biting through human skin.

A common species of moderate size (about 1 1/5 inches [3 cm]) is the house centipede, *Scutigera coleoptrata* Linnaeus, which is well adapted to human dwellings where it lives by feeding on various arthropods (for example, cockroaches, boxelder bugs, elm leaf beetles, etc.) that enter homes. It has very long legs and is usually observed running rapidly across the floor after a light has been turned on in the room.

Collecting Tips: Giant centipedes are most easily collected under boards, rocks and other protected sites, in particular, sites with increased humidity. However, since these areas are also used by such potentially dangerous species as rattlesnakes and scorpions, searches should always be made with great caution. As a minimum protective measure, always wear thick leather gloves.

Giant desert centipedes can bite, causing a painful reaction in many people, similar to that caused by a wasp sting. The claws on the legs may also cause scratches. Puncture wounds should be washed with soap and water and treated with a mild antiseptic to prevent infection.

All centipedes are best preserved for permanent display in alcohol.

Rearing Tips: Giant desert centipedes can be kept in captivity for several months or even years, maintained in an aquarium with loose soil or sand for digging. A moisture source should be included. They should be fed grasshoppers or a variety of other insects.

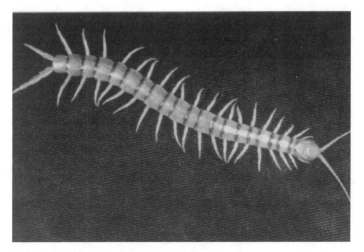

Giant desert centipede; photograph by Frank Peairs

Glossary
of Terms

Abdomen—the posterior of the three main body divisions of an insect.

Algae—a group of nonvascular plants, usually found in aquatic or highly moist environments. Algae contain chlorophyll but may be red or other colors because of the presence of pigments that mask the normal green coloration.

Antennae—a pair of segmented appendages used for sensing, located on the head above the mouthparts.

Anterior—front; in front of.

Aquatic—living in water.

Basal—at the base; near the point of attachment (of an appendage).

Brood—the individuals that hatch from the eggs laid by one mother.

Bud break—the time when dormant buds begin to expand and open.

Carrion—flesh of a dead animal.

Caste—separation of an insect colony into different groups, each of which has certain functions and different physical features (e.g., sterile workers and reproductive kings and queens).

Caterpillar—the larva of a butterfly, moth or skipper (order Lepidoptera).

Caudal filaments—threadlike filaments located on the posterior end of the abdomen of many insects.

Cephalothorax—a body segment of arachnids that combines the head and thorax, including the legs.

Cerci—a pair of appendages at the end of the abdomen.

Chrysalis—the pupa of a butterfly.

Class—a group of closely related orders.

Cocoon—the silken case in which the pupal stage of many insects is formed.

Conifer—a plant in the order Coniferales, which includes most of the evergreen species in the region, such as pines, spruce, Douglas fir and juniper.

Coxa—the basal segment of the leg.

Deciduous—as applied to plants, a perennial tree or shrub that sheds its leaves annually. Most deciduous trees are also considered to be "hardwoods."

Defoliation—the loss of leaves from natural shedding, or from the feeding activities of insects and other plant feeders.

Diapause—a period of arrested development and reduced metabolic rate that is not readily interrupted unless certain environmental stimuli (such as day length, critical chilling period) have passed. Diapause is used by many arthropods to survive periods of adverse environmental conditions, such as winter.

Diurnal—active during the day.

Dorsal—the back or upper side.

Drone—a reproductive male bee.

Elytra—the hardened or horny forewings produced by several insect groups (such as Coleoptera, Dermaptera, some Homoptera) to form wing covers that protect the hind wings and abdomen.

Eyespots—the prominent markings that resemble eyes on the wings of certain insects.

Family—a group of closely related genera. The suffix for such grouping is *idae.*

Femur—the third segment of the insect leg, located between the trochanter and tibia.

Forewings—the forward pair of wings.

Frass—solid insect excrement, typically mixed with chewed plant fragments.

Fungal spores—the reproductive stage of fungi, analogous to the seeds of higher plants.

Fungi—a large and diverse group of lower plants that lack chlorophyll and specialized conductive tissues. Singular: fungus.

Gall—the abnormal growth of plant tissues, caused by the stimulus of an animal, microorganism or wound.

Genus—a group of very closely related species. Plural: genera.

Gregarious—living in groups.

Grub—a general term that describes the larval stage of many insect larvae, particularly beetles.

Halteres—the small, knoblike balancing organs that replace the hind wings of adult Diptera.

Head capsule—the structure that contains the head and the appendages attached to it.

Herbivorous—feeding on plants; phytophagous.

Hibernaculum—a tiny cocoon spun by first- or second-instar caterpillars of some species for overwintering shelter.

Hibernation—a period of temporary dormancy, usually in winter, to avoid adverse environmental conditions.

Hilltopping—a behavior common among many insects (such as harvester ants) by which reproductive stages seek out prominent points to aggregate in search of mates

Honeydew—a sugary liquid waste product produced by insects that suck plant sap, such as aphids, soft scales and leafhoppers.

Host—the plant on which an insect feeds; the insect in which a parasite develops.

Instar—the stage of an insect between molts. Instar I is the stage that occurs immediately after egg hatch.

Kick net—a D-frame aquatic net or screen that is placed downstream while the collector dislodges rocks to capture aquatic insects.

Larva—the immature stage, between egg and pupa, of an insect with complete metamorphosis; also called caterpillar, maggot or grub. The term is now often used to describe the immature stage of all insects, supplanting the term *nymph* among insects with simple/gradual metamorphosis. Plural: larvae.

Legumes—plants in the pea family, Fabaceae, including peas, beans, alfalfa, caragana and honey locust.

Maggot—a legless larva without a well-developed head capsule, found among certain Diptera.

Mandibles—the anterior pair of mouthpart structures that make up the insect jaw. These are often hardened and used to crush, chew or puncture cells.

Maxillae—the pair of mouthpart structures located immediately behind the mandibles.

Membranous wings—the thin, more or less transparent wings found on insects such as flies, lacewings and dragonflies.

Mesothorax—the second, middle segment of the insect thorax.

Metamorphosis—the changes in form undergone by insects as they grow and develop.

Metathorax—the third, posterior segment of the insect thorax.

Molt—the shedding of the exoskeleton by an insect in the process of development.

Naiad—a term sometimes used instead of nymph to describe the immature stages of certain insects that develop in water—orders Odonata, Ephemeroptera and Plecoptera. The terminology is considered archaic.

Nocturnal—active at night.

Nymph—an immature stage of an insect with simple metamorphosis, such as aphids, bugs and grasshoppers. The term *larva* is now the preferred description for immature stages of all insects.

Ootheca—egg capsule produced by certain groups of insects, including the cockroaches and mantids. Plural: oothecae.

Order—a group of closely related families.

Osmeteria—glands containing defensive compounds that can be extruded from the head to deter predators.

Oviposit—to lay eggs.

Ovipositor—the egg-laying apparatus of a female insect.

Parasite—an animal that lives within or on another living animal, drawing sustenance from its tissues and causing injury to it. Many insects are parasites of other insects and actually kill the host, a relationship described as parasitoid.

Parthenogenesis—development of an egg without fertilization.

Pedipalps—structures attached to the mouthparts of an arthropod that may be leglike in form but that are actually used for sensing or holding prey. Male spiders, sun spiders and scorpions have very large pedipalps.

Posterior—hind or rear.

Predaceous—feeding as a predator; living by attacking and feeding on other animals.

Predator—an animal that develops by attacking and killing other animals (prey) on which it feeds. Arthropod predators typically must devour several prey in order to complete development.

Proleg—one of the fleshy abdominal legs located on the abdomen of certain insect larvae such as caterpillars.

Prothorax—the first, anterior segment of the insect thorax.

Pupa—the transitional stage, between larva and adult, of insects with complete metamorphosis. In moths and some other insects, the pupal stage usually takes place in cocoons. Plural: pupae.

Puparia—a case formed by a hardening of the skin from the last larval stage, in which the pupa is formed, produced by certain Diptera.

Pupate—to transform to a pupa.

Queen—a female insect capable of reproduction found in colonies of social insects such as ants, social wasps and bees.

Raptorial—designed for capturing and holding prey; used to described the forelegs of several insects that are predators, such as mantids, assassin bugs and mantidflies.

Reproductives—members of a social insect colony (such as termites and ants) that are capable of reproduction. The female reproductive stages (queens) typically disperse to form new colonies after mating with the male stage (drones).

Riffle—an area of small waves in a stream, produced by water flowing over a rocky, shallow streambed.

Sand blowout—an exposed area of sandy ground produced by wind action.

Scavenger—an animal that feeds on dead plants or animals, decaying materials or animal wastes.

Scutellum—small plates (sclerites) located on the back of the thorax.

Segment—a subdivision of the body or of an appendage.

Shelterbelt—an area of trees or shrubs, usually purposefully planted, that provides shelter from winds and/or habitat for wildlife.

Skeletonizing—the feeding pattern of certain leaf-feeding insects that leave only the veins of the leaf.

sp.—abbreviation for the singular form of species. Plural: spp.

Species—a group of organisms, capable of successfully interbreeding, that is isolated from all other such groups.

Spinnerets—structures on the posterior of most spiders through which silk is expelled for spinning into webs or other purposes.

Subfamily—a group of very closely related genera that is too small or specialized in features to be classified as a family. The suffix for such groupings is *inae.*

Systematist—a biological researcher who defines and classifies the interrelationships of species into hierarchical series.

Talus—a slope formed by the accumulation of rock debris.

Tarsus—the part of the leg beyond the tibia, consisting of one or more segments or subdivisions. Plural: tarsi.

Taxonomist—an individual who describes, names and classifies organisms.

Tegmina—the thickened, leathery forewings of Orthoptera, Montodea and several other insect orders.

Thorax—the middle section of an insect body, where the legs and wings are attached.

Tibia—the fourth segment of the leg, between the femur and the tarsus.

Tubercles—a rounded protuberance common on many insects, such as caterpillars.

Tymbal—a skinlike membrane covering a specialized sound-making organ found in certain insects, such as the cicadas.

Ventral—the underside of the body.

Wingspan—the measurement between tips of the extended forewings of an insect.

Pronunciation Guide

Scientific names are used to described insects and other organisms because the way they are spelled is the same throughout the world. This allows people from different places to read and write about a species even though local common names may be different.

For people not used to scientific names, pronunciation of them can be daunting. Although there are some general rules for pronunciation, there are differences in how a specific word is spoken. The following list will assist in using some of the scientific terms in this book. This guide to pronunciation is based only on the consensus of the authors.

Phylum, Class and Order Names

Names of animal classes and phyla end in the suffix *a*, pronounced "uh." Among the insects, many of the order names have either the suffix *optera* (op'-terr-uh) or *aptera* (ap'-terr-uh), which refers to characteristics of the wing (*ptera* in Greek).

Acarina	ak-uh-ry'-na
Anoplura	ann-o-pleur'-uh
Arachnida	uh-rak'-nid-uh
Arthropoda	ar-throp'-ah-duh
Blattaria	blat-tay'-ree-uh
Coleoptera	coal-ee-op'-terr-uh

Collembola	kol-lem'-bow-luh
Crustacea	krus-ta'-she-uh
Dermaptera	dur-map'-terr-uh
Diplopoda	dip-low-po'-duh
Diptera	dip'-terr-uh
Ephemeroptera	eff-em-err-op'-terr-uh
Grylloblattaria	grill-o-blat-tare'-ee-uh
Hemiptera	hem-ip'-terr-uh
Homoptera	ho-mop'-terr-uh
Hymenoptera	hy-men-op'-terr-uh
Isopoda	eye-so-po'-duh
Isoptera	eye-sop'-terr-uh
Lepidoptera	lep-id-op'-terr-uh
Mallophaga	mal-loff'-uh-guh
Mantodea	man-toe'-dee-uh
Megaloptera	meg-uh-lop'-terr-uh
Neuroptera	new-rop'-terr-uh
Odonata	o-don-ate'-uh
Orthoptera	or-thop'-terr-uh
Phasmida	phas'-mee-duh
Phthiraptera	thur-ap'-terr-uh
Plecoptera	plee-cop'-terr-uh
Scolopendromorpha	sko-low-pen'-dro-mor'-pha
Scorpiones	skorp-ee-oo'-nees
Siphonaptera	si-fon-ap'-terr-uh
Solpugida	sawl-pew'-jid-uh
Symphyla	sim'-fy-luh
Thysanoptera	thy-san-op'-terr-uh
Thysanura	thy-san-urr'-uh
Trichoptera	tri-cop'-terr-uh

FAMILY NAMES

Family names of insects typically end in the suffix *idae*, pronounced "id-ee." Subfamilies use the suffix *inae* (in-ee). The accent is usually on the syllable preceding this suffix.

Acrididae	ak-rid'-id-ee
Adelgidae	uh-del'-jid-ee
Aeolothripidae	ee-o-lo-thrip'-id-ee
Aeshnidae	esh'-nid-ee
Aphididae	a-fid'-id-ee
Apidae	a'-pid-ee
Araneidae	air-an-ee'-id-ee
Arctiidae	ark-tee'-id-ee
Armadillidiidae	ar'-ma-dill-id-ee'-id-ee
Asilidae	uh-sil'-id-ee
Belostomatidae	bell'-o-sto-mat'-id-ee
Braconidae	bra-kon'-id-ee
Buprestidae	bew-press'-tid-ee
Calliphoridae	kal-leh-for'-id-ee
Carabidae	kuh-rab'-id-ee
Cecidomyiidae	seh'-sid-o-my-ee'-id-ee
Cerambycidae	sair-am-biss'-id-ee
Ceratophyllidae	sur'-at-o-fill'-lid-ee
Chrysomelidae	cry-so-mel'-id-ee
Cicadidae	sick-a'-did-ee
Cicindellidae	siss-in-dell'-lid-ee
Coccinellidae	cock-sin-el'-lid-ee
Coreidae	ko-ree'-id-ee
Corydalidae	kor-ee-dal'-id-ee
Cossidae	cos'-sid-ee
Culicidae	kew-liss'-id-ee
Curculionidae	kir-kew'-lee-on'-id-ee
Cuterebridae	kew-tuh-ree'-brid-ee
Cynipidae	sy-nip'-id-ee
Dermestidae	dur-mes'-tid-ee
Diprionidae	dip-ree-on'-id-ee

Dytiscidae	dy-tis'-sid-ee
Elateridae	ee-lah-terr'-id-ee
Ephemeridae	eff-em-err'-id-ee
Ereomobatidae	air-ee-o-bat'-id-ee
Eriophyidae	air-ee-o-fi'-id-ee
Eriosomatidae	air-ee-o-so-mat'-id-ee
Erotylidae	air-o-til'-id-ee
Forficulidae	for-fik-u'-lid-ee
Formicidae	for-miss'-id-ee
Gerridae	jair-rid'-ee
Gryllacrididae	grill-ak-rid'-id-ee
Gryllidae	grill'-id-ee
Haematopinidae	heem'-at-o-pi'-nid-ee
Hesperiidae	hess-per-ee'-id-ee
Heteronemiidae	het'-er-o-nem-ee'-id-ee
Hydrophilidae	hy-dro-fil'-id-ee
Ichneumonidae	ik-new-mahn'-id-ee
Inocellidae	eye-no-sel'-lid-ee
Iuridae	i-ur'-id-ee
Ixodidae	ix-o'-did-ee
Kermesidae	kur-mess'-id-ee
Lampyridae	lam-peer'-id-ee
Limnephilidae	lim-neh-fil'-id-ee
Lucanidae	lou-kan'-id-ee
Lycosidae	ly-ko'-sid-ee
Machilidae	mah-kill'-id-ee
Mantidae	man'-tid-ee
Mantispidae	man-tiss'-pid-ee
Meloidae	meh-low'-id-ee
Mutillidae	mew-til'-lid-ee
Myrmeleontidae	mere'-mell-e-on'-tid-ee
Noctuidae	nok-too'-id-ee
Notonectidae	no-toe-nek'-tid-ee
Nymphalidae	nim-fal'-id-ee
Papilionidae	pah'-pill-ee-on'-id-ee
Pentatomidae	pen-ta-toe'-mid-ee

Phalangidae	fa-lan'-jid-ee
Phymatidae	fy-mat'-id-ee
Pompilidae	pom-pil'-id-ee
Pteronarcyidae	tair-o-nar'-sid-ee
Pyralidae	py-ral'-id-ee
Reduviidae	red-you-vi'-id-ee
Rhinotermitidae	ry-no-ter-mite'-id-ee
Saturniidae	sat-ur-nee'-id-ee
Satyridae	sat-eer'-id-ee
Scarabaeidae	skare-ah-bee'-id-ee
Scolytidae	sko-ly'-tid-ee
Sesiidae	sess-ee'-id-ee
Silphidae	sill'-fid-ee
Siricidae	syriss'-id-ee
Sphecidae	sfess'-id-ee
Sphingidae	sfin'-jid-ee
Staphylinidae	staff-ill-in'-id-ee
Syrphidae	seer'-fid-ee
Tabanidae	tuh-ban'-id-ee
Tachinidae	tak-in'-id-ee
Tettigoniidae	tet'-teh-gohn-ee'-id-ee
Theriidae	thur-ee'-id-ee
Therophosidae	thur-o-foss'-id-ee
Tipulidae	tip-u'-lid-ee
Vespidae	ves-pid'-ee

Common Mistakes Made in Insect Identification

Colorado potato beetle or sunflower beetle?

Two leaf-feeding beetles (Chrysomelidae family) that can easily be confused with each other are the sunflower beetle and the Colorado potato beetle. Both have a broad, curved body and are generally light colored with prominent striping.

However, feeding habits vary between these two beetles, so an easy way to distinguish them is to note on what plant they were feeding. Sunflower beetles feed only on sunflower; Colorado potato beetles feed only on certain plants in the nightshade family, such as potato, eggplant, hairy nightshade and buffalo burr.

Colorado potato beetle (left) and a sunflower beetle (right)

The Colorado potato beetle is larger and darker than the sunflower beetle. Another feature that can distinguish them is the striping on the side of the insect. On the sunflower beetle one of the stripes is broken and resembles an exclamation point; none of the stripes on the Colorado potato beetle are broken in this manner.

Stag beetle or larger ground beetle (*Pasimachus* species)?

One of the most prominent features of the stag beetles (Lucanidae family) is their large mouthparts, which are particularly developed in the male. The males use their mouthparts during courtship and mating, and the females use theirs to chew wood. Stag beetles are relatively uncommon in the region. The larvae develop as borers in dead and decaying wood.

Much more common, especially in grasslands of the region, are various large black ground beetles (Carabidae family) of the genus *Pasimachus*. They also possess very large, forward-projecting jaws used to capture and crush prey. They are predators of other insects and are most commonly observed as they walk rapidly across the ground while hunting for prey.

The dark black color of the ground beetles differs from that of the brown stag beetles. Antennae of the stag beetles are in the form

Stag beetle (left), ground beetle in the genus Pasimachus *(center) and a darkling beetle (right)*

of an elbowed, comblike club, while those of the ground beetles are threadlike and straight.

Darkling beetle or ground beetle?

Ground beetles are also commonly confused with the darkling beetles (Tenebrionidae family). Several members of both families are large, conspicuous, dark-colored insects that are frequently collected.

Ground beetles are predators of other insects and usually have large, forward-projecting jaws. Darkling beetles feed on plant materials and have smaller mouthparts that are often oriented downward.

Antennae of ground beetles are threadlike, without a club. Those of some darkling beetles are also threadlike, but most species have clublike antennae that are slightly enlarged at the terminal end.

The best way to distinguish the two insect families is to look where the hind legs appear to be attached to the body. Legs of darkling beetles are easily traced to the mid-stage of the body, or thorax. Those of the ground beetles appear to be much farther back on the body. This is because the body segment to which they are attached is a large plate that covers part of the abdomen. Although the legs are truly attached to the thorax (as with all insects), they appear to be part of the abdomen.

The most commonly collected darkling beetles are the "stink beetles" (*Eleodes* species), so named because they produce smelly defensive chemicals. However, many ground beetles also produce unpleasant odors.

Rove beetle or earwig?

The rove beetles are a rather unusual family of beetles (Coleoptera order). They are very elongate and lack the hard wing covers distinctive of most other beetles. Instead, rove beetles have short wing covers that cover only the thorax, under which a pair of membranous wings are folded. Most rove beetles are dark colored, and many are predators of other insects, particularly fly larvae.

Rove beetles are often mistaken for earwigs (Dermaptera order) since the general body shape and short wing covers are similar. Earwigs, particularly the European earwig, are very common and

*Rove beetle (left)
and earwig (right)*

familiar insects to most people in the region. They feed on many different things, including other insects and soft plant parts, and are often considered a nuisance because they commonly invade homes and sometimes eat flowers and tender seedlings.

Earwigs can be distinguished by the presence of a pair of forceps off the hind end. (The forceps are bowed in male earwigs, straight in the females.) These appendages are lacking in the rove beetles.

Damselfly or antlion?

The immature stages of damselflies develop in water and are closely related to dragonflies (Odonata order). The larvae of antlions (Neuroptera order) are predators that dig pits in sandy soils to trap prey, usually ants. However, adults of both have a very elongate body and delicate wings, causing them to be mistaken for one another.

The wings of the antlion fold flat or rooflike over their abdomen when at rest. Damselflies cannot fold their wings so they stay extended, pointing upward. Antlion wings also possess more veins, typical of other members of the Neuroptera. Furthermore, damselflies are day fliers. Antlions rarely fly during the day and are most frequently collected at lights during the evening.

The conspicuous clubbed antennae of the antlions (reduced to a short, bristlelike appendage on the damselflies) is also a useful way to distinguish these two insect groups.

Antlion (left) and a damselfly (right); under natural conditions the wings fold flat over the body, the damselfly's wings at an upright angle.

Green lacewing or mayfly?

The green lacewings (Neuroptera order) are one of the most beneficial groups of insects and are common inhabitants of gardens and fields. Their larval stage, sometimes known as "aphid lions," is a voracious predator of many kinds of pest insects.

The mayflies (Ephemeroptera order) are insects that develop in water, emerging for a brief period as winged adults. Adult stages of both mayflies and green lacewings are delicate insects with clear wings and may resemble each other superficially.

One way to distinguish these two groups of insects is the manner in which they hold their wings when resting. The lacewings

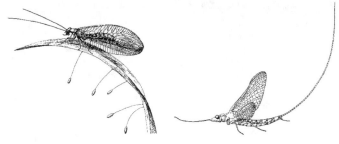

Green lacewing   *Mayfly*

fold their wings over their body, while the wings of mayflies remain erect and do not fold. Green lacewings possess long, beaded antennae that are reduced to small bristles in mayflies. Perhaps the most obvious difference is the presence of two or three long, filamentlike "tails" on the hind end of mayflies.

Peach tree borer or ctenuchid moth?

The peach tree borer is one of the most serious insect pests of fruit and ornamental trees, a member of the plant-damaging family known as the "clearwing borers" (Sesiidae family). Adult moths are frequently pictured in books, which illustrate the unusual dark wings of the female moth. However, another group of more commonly collected moths, the ctenuchid moths (Arctiidae family), also have dark wings. Both clearwing borers and ctenuchid moths fly during the day and mimic wasps.

Although the front wings of both moths are dark, the hind wings of the female peach tree borer are largely clear, lacking colorful scales. Also, the female peach tree borer has a bright orange band across the abdomen. Ctenuchid moths have a dark hind wing and lack the orange band.

Female peach tree borer, drawing by Tess Henn

Ctenuchid moth; photograph by Wendy L. Meyer from the Gillette Entomology Slide Collection

Harlequin bug or twospotted stink bug?

These two brightly colored stink bugs (Pentatomidae family) are commonly confused. However, habits of these two insects differ greatly. The harlequin bug is a well-known pest species, particularly damaging to plants of the cabbage family grown in the southern half of the United States. The twospotted stink bug is a predator of other insects and an important natural enemy of the Colorado potato beetle. The twospotted stink bug, and other relatives (*Perillus* species), are more generally distributed throughout the region.

Harlequin bugs are generally red-orange with numerous black and white markings. The twospotted stink bug is more variable in color and may be black, gray or red. However, it has a distinctive U-shaped pattern on its back, between the wings. It derives its name from the two dark patches behind its head, on the prothorax.

Harlequin bug   *Twospotted stink bug, mating pair*

Lygus (plant) bug or aphid?

The plant bugs (Hemiptera order; Miridae family) are very common insects on a wide variety of plants. They are usually associated with developing seed heads. One of the most common kinds of plant bugs is the Lygus bug, which is a pest of several crops grown in the region.

Immature stages of plant bugs are sometimes confused with aphids (Homoptera order; Aphididae family). Plant bug nymphs lack wings and often are generally the same size and shape as an aphid.

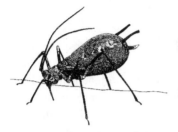

Aphid

A common lygus bug, the pale western legume bug

One of the easiest ways to differentiate the two groups of insects is by their behavior in the field. Plant bugs are usually active insects, particularly if disturbed, and can run rapidly over the plant. Aphids are always quite slow-moving. Furthermore, plant bugs are usually solitary insects, while aphids often occur in colonies.

Close inspection may reveal other differing characteristics. Most (but not all) aphids have a pair of pipelike cornicles protruding from the hind end. These are not present on any of the plant bugs. However, the piercing-sucking mouthparts of plant bugs are much more visible (with some magnification) since they project from the front of the head. The mouthparts of aphids appear as a small cone underneath the insect, between the front legs.

Box elder bug or small milkweed bug?

Two commonly collected bugs that are often confused are the box elder bug (*Boisea trivittatum*) and the small milkweed beetle (*Lygaeus kalmii*). Both are similarly shaped, about 1/2 inch (1.3 cm) long and marked with red and black. The box elder bug is a well-known household pest, sometimes moving indoors in large numbers for winter shelter during the fall. It develops primarily by feeding on seeds of the box elder maple. The small milkweed beetle feeds on a wide variety of plants and is primarily a seed feeder.

The small milkweed beetle has two white spots near the end of the front wings. Box elder bugs lack white markings.

Box elder bug   *Small milkweed bug*

Bees or bee-mimicking flies?

Bees, such as honeybees and bumblebees (Hymenoptera order), are capable of stinging when handled or attacked. Because of this defensive ability, many other insects, notably various kinds of flies (Diptera order), have developed as mimics of bees. The bee-mimicking flies are often colored and patterned very similarly to bees. Some of the flies even buzz, and many also visit flowers for nectar. However, none of them sting or bite.

Close inspection can distinguish the two groups. All bees and wasps have two pairs of wings, while flies have only one pair. Although this is a clear distinction between the orders, the wings of

A syrphid fly mimic (left) and a honeybee (right)

wasps and bees are often hooked together and may appear as a single pair.

Bees and wasps also possess a distinct constriction between the thorax and abdomen ("wasp-waist"). This attachment is usually broad among flies, although some even mimic this feature.

Perhaps the best distinguishing feature is the antennae. Antennae of flies are usually short, often only a tiny bristle. Bees and wasps possess long, conspicuous antennae that are elbowed with many segments.

Conifer seed bugs or assassin bugs?

The conifer seed bugs (*Leptoglossus* species; Coreidae family) are large brown insects that feed on seeds and leaves of plants. Occasionally they enter homes during the winter months and become a nuisance, particularly in forested areas.

Assassin bugs (Reduviidae family) are predators of other insects. Although one species, the masked hunter, sometimes occurs indoors, most limit their activities to outdoor plants.

Both conifer seed bugs and assassin bugs can be similar in size, and both possess a distinct "beak" containing the mouthparts. However, the head of assassin bugs is more elongate and the mouthparts are more clearly visible.

Perhaps the best feature to distinguish the two groups of bugs is the legs. Portions of the hind legs of conifer seed bugs are broad, sometimes leading to the name "leaffooted bugs." Assassin bugs have narrow hind legs and thickened front legs, used to grasp and hold prey.

Conifer seed bug

Assassin bug

Milkweed beetle or spotted asparagus beetle?

Two common orange-red beetles with distinct dark spots are the milkweed beetles (*Tetraopes* species) and the spotted asparagus beetle, *Crioceris duodecimpunctata* (Linnaeus). Milkweed beetles develop as borers in the stems of milkweed plants, while the spotted asparagus beetle develops in the fruit of asparagus. The type of plant on which the insect is found can be very useful in distinguishing them.

Although their general shape and coloration are similar, these two insects are dramatically different in size. Milkweed beetles are up to 1 inch (2.5 cm) long, while the spotted asparagus beetle is less than 1/2 inch (1.3 cm) long. The latter is more highly spotted (eleven spots) and darker red than the milkweed beetles.

Milkweed beetles will produce an audible squeak when picked up and held next to the ear; the spotted asparagus beetle will not.

Milkweed beetle (left); spotted asparagus beetle (right)

State
Insects

The monarch butterfly is being considered by the U.S. Congress for designation as the national insect. However, most states already have a designated state insect.

Alabama	Monarch butterfly
Alaska	None
Arizona	None
Arkansas	None
California	California dog-face butterfly
Colorado	None; Colorado hairstreak is under consideration
Connecticut	Praying mantis
Delaware	Convergent lady beetle
District of Columbia	None
Florida	None
Georgia	Honeybee
Hawaii	None
Idaho	None
Illinois	Monarch butterfly
Indiana	None
Iowa	Lady beetle
Kansas	Honeybee
Kentucky	None

Louisiana	Honeybee
Maine	Honeybee
Maryland	Baltimore checkerspot butterfly
Massachusetts	Ladybug
Michigan	None
Minnesota	None
Mississippi	Honeybee
Missouri	Spice bush swallowtail
Montana	None
Nebraska	Honeybee
Nevada	None
New Hampshire	Ladybug
New Jersey	Honeybee
New Mexico	None
New York	Ladybug (*Coccinella novemnotata*)
North Carolina	Honeybee
North Dakota	None
Ohio	Ladybug beetle
Oklahoma	None
Oregon	Swallowtail butterfly
Pennsylvania	Lightning bug
Rhode Island	None
South Carolina	None
South Dakota	None
Tennessee	Firefly, ladybug
Texas	None
Utah	Honeybee
Vermont	Honeybee (monarch is the state butterfly)
Virginia	Tiger swallowtail
Washington	None
West Virginia	None
Wisconsin	Honeybee
Wyoming	None

Entomology Organizations, Museums and University Departments

Organizations

Entomological Society of America
9301 Annapolis Road
Lanham, MD 20706
(301) 731-4535

The national organization of entomology in North America. In addition to holding several national and regional conferences annually, it has reference books, slides and other materials useful to individuals interested in the insect sciences. Among their publications are *Journal of Economic Entomology, Environmental Entomology, American Entomologist* and *Insecticide and Acaricide Reports.*

In 1994, the Society created a Youth Membership Program. For nominal annual dues (around $10), members receive the quarterly magazine *American Entomologist;* monthly association newsletters; a youth-oriented magazine, *Beeswax;* and various information materials.

Entomological Society of Canada
395 Winston Avenue
Ottawa, Ontario
Canada K2A 1Y8

The Entomological Society of Canada publishes several high-quality journals and bulletins, and helps coordinate much of the entomological pursuits in Canada.

Butterfly Pavilion and Insect Center
6252 West 104th Avenue
Westminster, CO 80020
(303) 469-5441

This new learning center designed around insects opens in June 1995 and includes an open, walk-through area with free-roaming butterflies, various live insect displays and educational classroom facilities. Group tours can be arranged.

Sonoran Arthropod Studies, Inc.
P.O. Box 5624
Tucson, AZ 85703
(602) 883-3945

A learning center dedicated to the study of arthropods, particularly those found in the southwestern desert region. The organization produces many publications related to arthropod habits, rearing and use of arthropods in teaching.

The Xerces Society
10 SW Ash Street
Portland, OR 97204
(503) 222-2788

An organization dedicated to conservation of invertebrates, primarily butterflies. They produce a magazine, *Wings: Essays on Invertebrate Conservation*, and are involved in organized butterfly counts in early summer, similar to the bird counts conducted by the Audubon Society.

Young Entomologists Society, Inc.
1915 Peggy Place
Lansing, MI 48910
(517) 887-0499

An organization for young entomologists that serves as a resource for many publications and supplies useful to the budding entomologist. The society also produces several magazines and newsletters, including *Insect World, Y.E.S. Quarterly* and *The Flea Market.*

Museums

Denver Museum of Natural History
2001 Colorado Boulevard
Denver, CO 80205
(303) 322-7009

The largest natural history museum in the region, it features a wide variety of subjects and continually adds new exhibits. The displayed entomology collections are fairly small, but are growing in prominence and often feature unique themes (e.g., insect mimicry and camouflage, urban insects).

May Museum of Natural History of the Tropics
710 Rock Creek Canyon
Colorado Springs, CO 80926
(719) 576-0450; (800) 666-3841

The May Museum displays large collections made at the turn of the century featuring most of the largest and more spectacular tropical species of insects. Open to the public from May 1 through October 1. The museum is associated with an RV park and a camping area.

The Monte L. Bean Life Science Museum
Brigham Young University
Provo, UT 84602
(801) 378-6356

Established in 1977, this growing natural history museum is associated with Brigham Young University. It is a full-service museum that also produces educational programs. Entomology collections include in excess of 1.5 million specimens, making it one of the most complete collections in the region.

University of Colorado Museum
Henderson Building
Campus Box 218
Boulder, CO 80309
(303) 492-6270

A natural history museum associated with the University of Colorado, Boulder, that is open to the public. It is also involved in public outreach programming. Entomology exhibits are among the displays, and the university maintains a separate reference collection.

University Departments

Each state in the region supports at least one university department or department section involved in entomology, usually within the land grant institution. Extension programs in entomology are developed within these departments, and each department supports insect collections that aid research in arthropod studies. Although these collections are not generally open to the public, they usually can be visited if prior arrangements are made.

Colorado
Department of Entomology
Colorado State University
Ft. Collins, CO 80523
(303) 491-7860

Idaho
Department of Plant, Soil and Entomological Sciences
University of Idaho
Moscow, ID 83843-4196
(208) 885-7544

Montana
Entomology Research lab
Johnson Hall
Montana State University
Bozeman, MT 59717
(406) 994-3861

Utah
Department of Biology
Entomology Division
Utah State University
Logan, UT 84322
(801) 750-2516

Wyoming
Department of Plant, Soil and Insect Sciences
Box 3354, University Station
Laramie, WY 82071
(307) 766-2115

Sources of Insect-collecting Supplies

Aztec Biologicals
311 Bernadette Drive
Columbia, MO 65201

Bio-Quip Products
17803 LaSalle Avenue
Gardena, CA 90248

Blue Spruce Biological Supply
221 South Street
Castle Rock, CO 80104

Carolina Biological Supply
2700 York Road
Burlington, NC 27215

Ianni Butterfly Enterprises
P.O. Box 81171
Cleveland, OH 44181

Ward's Natural Science Establishment
11850 E. Florence Avenue
Santa Fe Springs, CA 90670

Bibliography

Book Series

Audubon Society Field Guide series. Alfred A. Knopf, New York, NY. This series is most notable for its extensive use of color photographs, moderate price and wide availability.

The Audubon Society Field Guide to North American Butterflies. R. M. Pyle. 1981.
Lavishly illustrated with more than one thousand photographs illustrating more than six hundred butterflies found throughout North America, this is an excellent butterfly guide. Many local species are not included, however, and it is not always clear which features are used to identify the insect.

The Audubon Society Field Guide to North American Insects and Spiders. L. J. Milne and M. Milne. 1980.
Superlative pictures illustrate some 600 species of North American insects, with notes on some 250 others. A little difficult to use since size and range of insects are not easily determined, and many local species are not included. However, a brief appraisal of the color plates is an excellent introduction to insect diversity.

Golden Guides. Golden Press, Western Publishing, Racine, WI. These are good, inexpensive guides to specific groups of insects and relatives, and are widely available in bookstores. The following titles are recommended:

Butterflies and Moths. R. T. Mitchell and H. S. Zim. 1977.

Quite useful for identification of the more showy species of moths and butterflies. It also contains pictures of some economically important caterpillars. However, it is not particularly complete for this region, as it emphasizes eastern species.

Insect Pests. G. S. Fichler. 1966.

A large number of important plant pests are included and illustrated. Although it doesn't allow identification of all pest species, generally one can get close.

Insects. C. Cottam and H. S. Zim. 1987.

A general overview of North American insects, their arthropod relatives and basic information on collecting.

Pond Life. G. K. Reid and H. S. Zim. 1967.

An excellent introduction to familiar pond animals, including the common aquatic insects.

Spiders and Their Kin. H. W. Levi and L. Z. Levi. 1969.

Aids in identification of many common spiders up to the family level and even sometimes to species. It is less accurate but much easier to use than *How to Know the Spiders* because of the many color illustrations. On account of its low cost and ease of use, this is probably the best nontechnical guide to spider identification.

How to Know the … series. William C. Brown Co. Dubuque, IA. These books provide identification keys to various groups of organisms. Several of them deal with insects or other arthropods. The following are particularly good:

How to Know the Beetles. 2nd edition. R. H. Arnett, Jr., N. M. Downie and H. E. Jaques. 1980.

Illustrates many of the beetles found in the United States and provides keys to common species.

How to Know the Grasshoppers, Crickets, Cockroaches and Their Allies. J. R. Helfer. 1987.

An excellent overview of the taxonomy and distribution of termites, cockroaches, mantids, grasshoppers and crickets found in the United States.

How to Know the Insects. R. G. Bland and H. E. James. 1978.

An inexpensive alternative to *Introduction to the Study of Insects* without the comprehensive descriptions of insect biology. Some of the taxonomy is out-of-date and incomplete, however.

How to Know the Spiders. B. Katson. 1982.

A rather technical book that reflects the difficulties in spider identification, but a useful glossary is provided. Some magnification is needed to observe characters used in these keys. Spider identification is difficult, but this book is unsurpassed as a tool for preliminary spider determination.

How to Know the True Bugs. J. A. Slater and R. M. Boronowski. 1978.

An excellent key to the families in the order Hemiptera. Includes keys to the generic level. Common and economically important species are illustrated.

Keeping Minibeasts series. Barrie Watts. Silver Burdett Press, division of Paramount. Morristown, NJ. These series of small books (generally twenty-five to forty pages) contain information on rearing and observing various animals, including arthropods. They are generally written for elementary school–aged children. The following titles are included:

> *Ants*
> *Beetles*
> *Butterflies and Moths*
> *Grasshoppers and Crickets*
> *Ladybugs*
> *Spiders*
> *Stick Insects*
> *Wood Lice and Millipedes*

Peterson Field Guide series. Houghton Mifflin, Boston. These books are more expensive and more complete than the *Golden Guides*. More species and brief descriptions of insect habits are included.

A Field Guide to the Beetles of North America. R. E. White. 1983.

A selection of the 27,000 species of beetles in North America north of Mexico are illustrated in this more specialized guide. Provides excellent diagnosis sections for distinguishing beetle families and even genera. Collecting hints for each family are given.

A Field Guide to Eastern Butterflies. P. A. Opler and V. Malikul. 1992.

An all-new edition of the original classic guide to eastern butterflies, describing 524 species found east of the 100th meridian. Well illustrated with distribution maps. Many species included in this book are commonly found east of the Rocky Mountains.

A Field Guide to Insects of America North of Mexico. D. J. Borror and R. E. White. 1970.

Contains illustrations and information about insects of all the major orders. Does not have many keys, but important characteristics of each group are emphasized. Color plates of some of the more common or showy species are included.

A Field Guide to Western Butterflies. J. W. Tilden and A. C. Smith. 1986.

Provides photographs of 524 species of butterflies found in western North America.

Individual Books

Arachnomania: The General Care and Maintenance of Tarantulas and Scorpions. Phillipe de Vosjoli. Advanced Vivarium Systems, Lakeside, CA. 1991. Also available through many pet stores.

An excellent publication on the care and maintenance of scorpions and tarantulas that is also useful for rearing several other arthropods.

The Bugs in the System: Insects and Their Impact on Human Affairs. M. Berenbaum. Helix Books; Addison-Wesley Publishing Company. 1995.

    Packed with interesting information on a wide variety of topics related to insects: how they develop, their importance in natural ecosystems and in agriculture, historical events involving insects—a bit of everything. Written well and very entertaining.

Butterfly Gardening: Creating Summer Magic in Your Garden. Xerces Society in association with the Smithsonian Institution. Sierra Club Books, San Francisco, CA. 1990.

    Probably the best single reference on the practice of purposefully gardening to attract butterflies. Well illustrated, with good lists of attractive nectar plants as well as larval food plants used by most of the more common North American butterflies.

Butterflies of the American West: A Coloring Album. P. A. Opler and S. W. Strawn. Roberts Rinehart, Niwot, CO. 1988.

    An inexpensive and entertaining way to learn the common "backyard" butterflies of the western United States.

Butterflies of the Rocky Mountain States. C. D. Ferris and F. M. Brown, eds. University of Oklahoma Press, Norman, OK. 1981.

    A standard reference for butterflies in the region. One of the most complete guides available. Distribution maps for the species in the back of the book are especially helpful.

Caring for Insect Livestock: An Insect Rearing Manual. G. A. Dunn. Young Entomologists Society, Inc., Lansing, MI. 1993.

    A comprehensive, well-prepared book on rearing many of the insects used in displays and classrooms. An introductory section gives general instructions related to rearing techniques, followed by specific intructions on forty-nine insects and ten arthropods.

Florissant Butterflies: A Guide to the Fossil and Present-Day Species of Central Colorado. T. C. Emmel, M. C. Minno and B. A. Drummond. Stanford University Press, Stanford, CA. 1992.

    A description of all the butterflies, fossil and current, that have been associated with this important geological site in central Colorado. Brief biologies and collecting records are given for present-day species.

An Illustrated Guide to the Mountain Stream Insects of Colorado. J. V. Ward and B. C. Kondratieff. University of Colorado Press, Niwot, CO. 1992.

A guide to aquatic insects written for a nontechnical audience. The best single source for information on aquatic insects found in Colorado. Illustrated with excellent line drawings.

Insects of the Southwest. F. Werner and C. Olson. Fisher Books, Tucson, AZ. 1994.

A review of the most commonly encountered insects found in the southwestern states. Sections discuss insects found in different settings—home, patio, desert and crops. A bit short on illustrations but contains a wealth of interesting information on a wide range of species.

Introduction to the Aquatic Insects of North America. R. W. Merritt and K. W. Cummins. Kendall Hunt, Dubuque, IA. 1983.

One of the most comprehensive books dealing with aquatic insects. Excellent keys to adults and immatures are provided, as well as information on the biology and ecology of North American species. A special feature is an extensive literature review.

An Introduction to the Study of Insects. D. J. Borror, C. A. Triplehorn and N. F. Johnson. Saunders College Publishing/HBJ College Publishing. 1989.

The standard text for introductory college entomology courses that emphasize insect identification. Excellent keys to adult stages of all North American insect families. Illustrations are among the best for completeness and clarity. A brief description of the biology of each insect family is included. The use of a microscope is usually necessary for most identifications.

Life on a Little Known Planet. H. E. Evans, Lyons and Burford, New York, NY. 1993.

Probably the best introduction to the world of living insects available. Full of well-written, fascinating stories about common insects, with a healthy dose of philosophy.

Pests of the West. W. S. Cranshaw. Fulcrum Publishing, Golden, CO. 1992.

A book about diagnosing and correcting garden pest problems of the high plains, Rocky Mountain and intermontane West region. The biology and management of insects are heavily featured.

The Pleasures of Entomology: Portraits of Insects and the People Who Study Them. H. E. Evans. Smithsonian Institution Press. 1985.

Delightful accounts of twelve common insects, plus some entomological history and philosophy.

Extension/University Publications

An excellent source of information on the habits of many of the more economically important insects is the Cooperative Extension offices, located in most counties. Each state produces a series of information sheets on insects that is available for free or a nominal cost. More extensive publications that may be of interest to the bug-collector include the following:

Field Guide to Common Western Grasshoppers. R. E. Pfadt, 1991. Available for $15.00 from the Bulletin Room, University of Wyoming, P.O. Box 3313, Laramie, WY 82017. Phone: (307) 766-2115.

Household Insects of the Rocky Mountain States. W. S. Cranshaw, S. Armbrust, M. Brewer and S. LaJeunesse. Colorado State University Cooperative Extension Bulletin 557. 1995. Available for $8.50 from the Cooperative Extension Media Resource Center, 115 General Services Building, Colorado State University, Ft. Collins, CO 80523. Phone: (303) 491-6198.

Insects That Feed on Colorado Trees and Shrubs. W. S. Cranshaw, D. A. Leatherman and B. A. Kondratieff. Colorado State University Cooperative Extension Publication 506A. 1993. Available for $6.75 from the Cooperative Extension Media Resource Center, 115 General Services Building, Colorado State University, Ft. Collins, CO 80523. Phone: (303) 491-6198.

Venomous Animals of Arizona. R. L. Smith. The University of Arizona Cooperative Extension Bulletin 8245. 1982. Available for $10.00 from Publication Distribution Center, 4042 N. Campbell, Tucson, AZ 85719. Phone: (602) 621-7176.

Index